Reflection in Sequence

Reflection in Sequence

Novels by Spanish Women, 1944–1988

Sandra J. Schumm

Lewisburg
Bucknell University Press
London: Associated University Presses

Associated University Presses
440 Forsgate Drive
Cranbury, NJ 08512

Associated University Presses
16 Barter Street
London WC1A 2AH, England

Associated University Presses
P.O. Box 338, Port Credit
Mississauga, Ontario
Canada L5G 4L8

The paper used in this publication meets the requirements of the American National Standard for Permanence of Paper for Printed Library Materials Z39.48-1984.

Library of Congress Cataloging-in-Publication Data

Schumm, Sandra J., 1947–
    Reflection in sequence : novels by Spanish women, 1944–1988 / Sandra J. Schumm.
        p.   cm.
    Includes bibliographical references and index.
    ISBN 0-8387-5400-7 (alk. paper)
    1. Spanish fiction—Women authors—History and criticism.
    2. Catalan fiction—Women authors—History and criticism.
    3. Spanish fiction—20th century—History and criticism.   4. Catalan fiction—20th century—History and criticism.   5. Women in literature.   6. Self-realization in literature.   I. Title.
PQ6055.S27   1999
863'64099287—dc21   98-33980
                                                                                           CIP

PRINTED IN THE UNITED STATES OF AMERICA

For Bob . . .
and our children,
Christopher,
Carolyn,
Stephanie, and
Marguerite

Contents

Preface

While women in the United States talk of breaking through the "glass ceiling" that still limits job advancement and pay scales for them, women in Spain during the twentieth century have experienced a much more opaque barrier. Even though Spanish women began to acquire more equal rights during the liberal Second Republic (1931–39), the Spanish civil war (1936–39) interrupted their hopeful possibilities. After Generalissimo Francisco Franco seized control of Spain in 1939, he maintained his role as dictator until his death in 1975. In the early years of his dictatorship, Franco rewrote Spain's civil and penal laws, giving husbands all legal authority in the family and denying women all sorts of familial, societal, and conjugal rights. Franco even established a special Feminine Section, dedicated to instruct women about proper comportment. After Franco's death, the democratic monarchy of Juan Carlos I, the general elections in Spain, and the Spanish Constitution of 1978 reinstated many rights for women, but the process of women's social autonomy is a slow one. The haunting effects of dictatorial control, censorship, and more subtle propaganda to dominate women are difficult to eradicate, as evidenced by the novels I examine in this study.

Despite all the barriers against women's development during Franco's dictatorship, or—more conceivably—in retaliation to them, novels by women in Spain began to flourish soon after Franco took control. A great many of these works concern female identity. While many of these novels have been tremendously popular, especially among Spanish women, most of the novels and their authors are relatively unknown outside Spain (except for scholars of twentieth-century Spanish literature). This is true even though five of the seven novels I analyze at length in this study have been translated into English. Moreover, books of criticism about Spanish novels by women had been very sparse until the mid-1980s. With this study I hope to add to the body of work about women writers by emphasizing the thread of discourse and social evolution precipitated by Spanish women's writing.

9

To make my analysis of these novels more accessible to English speakers, I have translated quotes extracted from the texts into English. I have also translated their titles the first time they are mentioned; in some cases my translation of a title coincides with the published title of the translated version of the novel. Two of the novels I examine were originally written in Catalan, a language spoken by millions of people principally in the eastern portions of Spain. (During his dictatorship, Franco prohibited the use of the Catalan, Galician, and Basque languages in Spain.) I have used the Catalan original as the basis of my English translation of quotations from these two novels, although both works have also been translated into Spanish. I apologize to readers who would rather read quotations from the novels in the language in which they were written.

My husband, Bob, and my family were constantly patient and very supportive while I worked on this project. I would also like to give a very special thank you to Robert C. Spires for his invaluable advice and encouragement. I thank Roberta Johnson, John T. Booker, and Sharon G. Feldmen for reading my manuscript and giving me insightful suggestions. Immaculata Pineda and Julián Companys helped me with some words and phrases I had difficulty translating from Catalan. Additionally, I am grateful to Andrew P. Debicki, for inspiring my interest in metaphor and metonymy, and to John S. Brushwood, for suggesting the title of my book.

Reflection in Sequence

Introduction: Tools of Self-Discovery and Change

Following a dearth in the early decades of the twentieth century in Spain, novels by women began to proliferate after the civil war (1936–39). Many of these works reveal a tendency to explore self and identity. Carmen Martín Gaite, for example, notes that following the publication of Carmen Laforet's *Nada* (1944 Nadal Prize winner), female novelists began to project a new and dynamic view of women and their development as individuals.[1] In the works examined in this study—*Nada* (Nothing), *Primera memoria* (First memory), *La plaça del Diamant* (Diamond Plaza), *Julia, El cuarto de atrás* (*The Back Room*), *El amor es un juego solitario* (*Love Is a Solitary Game*), and *Qüestió d'amor propi* (A question of self-pride)—the female protagonists struggle for self-realization, and interestingly, these protagonists are often writers whose writing serves as a self-reflective device.

Women's novels of self-realization—which imply a position of subordination and the desire to improve one's individuality—are certainly not exclusive to Spain.[2] However, the politically repressive situation in Spain for more than forty years under Francisco Franco's dictatorship (1939–75) greatly complicated Spanish women's strides toward autonomy. The labor of identity formation in these texts, as well as the aforementioned surge of novels by women after the inception of Franco's dictatorship in Spain, hints at a connection between women's oppression and their need to assert themselves through writing. The novels of self-reflection I analyze here are not merely narcissistic and ineffective contemplation of the individual ego but, rather, have worked together as a powerful tool to change women's role in Spanish society. Moreover, the reflection of females in these and other novels by women in Spain has served as an instrument of discourse to further that evolution.

Women's self-reflection immediately suggests mirrors, and Biruté Ciplijauskaité sees the mirror as an image in women's literature that nearly always indicates self-identification, or "el proceso de

13

concienciación" (the process of the formation of consciousness). In fact, Jenijoy La Belle argues that the mirror plays an important role in the very formation of feminine identity. Likewise, Patricia Spacks observes that both Simone de Beauvoir and Virginia Woolf are interested in "the mirror, metaphor and reality, as a key to the feminine condition."[3] All these women see a difference between the way women and men employ mirrors.

Spacks claims there is a distinction because women "concern themselves with their own images," while "men require the enlarged self-image provided by their reflection in a woman."[4] Woolf, too, feels that men employ women to augment their self-image: "Whatever may be their use in civilized societies, mirrors are essential to all violent and heroic action. That is why Napoleon and Mussolini both insist so emphatically upon the inferiority of women, for if they were not inferior, they would cease to enlarge."[5] In the preceding quotations, both Spacks and Woolf convey the idea that men have used women as objects to aid in the men's self-perception as subjects.

De Beauvoir further develops the subject/object contrast between men and women: "Man, feeling and wishing himself active, subject, does not see himself in his fixed image; it has little attraction for him, since man's body does not seem to him as object of desire; while woman, knowing and making herself object, believes she really sees *herself* in the glass."[6] Women tend to visualize themselves as objects—a perception precipitated by male consideration of the female as an *object* of desire. Therefore, most women regarding themselves in a speculum see their own objectified *selves* as the recipient of their gaze.

This intense scrutiny of the self as object helps to explain the difference that the critics cited see between men's and women's use of mirrors. La Belle elaborates on this contrast:

> What women do with mirrors is clearly distinct from and psychically more important that what men do with mirrors in their pursuit of generally utilitarian goals. . . . Men look at their faces and their bodies, but what they *are* is another matter entirely.

Women communicate with the mirror about their inner selves; the resulting exchange implies a duality rather than a simple reflection. According to La Belle, the image women see in a mirror is like a metaphor, because it is "inscribed with both identity and difference."[7]

This metaphoric aspect of the mirror for women, and de Beauvoir's and Woolf's interest in it as a "key" to feminine identity, also intimates the significance of metaphor in women's writing and self-expression. For Domna Stanton, metaphor reveals "la différence féminine" in the works of the French feminine theorists Hélène Cixous, Luce Irigaray, and Julia Kristeva; metaphor has been "the optimal tool for transporting meaning beyond the known" since classical times.[8] Since de Beauvoir emphasizes that many women feel misunderstood,[9] metaphors could be very important communicative implements for them.

Metaphor has been understood as an important means of expression from Aristotle to modern times.[10] Roman Jakobson, for instance, defines metaphor as a "substitution" of one item for another. In Jakobson's example, metaphors of "hut" might be "den" or "burrow," the synonyms "cabin" or "hovel," or the antonym "palace."[11] (While some theorists distinguish between prototypes of metaphor—differentiating between metaphor, simile, and allegory, for example—these differences are not important in this study. I consider all of these as metaphoric expressions.)[12] In terms of aesthetic literary expression, however, Umberto Eco points out that simple metaphors (such as the substitution of "hovel" for "hut")—in which the two elements are evidently related—are "acceptable," but not "rewarding." Eco describes a "merely acceptable" metaphor in this way: "No one would say that it is 'beautiful'; it is missing the tension, the ambiguity, and the difficulty which are characteristic of the aesthetic message."[13]

Paul de Man also finds the ambiguous metaphor that unites dissimilar ideas intriguing because it creates a new type of reality for the reader and, according to de Man, actually "freezes hypothesis, or fiction, into fact."[14] By stating the terms of the comparison as an equivalence, the metaphor transmits a new concept that could be considered as improbable or fictitious. According to Michael Cabot Haley, a metaphor that involves an analogy of dissimilar items does not remain in a balance of appositions; rather, the items interact and generate a new reality from two diverse ideas.[15] Perhaps the need to express a "new reality" also helps explain the prominent role of metaphor in literature written by women.

While Haley describes the reader's tendency to relate the dissimilar items conveyed through a metaphor,[16] Eco describes this process in terms of the reader's tracing the metaphor back to a "subjacent chain of metonymic connections which constitute the framework of the code."[17] Whereas Jakobson defines metaphor as a "substitution" (citing examples of "hovel" and "palace" as metaphors of "hut"), he explains metonymy in terms of "association." He says metonymic responses to "hut" might be "thatch," "litter," or "poverty."[18] Metaphors compare or substitute, while metonymy moves on to an associated idea. Thus Jakobson sees metaphor and metonymy as opposites: Metaphor represents a vertical pole, while metonymy is on a horizontal pole. (As with metaphor, the prototypes of metonymy—such as synecdoche, where a part represents a whole—are not important in this study.)

Although Jakobson's distinction is extremely helpful in establishing the difference between metaphor and metonymy, it also isolates the two functions, ignoring the way they work together. David Lodge, for example, highlights the fluidity between metaphor and metonymy; he notes that on occasion in modernist prose "an essentially metonymic style is made to serve the purposes of metaphor." Lodge also points out that extremely "weak" metaphors, where "the terms of comparison are not widely separated," are actually more related to metonymy because "they depend on contiguity and context."[19] Jakobson's own substitution of "hovel" for "hut" is a good example of a "weak" metaphor that has its basis in a proximate meaning, and thus actually blurs the distinction between metaphor and metonymy. In some cases, metonymy is even considered to be a prototype of metaphor.[20]

Other theorists, such as Michael and Marianne Shapiro, emphasize the dynamic, circular aspect of the function of metaphor and metonymy. They stress that the two tropes are interdependent, with metonymy being "the more basic, less complex" of the two, always having "the potential for sliding into metaphor."[21] A metonymic association suggests a metaphor in the mental process, while further metonymic associations might change the original metaphoric concept. Indeed, their circular theory would help to explain the difficulty that sometimes results from trying to isolate metaphor and metonymy to illustrate cognitive procedures. The Shapiros point out that only when localized in texts are metaphor and metonymy sometimes preserved as separate entities—in normal thought processes they fuse and cannot be clearly separated.[22]

Because Eco feels the "merely acceptable" metaphor is essentially boring to the reader, metonymic displacement is imperative in the more ambiguous and dynamic metaphor that Eco finds more interesting. Complex metaphors require greater reader participation; readers must make metonymic associations based on what they have read or know. While metaphor "freezes" a concept, as de Man has stated, metonymy moves it on to other areas, demonstrating expansion and growth, and creating new metaphorical perceptions. Therefore, metonymy seems essential to show dynamism and to keep a metaphor from becoming a static concept arrested in the balance of opposites, or a "merely acceptable" expression.[23]

In literature a metaphor serves to transport meaning between the literary work and the reader. However, a lack of metonymic connections to transport the original metaphors to other areas would tend toward stagnation instead of growth. Stanton criticizes the abundance of metaphorical images without metonymic connections in the work of Cixous, Kristeva, and Irigaray, saying that the repetition of metaphors depicting masculine and feminine notions (specifically the maternal metaphor for women) leads to separation into binary opposites. In other words, the metaphors contained therein have become static clichés, and no longer interact to form new meaning. She feels that displacement from metaphor to metonymy in their work would resolve this static separation: "Metonymy underscores the desire for the other, for something/somewhere else, a desire extended along an indefinite chain of signifiers by substitution, by a displacement that wanders off the subject."[24]

In the same manner, literature about women that does not incorporate metonymy to show change in the original metaphors would tend to depict women as static. Conversely, writing that employs metonymy to displace and expand initial metaphorical concepts would show progress in women's meditations on identity and self-realization. Thus, the "dynamic view" of women that Martín Gaite has noticed in novels written by women might well arise from the effect of metonymic expansion in those works.

The circularity of the process of metaphor and metonymy, noted by the Shapiros, results when metonymy is converted into metaphor. The metaphor is then metonymically linked to other areas and concepts, causing the mind to form a new metaphor. This "life cycle" of a metaphor might also be compared to the often circular process that many feminine theorists have seen in female development.[25] While male development is customarily viewed as linear or a spiral, female development is frequently depicted in a circular manner. However, to fit into the concept of dynamic growth (like that of the metaphor augmented by metonymy), the circle would need to expand rather than retract, as retraction would indicate regression rather than growth.

If, indeed, metaphor and metonymy can be thought of as dynamic, cyclical processes, these tropes may serve as useful areas of analysis to help explain the underlying forces at work in novels of female self-realization.[26] Lacan's theory that metaphor and metonymy are expressions of the unconscious, and that the unconscious is structured like a language,[27] serves to reinforce the notion that these tropes are basic, underlying concepts in all literary creations.[28] Therefore, the specific use of metaphor and metonymy within a work tends to reveal not only the subconscious of its characters but also (indirectly) the subliminal thoughts of the implied author of that work. M. M. Bakhtin calls this refraction of the author's intentions through its characters or narrative voice the "double-voiced discourse" of a novel.[29] The "double-voicing" that occurs between the author and her female protagonist in novels written by women echoes Gardiner's claim that "the hero is her author's daughter."[30] (Gardiner apparently feels the word "heroine" has an undesirable connotation.)

Gardiner metaphorically concludes the "hero" is the author's daughter because of female identity formation based on the mother-daughter bond: "The maternal metaphor of female authorship clarifies the woman writer's distinctive engagement with her characters and indicates an analogous relationship between woman reader and character."[31] The mother-daughter affinity that Gardiner describes in women's writing parallels what others call a "mirror" image between mother and daughter. According to Madonna Kolbenschlag: "We come into the world as mirror images of our mother—destined to be not only her reflector, but also her silent inquisitor." She calls the mother-daughter relationship the most "symbiotic and symmetrical bond known to humans."[32]

Similarly, Marianne Hirsch finds that most female development is "the gradual and not always successful process of identification with and differentiation from a mother who remained an important inner object for the maturing daughter." Hirsch's observation is supported by Nancy Friday's exploration of such complex bonding in her book with the catoptric title *My Mother/My Self,* while Nancy Chodorow asserts that the traditional societal family structure creates "permeable ego boundaries" between mother and daughter that makes self-identity difficult.[33]

Thus the mother-daughter relationship between the characters of the novel (as well as the affinity between the female protagonist, author, and a female reader) creates an intimate affiliation, but one that also hints at a perplexing *mise en abyme.* The mirrorlike connections between mother and daughter (and sometimes author, protagonist, and reader) create symmetry, but—like images that contain the same form reflected in smaller and smaller proportions ad infinitum or wooden dolls stacked one inside another—individual differences become hard to discern. The indistinguishability becomes dizzying.

While differentiation from one's own mother can be problematic for women, other writers speak of a metaphoric mother, representing the solidarity of feminine concerns against the patriarchal power dominant in most societies. Hélène Cixous explains that, in order to increase their virility and control, men have led women to be their own enemies: "They have made for women an antinarcissism." Cixous's comments expand Spacks's and Woolf's observations about men needing women as a magnifying mirror. In defense against this self-hatred, Cixous implores women to support each other: "Everything will be changed once woman gives woman to the other woman. There is hidden and always ready in woman the source; the locus for the other. The mother, too, is a metaphor."[34]

Clarissa Pinkola Estés also confirms the importance of a metaphoric mother, or the "woman-to-woman circle," of feminine solidarity and wisdom, and writes about the importance both of a wise mother and her support from other women: "The woman who has a child-mother or unmothered mother construct in her psyche . . . is likely to suffer from naive presentments, lack of seasoning, and in particular a weakened instinctual ability. . . ." Estés explains that a "child-mother" often gives destructive attention to her child, making identity formation difficult.[35]

The formation of a "child-mother," however, is partially caused by dominant male influence that induces feminine "antinarcissism." Martín Gaite explains that in postwar Spain Franco directed special programs at women to instill "a passive attitude and spirit of sacrifice."[36] The qualities of submission and obedience—normally expected of children—would magnify male hegemony over both mother and daughter. Thus, Franco's dictatorship not only served to augment patriarchial domination and authoritarian influence in Spain, but also especially complicated identity formation for Spanish women.

According to Madonna Kolbenschlag and Ellen Cronan Rose, fairy tales also elicit childlike compliance of women, while Emilie Bergmann highlights their importance as intertexts in many of the same novels included in this study. Virginia Higginbotham draws attention to the subtle, but powerful, persuasion of fairy tales by asserting that they function subliminally: "Recent studies in psychiatry discuss fairy tales as repositories of the collective unconscious which parallel and often illuminate individual, as well as collective behavior." Thus fairy tales function on the same level of consciousness as in Lacan's notion of the metaphor. Kolbenschlag feels they often express women's desire for change and liberation: "Most fairy tales . . . celebrate the metaphoric death of the old inadequate self as it is about to be reborn on a higher plane of existence. . . . Fairy tales are thus primarily metaphors of the human personality, of the individual psyche's struggle to be free of fear and compulsion."[37]

But the subconscious metaphoric influence of fairy tales can also make them tools of enslavement when they present models of patriarchal submission. For instance, the story of Cinderella acts metaphorically as a subversive mirror and model for women. Because Cinderella accepts her position of servitude, the story mirrors women's acknowledgment of their worthlessness and inadequacy, and although Cinderella provides a model of change and escape, it is only within patriarchal norms—by marrying the Prince.[38]

While fairy tales can serve as entrapping models for women, women's writing is a metaphorical mirror that can both liberate and create the self.[39] Anaïs Nin sees writing as a continuation of the mirror, but it also offers opportunities for women to identify themselves as subjects who reach beyond the self, rather than as mere objects. Cixous says that by "writing herself" woman will be able to reclaim that which has been confiscated from her identity and strength. Because many of the protagonists in this study are also writers, they too share this liberating and powerful aspect of identity formation that Woolf lauds in *A Room of One's Own*, and that Pratt believes will change others, in addition to being a "pathway to the authentic self."[40]

These metaphorical allusions to mirroring underscore why the mirror is such an important trope of self-formation in women's literature. Indeed, we might consider that the mirror itself functions both as a metaphor and a metonymy, making it a forceful tool. The mirror reflection serves as a metaphor of the self for a woman, but as La Belle indicates, it works in a far more important way than in the aforementioned duality of communication with the self.

The mirror also implies the judgment of the "other" to women, according to La Belle: "What a mirror stands in place of (men, society, the world) does impose on the woman these various faces she exhibits. The medium of reflection *does* have enormous power, the power of the world to determine self."[41] Thus instead of only a "substitution" of self (simultaneous identity and difference—which would describe a metaphor), the mirror also indicates the "combination" of ideas of others—in other words, a metonymy. It is helpful to remember that "substitution" is one of the key words that Jakobson uses to define metaphor, while he says that metonymy would "combine and contrast."[42] Scenes of women looking into mirrors—as metaphoric and metonymic expressions of the self—can reveal vital subconscious development of self perception.

In addition to the growth of self indicated by a female protagonist's use of metaphors expanded by metonymy, the mirror also reveals change. Since the mirror images exhibit both a metaphoric and a metonymic process, they form a network of substitution and association throughout the text, revealing the development of the key female personality. In the analyses that follow, I demonstrate how this relationship functions within individual novels, and how female development evolves through the postwar to the post-Franco period. Because of the fluidity between metaphor and metonymy in the thought process, often it is difficult to completely isolate these tropes. Thus I differentiate the metonymic associations only when they are meaningful in the cognitive processes of the protagonist, or when they are significant in the reader's perception of the novel. In all the works analyzed, the examination of these literary devices and of mirror scenes reveals subtle aspects with regard to the protagonist's problem of self-realization.

For instance, the first two novels, *Nada* and *Primera memoria,* present precocious young protagonists who also serve as first-person narrators. Andrea and Matia, the respective protagonists, express their fears and hopes in new situations through metaphors and metonymy. They also demonstrate transitions in their process of maturation by describing themselves looking into mirrors. Although *La plaça del Diamant* also presents a young protagonist, Natàlia, the novel traces her development through most of her lifetime. While Natàlia is not as well educated or aspiring as the first two young women, she uses metaphors (which become increasingly complicated because of new metonymic associations) to comprehend the dilemmas in her life. Natàlia's refusal to regard herself directly in the mirror for many years demonstrates her timid nature and the abnegation of her own needs.

Although the protagonist of Moix's *Julia* is also a young woman, the third-person narrator is a distinct change from the previous novels. Metaphorical expression is frequently less direct because Julia has subconsciously repressed being raped when she was six years old. Her troubled personality is evident since she often does not recognize her own reflection in the mirror. Sexual descriptions, metonymically suggested in *Julia,* are overtly described in *El amor es un juego solitario,* when Elia (the older protagonist) escapes from self-reflective contemplation by indulging in a gamelike mé-

nage à trois. Mirrors aid in Elia's sexual games, but she is afraid to regard herself directly.

While Carmen, in *El cuarto de atrás,* and Àngela, in *Qüestió d'amor propi,* are also older protagonists, they seem to overcome the insecurities that plague them (and most other women) various times in their lives. Carmen employs many types of mirror reflections to bolster her self-confidence, while Àngela mirrors her thoughts off a friend. Both of these mature protagonists are writers, suggesting another dimension to the importance of metaphor and metonymy in their self-expression.

The positive development in *El cuarto de atrás* and *Qüestió d'amor propi,* as well as the change from younger protagonists in the earlier novels to adults in the more recent works, suggests a progressive change in the status of women in Spain between 1944 and 1988. Older protagonists imply that there is no longer a need to struggle for independence either from parental authority, or from those who wish to treat them like children. Although *El amor es un juego solitario* indicates that not all women successfully accept their transition into adulthood, the other older protagonists fit into the positive position of cyclical development that Pratt sees in women's development. Pratt explains that older, mature women often begin to recognize and reject the constraints patriarchal society has placed on them, and thus regain the freedom they felt as children.[43] The maturity of the more recent protagonists, therefore, contributes to their progress.

In fact, several critics have seen various forms of progression in female self-realization as reflected by contemporary Spanish novels written by women. Phyllis Zatlin illustrates a "process of defamiliarization" in post-Franco novels by women that makes readers more aware of the female perspective. Likewise, Bergmann finds that in many of the same novels employed in this study "women authors seek narrative strategies to express what has not been expressed before." Ciplijauskaité, too, notices a gradual evolution of the protagonists beginning with *Nada,* as well as an increasing search for free expression that would indicate advancement in contemporary Spanish novels written by women.[44] However, the number of novels that manifest negative development of their female protagonists demonstrates that the path toward female autonomy is not a steady linear progression. Instead, the sequence fits better into a cyclical expansion—much like the circular process feminine theorists see in the personal formation of women.

But within this expanding cyclical development, Geraldine Nichols notices a clear sense of dialogue between the works of Rodoreda, Laforet, and Matute (writers of the "first generation") and the later writers—Riera and Tusquets. She classifies Moix as a curious bridge between the two generations.[45] While Martín Gaite's earlier novels—such as *Entre visillos* (Between curtains)—seem to fit better within the first generation, there are many qualities in *El cuarto de atrás* that locate it with works of the second generation, making Martín Gaite a bridging author as well. In addition to this dialogue and connection between generations, however, there are elements within the individual novels that create an ongoing discourse with the others.

The common theme in all the novels is a woman in search of her autonomous identity. In addition to this mutual theme, many of the novels contain images that echo those of the novels before it, creating more similarities. For instance, in *Nada,* after arriving in Barcelona at midnight, Andrea expresses her apprehensions about beginning her university studies while living there by comparing her grandmother's apartment and her relatives to situations in nightmares. Similarly, the beginning pages of *Julia* depict Julia waking terrified from a recurring nightmare—also populated by ghosts and monsters.

But while the nightmare motif creates a situation of sameness between the two novels, there are also distinct differences. Andrea eventually discards her nightmare metaphor as she becomes more confident of herself, but Julia is more and more convinced that the nightmare is her reality. This simultaneous sameness and difference is reminiscent of the definition of metaphor itself. For instance, the metaphor "your eyes are diamonds" expresses that one thing "is" another, while—at the same time—it inherently communicates that eyes and diamonds are distinct things.[46] The novels, likewise, portray situations that are and are not like the ones before them.

However, instead of mere comparisons and substitutions between the novels (Jakobson's definition of metaphor), the advancement in literary techniques, as well as evidence of social progress of the protagonists, indicates a combination that moves on—like a metonymy. The metaphoric and metonymic qualities between these novels by women is similar to the way women often use reflections of self and others to aid in their identity formation. Thus, this dynamic movement among the novels functions like the mirror, as a tool of self-discovery and creation.

Therefore, the dialogue between these contemporary Spanish novels written by women suggests the sort of female "mirroring" that has the power to effect a changing, dynamic social identity for women. As Pratt has observed, novels by women "become vehicles for social change."[47] The novels highlighted within this study (as well as other novels by the same and other female novelists) demonstrate a positive interaction among themselves—a reflection in sequence—that reflects change in the creative and social identity of women in Spain between 1944 and 1988 and also indicates the potential for more change.

1

Subjective Devices to Reveal the Feminine Psyche in Carmen Laforet's *Nada*

Carmen Laforet's 1944 Eugenio Nadal-Prize-winning novel *Nada* (Nothing), along with José Camilo Cela's novel *La familia de Pascual Duarte* (1942, *The Family of Pascual Duarte*), were acclaimed by critics as the prototypes of *tremendismo* in Spain.[1] According to Margaret Jones, the term *tremendismo* is used to define the "stylistic and structural devices" used by an author to convey the deprivation, despair, and negative attitude that was prevalent after the Spanish civil war.[2] Because of its extremely negative posture, *tremendismo* is felt to transmit a more *subjective* view than conventional realism. In the case of *Nada,* the protagonist, Andrea, subjectively relays her interpretation of her experiences and feelings during one year of her adolescence. By relying on metaphoric expression, or language in which "ordinary objects are charged with negative emotional values,"[3] Andrea allows the reader to experience with her a personal, subjective recreation of this pivotal year of her life.

These same stylistic and structural techniques also reflect Andrea's personality and identity, since the dominant theme of the novel is Andrea's search for her own individuality as an adolescent female from a small town in Franco's postwar Spain. As Andrea pursues her own sense of self, she involves the reader in her pursuit by expressing her impressions through metaphor and metonymy. Images of Andrea reflected in a mirror serve as a reinforcement of these metaphoric and metonymic expressions and show the development and changes she undergoes.[4] Moreover, the use of metaphoric tropes and mirrors in *Nada* conveys a specifically feminine quest for identity.[5] Laforet's techniques reveal Andrea's feelings before the character herself is consciously aware of or can rationally explain her state of mind, enabling the reader to experience the process of development as Andrea experiences it.

25

Nada begins as Andrea arrives late at night at her grandmother's apartment on Aribau Street in Barcelona to begin her university studies. She is shocked by the run-down, dingy condition of her relatives' home that was luxurious before the war. In spite of the depressing atmosphere and constant physical and verbal conflicts between members of the family, Andrea is initially optimistic. Although she attempts to isolate her problematic family life from her friends at the university, these two distinct areas begin to intertwine when her friend Ena expresses interest in Andrea's neurotic uncle, Román. Andrea's insecurity about her heritage and her feelings of rejection ultimately lead her to a key moment of self-revelation. Although Andrea is able to save Ena from a perilous association with Román, his subsequent suicide leaves Andrea feeling guilty and as if she had gained nothing from her year in Barcelona. After Ena's parents move to Madrid, they offer Andrea the opportunity to work and study there. Andrea again senses hope and liberation, but without the same illusions that she had upon arriving in Barcelona.

In the first chapter of the novel, which describes the night of her arrival in Barcelona, Andrea metaphorically reveals her initial aspirations of liberty, as well as her disappointing perception of reality. These metaphors illustrate what James Olney describes as a "psychological process . . . to grasp the unknown through the known" and to fit it into one's experiential knowledge:[6] they define the unknown in Andrea's new life and link her unconscious perceptions with her rational world. Andrea expresses her hopes for autonomy by brief references to stars and drops of water.[7] However these articulations are so brief and tentative that one might classify them in Lacanian terms of "repressed desire," as if she were afraid or unable to admit them directly.[8]

The reader is aware of Andrea's initial optimistic sensation of independence when she stresses that she is not afraid on arriving alone at the train station late at night but, rather, that everything seems like a pleasant and exciting adventure. She expresses in positive terms that she is "a drop in the current" as she moves among the crowds in the station,[9] like an independent particle in the infinite sea of humanity. Although this metaphor expresses only a subtle and somewhat tentative notion of independence and hope at this point, it serves as a contrast to the negative imagery that follows.[10]

The metaphor of the drop of water, with its suggestion of liberty, serves as the first link in a metonymic chain in which water becomes an enchanted and protective shield for Andrea. While the metaphor compares things that are different—a drop of water and liberty—metonymy connects concepts that are related to these entities. For example cleanliness, brilliance, and renewal are concepts that might be associated with a drop of water, whereas liberty might connote freedom, protection, and strength. The comparison of the drop of water and liberty also solicits the association of their respective metonymic connotations. Indeed, Lacan feels that metaphors are only fully understood when their metonymic connections are explored.[11] For example, as Andrea showers in cold water in the grimy bathroom of the apartment she exclaims: "What a relief to feel the icy water on my body!" (17). The water of the shower is described as "the brilliant threads of water" and "the crystalline and protective spell" (17–18). Thus Andrea's expanded view of her metaphor, including its metonymic associations, magnifies the drop of water into a flow that offers liberating renewal and magical protection.

By the end of the first chapter the subtle positive aspect of the "drop in the current" is metonymically and metaphorically expanded even further by the appearance of other particles among the infinite—which are kindred spirits of Andrea—and, like the water, are shiny. Andrea reveals her thoughts as she looks out the gallery door that she has opened to relieve the oppressive atmosphere of the room where she will sleep: "Three stars trembled in the soft blackness above me and on seeing them I suddenly felt like crying, as if I saw old friends, unexpectedly rediscovered" (190). The fleeting and evasive vision of herself as an independent particle in the infinite is reawakened in Andrea by the view of the three stars, even though they seem nearly unattainable and very distant, perhaps as a result of her entering the nightmarish world of her grandmother's house. The metonymic characteristics in common between drops of water and stars allow the reader to form a new metaphorical substitution expressing Andrea's quest for autonomy: Stars also equal liberty.

The increasingly strong positive characteristics of the stars and drops of water in comparison to Andrea's negative perception of her surroundings manifests an emerging dichotomy in her life. She reveals the sense of conflict she already perceives between her aspirations of liberty and her reality when she muses: "That illuminated flickering of the stars suddenly reminded me of all my anticipation about Barcelona, up until the moment I entered into this atmosphere of diabolical people and furniture" (19). Even though the realization of liberty seems improbable and remote at this point, the contrast between her hopes and her reality reignites and strengthens her desire to attain them.

Yet while the reader becomes more conscious of her hopes, Andrea merely expresses them on an unconscious level. Previously she minimized the expression of her aspirations, but the metonymic process we have been following suggests that she feels increasingly determined to realize them—a star in the darkness is a much more positive and strong expression of hope than a drop in the current. By her subconscious metonymic association of her hopes with stars, the hopes themselves change and take on additional meaning, even though they are distant and trembling. Like feminine theorist Hélène Cixous, Andrea senses the positive cosmic libido of "astral space not organized around any one sun that's any more of a star than the others."[12] In this context, the metaphor of "a drop in the current" also becomes a much more positive expression.[13]

Whereas Andrea initially relies on subtlety and understatement to express her aspirations, she resorts to exaggeration when describing her grandmother's house and its occupants. After her trip from the train station to the house on Aribau Street, Andrea introduces a new metaphor the minute the door to her grandmother's apartment is open: "Then it all seemed like a nightmare to me" (13). Inspired by the late hour of her arrival, Andrea establishes the obvious substitution of a bad dream. With the basic metaphor in place, the other descriptions she employs fit metonymically with that scary idea. For instance, phantoms, haunted houses, darkness, and death are all ideas that might be associated with a nightmare. By a similar process of associations, Andrea notes how the chandelier is dimly lighted and covered with cobwebs, how her uncle Juan "had a hollowed-out face, like a skull" (14), while the maid takes on characteristics of a witch with her black clothing and "greenish teeth" (15). The black dog that constantly follows the maid is "a prolongation of her mourning" (15), alluding to an evil aftermath of death. The other women in the room also seem phantomlike: Gloria (the wife of her skull-like uncle Juan) is thin with a sharp white face and "the lethargy of a hanging sheet" (15), suggesting a ghostlike character, and all appear "elongated, quiet, and sad, like the lights at a funeral wake" (15).

Andrea often creates new metaphors based upon metonymic associations with the nightmare. For example, the covered, unused furniture, which was moved from other rooms that had to be rented out, is ghoulishly personified as "a funeral tomb surrounded by mourners" (18). She even calls the bed that she is afraid to enter a coffin, adding to the incubus of death. All of the expressions presented can be linked with the idea of a nightmare and death, revealing Andrea's exaggerated and fearful state of mind upon confronting her new situation.

Laforet employs metaphor and metonymy in the first chapter of *Nada* to help achieve the effect of the subjective negativity that we associate with *tremendismo*. But perhaps more significantly, Andrea relies on them to establish the perimeters of her aspirations and the perception of her reality in her adolescent quest of self-concept and identity. While the metaphor of the "drop in the current" timidly expresses Andrea's "repressed desire" in Lacanian terms, the exaggerated metaphor of the nightmare represents the fear and obstacles that stand in her way as she tries to fulfill her aspirations. These two metaphors function as the frame of the fundamental conflict that Andrea subconsciously perceives. Metonymic associations then combine the original perceptions with other ideas, expanding or altering the precursor (often resulting in a new metaphoric expression) and demonstrating maturation.

Further metonymic extension of the nightmare begins in the second chapter when Andrea awakens the day after her arrival. Memories of her visits to prewar Barcelona as a child flood over her, and Andrea begins to consider her perception of the night before as *only* a nightmare: "It seemed to me I had dreamed about bad things, but now I rested in this cheerfulness" (21). The horror of the previous night seems to have disappeared just like a bad dream, although everything about the house conserves its "frightening disorder" (23). Andrea feels as if her imagination had played tricks on her the night before.

Andrea's relief is short-lived, however, when her aunt Angustias enters to talk to her and set up rules and restrictions limiting Andrea's liberty. Just as Andrea at first perceived the nightmare as a confrontation to her freedom (represented by the drop of water and the stars), now Angustias thwarts that aspiration. Andrea resents Angustias's limiting and spiteful attitude, and looks for some repugnant physical aspect of her aunt: "at last, when she was about to let me leave, I saw her dirty-colored teeth" (27). This distasteful detail is underlined by Angustias's request for a kiss. The dark teeth become a sign of evil and metonymically link Angustias with the previous night when Juan referred to her as "Angustias, the witch" (16), with the stained and grimy bathroom that Andrea perceives as "a house of witches" (17), and with the "greenish teeth" (15) of the black-clad maid that Andrea observed on arriving.

Angustias becomes a concrete manifestation of the nightmarish threat that Andrea sensed upon arriving at the house on Aribau Street. When Andrea and Angustias go for walks, even the streets seem to lose their brilliance: "As I went through the streets, linked by her arm, they seemed less brilliant and less fascinating than I had imagined" (32). In contrast, everything that Angustias forbids seems then to become more alluring. When the aunt condemns the *barrio chino* (an older, undesirable area of the city) as the "shine of the devil" (58), Andrea imagines it as an attractive place: "(At that moment, I imagined the *barrio chino* illuminated by a spark of great beauty)" (58–59). That "spark of great beauty" then becomes linked metonymically with Andrea's image of stars and their connotation of liberty. The dichotomy between her aspirations and the confines of her family becomes clearer with these metonymic extensions of her original metaphors.

While her family, and particularly Angustias, represents the negative element in her life, the other more positive world in which Andrea lives consists of people associated with the university. Andrea voices the polarity she feels:

> The truth is that an undefinable urge that I now can concretely define as an instinct of defense attracted me to them: only those people of my own generation and of my same tastes could support me and protect me against the phantasmal adult world. (59)

Forming another link in the metonymic chain, her university friends represent the same shining support against the frightening atmosphere of her family as the protective drops of water of the shower and the three stars. One friend in particular, Ena, seems to offer the most support.

Even though Andrea describes Ena as her preferred friend of all the students, she portrays Ena with complicated metonymic associations that do not fit completely into the division of two worlds she has established. One association is dark, limiting and frightening, and the other liberating, bright and promising, but Andrea's comments about her friend encompass both qualities:

> Ena had an agreeable and sensual face, from which her frightening eyes stood out. It was rather fascinating, that contrast between her soft gestures, the youthful aspect of her body and her blond hair, with that look of brilliance and irony that her big, green eyes had. (60)

Shortly after, Andrea similarly describes the eyes of Antonia the maid and Trueno, Román's dog (two of the more diabolical figures in the house on Aribau Street): "The animal's yellow eyes shone looking at the woman, and her eyes glittered too, small and dark" (64). Ena's eyes acquire the same foreboding, unsettling characteristics as those of the dog, and their color echoes Antonia's "greenish teeth" and the "greenish, emaciated lights" (17) throughout the house. This link to the negative aspects of Andrea's life, as well as the fact that Ena asks Andrea from the very first if Román is her uncle, foregrounds the transition that Ena represents between Andrea's two separate worlds. Later references to Ena as a cat playing with mice and the feline glow of her eyes confirm the more sophisticated perspective that Andrea is beginning to acquire. She seems to sense that people are not either completely good or evil.

Although at first Andrea associates all her difficulties in attaining her ideal with her aunt, after Angustias leaves the house on Aribau Street to become a nun, Andrea realizes in part two of the novel that her problem is not as simple as the mere confinement imposed by her aunt.[14] Andrea begins to make metonymic ties previously associated only with Angustias and the nightmarish situation of her house with circumstances outside the house, illustrating other forces impeding the liberty she desires. For instance, when Andrea establishes a date with Gerardo (a young man she met at Ena's house) the unsolicited and offensive kiss he bestows on her links him with the negative force once represented only by Andrea's family. Gerardo's protective ideas connect him further to Angustias.

Gerardo's kiss is one of several situations, like the description of Ena, where diverse metonymic associations begin to fuse the division of two worlds that Andrea had established. Even the *barrio chino,* that seemed attractive simply because Angustias criticized it, takes on frightening qualities when Andrea follows her Uncle Juan there one night: "All of that was no more than the frame of a nightmare, unreal like everything outside of my pursuit" (175). The city, which once represented a liberating force for Andrea, is converted here to a nightmarish hell similar to what she described the first night at the house on Aribau Street.

Additionally, as the specific threat that Angustias posed diminishes, the well-defined goal toward liberty represented by the stars also seems to become more nebulous, suggesting that Andrea no longer clearly delineates the exclusively negative and positive aspects of her life. After leaving Ena's house one night when the sound of Ena's mother singing leaves Andrea with a "nearly anguishing thirst for beauty" (114), Andrea wanders toward the cathedral in the *barrio gótico* (gothic area of the city). The cathedral is

illuminated by the Milky Way and the street lights, which Andrea
describes as "romantic and gloomy" (115). Although Andrea mar-
vels at the beauty of the cathedral in that light, she also describes
the scene with words that are reminiscent of her "nightmare":
"There was an impressive loneliness, as if all the inhabitants of the
city had died" (115). She speaks of the cold being trapped there in
the twisted streets, of a sinister sound, and of the "shipwrecked
gothic city" (115). The diffused light from the Milky Way is mixed
with the red of the artificial lights and seems very bizarre and
different from the three stars that shone like old friends on the first
night in Barcelona. Disparate metonymic associations to Andrea's
original metaphor convey the change and loss of direction that
Andrea feels without the concrete manifestation of obstacles Angustias had represented.

Once again Andrea describes the change effected by this metonymic transfer with a new metaphor: "I felt like I was functioning
like a fool that night, acting without will, like a sheet of paper in
the wind" (115–16). Although one might also consider a sheet of
paper in the wind as an independent particle in the infinite, this
metaphor conveys lack of direction rather than a positive connotation of liberty. While the adoption of the metaphor of the stars
showed a strengthening of Andrea's aspiration of liberty (first expressed as a drop of water), the metaphor of the sheet of paper in
the wind conveys a negative facet.

After Andrea expresses her complete lack of direction by comparing herself to a sheet of paper in the wind, she turns to universal
fairy tale models of change and liberation in an attempt to flee the
oppressive situation of her family. Bergmann explains that Andrea
identifies herself both with the fairy tale of the Ugly Duckling (who
undergoes a transformation into a beautiful swan) and with Cinderella, but that she rejects these patriarchal role models to form her
own identity.[15] The problem with the Cinderella story, of course,
is that it requires submission of feminine aspiration and identity to
the patriarchal norms: " . . . we know that for the Prince we should
read 'Patriarchy.'"[16] And in Andrea's case the Prince is represented by Pons (marrying him would place Andrea squarely within
the patriarchal ideal).[17]

Although Andrea's first dance party at Pons's house seems
analogous to Cinderella's going to the ball, Andrea never conforms
totally with that fairy tale. When she expresses her feelings towards
Pons—"I desired with all my strength to be able to fall in love with
him" (202)—one can see Andrea is trying to mold herself to the
Cinderella model. However, from the very beginning of Pons's

party, incompatible metonymic images show that Andrea is not going to fit into this patriarchal model. Just as the description of Ena's green, feline eyes did not fit within Andrea's completely positive view of the students, Andrea's comments about the party do not correspond to the fairy tale. For example, looking back on the party she remembers: "The odor of a woman with too much jewelry came to me as Pons's mother stretched out her hand, and her undefinable gaze, directed at my old shoes, crossed Pons's yearning gaze as he watched her" (218). Andrea feels as if she were Cinderella who had arrived at the ball without the visit of the fairy-godmother to change her rags to a beautiful gown and her old shoes to glass slippers.[18]

Also diverging from the fairy tale is Andrea's sense of rejection at the party. Andrea thinks she sees disapproval reflected in Pons's mother's eyes (alluding to the importance of the mirror in *Nada,* which we will examine later). But Andrea's interpretation of the mother's attitude reflects much more of her own doubts about the situation and her lack of confidence than it does about what others are thinking of her. As Rabindranath Tagore explains: "We imagine that our mind is a mirror, that it is more or less accurately reflecting what is happening outside us. On the contrary, our mind itself is the principal element of creation."[19] While she feels insecure at the party, it is apparent from her observation of Pons's mother ("smell of a woman with too much jewelry") that she has a nagging feeling that her "Cinderella" goal is not in keeping with her primary objectives.[20] The role of a rich wife—with its sublimation of goals to the masculine order—is distasteful to Andrea.

In this second section of the novel, Angustias's absence causes Andrea to reconsider her goals and redefine the obstacles in her life. However, her consideration of the metaphorical role model of Cinderella does not fit metonymically with her goals and self-concept. The third section of the novel, however, reveals a different metaphoric model for Andrea by way of her relationship with Ena and Ena's mother. Neither Gerardo's kiss, nor the dance at Pons's house fit into Andrea's aspirations; however, the challenge voiced by Ena's mother evokes an interchange of feminine ideals in Andrea and clarifies her goals.

While it was the sound of Ena's mother's singing that awakened an anxiousness in Andrea that inspired her to visit the cathedral at night, the conversation at the beginning of part three arouses an immediate compenetration between Andrea and her friend's mother.[21] Andrea relates: "I understood. More from the ardor of her voice than from what she was saying. It scared me a little"

(230). The voice of Ena's mother contains metaphoric qualities for Andrea that are similar to Cixous's description of woman's voice as "song" that "retains the power of moving us" and is "the first music from the first voice of love which is alive in every woman."[22]

As a prelude and explanation of her plea to help Ena, Ena's mother confesses that as a young woman she cut off her long golden braid and gave it to Andrea's uncle Román because he desired it so fervently. (This episode contains the same metaphoric and symbolic qualities as Alexander Pope's poem "The Rape of the Lock," where the shearing of Belinda's curls is nearly tantamount to the loss of her virginity.) After submitting to Román's wishes, Ena's mother regrets her action. Román confirms her imprudence when he says: "I have the best of you at home. I've robbed you of your charm. . . . Why did you do that stupid thing, woman? Why do you act like a dog for me?" (235). This outlandish demand by Román served as a way to denigrate Ena's mother while making himself feel powerful, echoing Cixous's remarks about antinarcissism.[23] Ena's mother's comments suggest an insightful concern about Andrea and a warning for her not to submit to the denial and hatred of self demanded in many traditional relationships with men. The more obvious reason for relaying the incident, of course, is to illustrate the danger to Ena that Román represents.

In fact, the conversation reveals the mirrorlike affinity between Ena and her mother and foregrounds the importance of the mirror in feminine development. The relationship between Ena and Román echoes that of her mother years earlier and intensifies their catoptric correspondence.[24] Ena's mother even feels that Ena is the completion of her personality: "I understood, humbly, the meaning of my existence when I saw all my pride, my strengths, and my best hopes of perfection come to life in her so magically" (239).

In a sense, Ena's birth re-forms her mother's identity, metaphorically mirroring the mother's creative role: "Because before I created her, nearly forcibly, with my own blood and bones, with my own bitter substance, I was a disoriented and wretched woman" (240). While Ena creates a mother who is more balanced and loving, she is also very similar to her mother and might, therefore, be vulnerable to the same things. But instead of vulnerability to Román, Ena professes that her relationship with him was to avenge her mother: a conscious attempt to improve and fulfill her mother.

Feal Deibe states that Andrea becomes the adoptive daughter of Ena's parents;[25] however, within the idea that she is an adopted daughter of Ena's mother evolves the same metaphoric reflection, the same sensitivity between mother and new daughter. Andrea expresses her understanding of her new creative role after hearing the mother's words: "it was easy for me to understand this language of blood, pain, and creation that begins with the same physical substance when one is a woman. It was easy to understand it, knowing that my own body was prepared—as if packed with seeds—for this labor of continuation of life" (240). Andrea's words suggest the same metaphoric relationship in which Cixous calls woman "the source" for other women.[26] Metaphorically then, Andrea becomes Ena's mother and gives of herself in order to help Ena; her thoughts are the same as those of Ena's mother: "When Ena's mother stopped talking, my thoughts harmonized entirely with hers" (240).

The effect of the conversation in which Andrea's and Ena's mother's thoughts harmonize so perfectly is similar to the effect of the sidereal forces that lead Andrea to look at herself in the mirror in part two (a scene that will be analyzed more closely later). Andrea again speaks of a thread, reminiscent of the attraction of the stars and the threads of water in the shower, forming a metonymic link with the previous events:

> But it seemed that an invisible thread was pulling at me as the hours unfolded, from Aribau Street, from the front door, from Román's room at the top of the house. . . . Half of the afternoon had already passed when that force became irresistible and I entered our front door. (255)

Andrea is motivated into action and arrives at Román's room just after Ena has jilted him. Andrea perceives that he is about to rape or kill her friend, a magnified echo of his treatment of Ena's mother. For Bergmann, Andrea rescues Ena from the "monster," a symbolic entity that represents male oppression, and by doing so also symbolically rescues herself.[27] This idea also supports the network of metaphoric duplications that exists between Ena, her mother, and Andrea. By rescuing Ena she rescues herself and rescues (avenges) Ena's mother.

Andrea's forceful action, resulting from her interchange of feelings with Ena's mother, is inconsistent with the more passive character Andrea has exhibited up to this point and is indicative of a change. Andrea realizes that her action will "open the horizons for me again," while before she had been "accustomed to let the current of events pull me on its own" (255). She has achieved a degree of autonomy, responding to the forces that represent liberty to her, rather than drifting through an otherwise male-controlled society. No longer is she like a sheet of paper carried by the wind, but exhibits more positive aspects of liberty. The "adoption" of a mother figure reunites Andrea with the fundamentals of feminine consciousness, freeing her from oppressive patriarchal "monsters."

Although Andrea has changed and become more autonomous, that does not mean that her change was easy, nor that it is permanent. A one-time linear achievement of self is inconsistent with the circular and shifting development of women. Additionally, the permeable ego boundaries that Chodorow identifies in women permit Andrea to empathize greatly with Román. Critics have mentioned the identification that Andrea feels with Román,[28] and in a sense, his death is symbolic of the death of her old self. The "monster" that Bergmann says Andrea destroys is partially a monster within herself and is part of herself; it is her own acceptance of the antinarcissism imposed on her by the norms of a male-dominated society. Kolbenschlag speaks of the fear and guilt that women suffer after beginning to acquire autonomy and attributes this feeling to their "other-centered conditioning."[29] For Andrea, this fear and guilt surfaces because of Román's suicide and her empathy with him.

Andrea conveys her associations of Román's death with her own state of being as she showers just after his death. The shower, with its protective drops of water that imply liberty and autonomy, was depicted at first as a purely positive force. However, after Román's suicide Andrea metonymically links the liberty represented by the water with his violent death:

> The drops were slipping over my shoulders and chest, they formed canals in my belly, they swept over my legs. Román was stretched out above, bloody, with his face parted by the gaping grimace of those who die condemned. The shower continued falling over me in fresh, unending waterfalls. (278)

The water of the shower rushes over her body in an endless, violent gushing that recalls the blood spilling from her uncle's body. Her freedom—the drops of water—is linked with Román's blood. The metonymic link between the death of her old self and Román's death is compounded when Andrea faints in the shower.

As a result of her fear and blame, Andrea begins to deny change and to see it as negative, an attitude she reveals with subsequent metonymic associations. The link between Román's death and Andrea's change precipitates a nearly catatonic state; she sleeps for two entire days and then experiences death wishes. Even her view of the stars becomes a wish for death: "I lifted my eyes to the sky, which was becoming softer and bluer with the first stars, and the impression of a nearly mystic beauty came to me. Like a desire for me to die up there" (287). In mourning for Román and the alteration in herself, Andrea denies these transformations by repeatedly affirming that nothing has changed in the house on Aribau Street: "Soon life seemed completely the same to me" (288). She denies any effect of his death on Gloria and Juan, and even on her grandmother: "But there wasn't much difference between this grandmother and the little old one from before. She didn't even seem sadder" (288). Andrea repeats her nightmare and deathlike metaphors of the first chapter and seems to regress to the same passive and oppressed state as when she first arrived, again blaming her lack of liberty on her environment.

However, after receiving Ena's letter inviting her to live and study in Madrid, the atmosphere of the house on Aribau changes for Andrea. Johnson points out three reflective images of light in the last chapter of *Nada;* light from the lamp, the streetlight, and the sun against the windows.[30] These reflections of light can be linked metonymically with the stars that have represented liberty throughout the novel. Kolbenschlag explains that liberation for women means rescue of the spirit "from repressive coercion, from inner compulsion and from the hazards of freedom itself."[31] Andrea's guilt and self condemnation after Román's death remained as obstacles to her autonomy, but Ena's letter acts as the powerful "voice" that moves her. The reflected light, the morning departure, and the words "that departure excited me like a liberation" (294) show that Andrea has achieved a degree of emancipation as she leaves Barcelona.[32]

As we have seen, the metaphoric images Andrea expresses reveal a definition of her perceptions, while the metonymic associations of these metaphors divulge the expanded connections that she senses as she matures and observes more about life. The scenes of Andrea looking into a mirror in the novel also serve as an indication of her development that reinforces the observations made upon examining the use of metaphor and metonymy throughout *Nada.* And, as previously noted, the use of mirrors is essentially another expression of metaphor and metonymy. The mirror reflection is a metaphor of the self in that it represents Andrea's own perception of herself, while it also serves as a refracted judgement of the "other."[33]

In *Nada* the scenes with mirrors have an added metonymic effect in that the reader sees Andrea's reflected image in various stages of her development. Each scene, therefore, acts as a frozen perspective of Andrea at a certain point in time. Just as the painting *Nu descendant un escalier* by Marcel Duchamp shows successive temporal images of a person descending a staircase, the ensuing images of Andrea in the mirror show a temporal change that Jakobson would define as a metonymy.[34] By functioning as both metaphor and metonymy, the mirror scenes in *Nada* reinforce the process we have been observing.

For example, it is significant that within the first chapter of the novel Andrea speaks of a mirror in her grandmother's house. As with her first metaphor of the drop of water and liberty, her first glimpse into the mirror is tentative and expressive of the frightening situation in which she finds herself:

> The stained mirror above the sink—what emaciated, greenish lights there were throughout the whole house!—reflected the low ceiling covered with cobwebs, and my own body between the brilliant threads of water, trying not to touch those dirty walls, on tiptoes in the filthy porcelain bathtub. (17)

Andrea is impeded from looking at herself as she concentrates on other objects surrounding the mirror and reflected by it. Additionally, the mirror seems at this point to be distorting the images it reflects, causing her to feel disoriented: "I began to see strange things, like people who are drunk" (18). She quickly finishes her shower so as not to have to see them anymore.

Andrea's refusal to look at her face in that eery situation is a defensive action on her part. La Belle points out that very often in Western culture part of a woman's identity is connected to her image in the mirror: "for a woman whose basic idea of self is intimately tied to the mirror, to have one's face changed . . . is to have the self changed."[35] This change of concept of self is disturbing and even terrifying, and in this case Andrea has already noticed the distorted light and appearance of things in the bathroom:

> That bathroom seemed like a house of witches. The smudged walls conserved the fingerprint of gnarled hands, of screams of desperation. All around, areas with missing tiles opened their toothless mouths, oozing with moisture. . . . Madness smiled in the twisted spigots. (17)

The metaphors within her description convert the inanimate objects of the bathroom into ghoulishly human creatures, conforming with her original metaphor of the nightmare. But if her surroundings are so dramatically changed, it is probable that her own face would also appear distorted. Therefore, it seems a prudent measure for her not to gaze at her face in the mirror. A frighteningly contorted face indeed would have been more than she could have handled at that moment.

The avoidance of a confrontation of her own self within the mirror also indicates that Andrea as yet does not have a strong self-identity, a phenomenon that is not surprising in an adolescent. Andrea's undeveloped self-concept was previously noted by her tentative metaphors that expressed her aspirations of autonomy, but which became stronger as her situation changed. One of the principal alterations of Andrea's perspective was the surprising confusion resulting from Angustias's departure from the house.

Just before her aunt leaves, Andrea begins to note this change and confusion from their reflection in a mirror:

I saw in the mirror, sideways, the image of my arid eighteen years enclosed in an elongated figure and saw Angustias's beautiful and reflected hand becoming tense on the back of the chair. A white hand, with a large and soft palm. A sensual hand, now tearing at the chair, shouting more with the tenseness of its fingers than my aunt's voice. (104–5)

Here the reflected image seems to communicate truths that are not normally visible to Andrea: Andrea is the dull and barren being, while Angustias's sensuous hand screams out for its lost youth and productivity. This scene illustrates the way the mirror often reflects perspectives that are not merely metaphoric reproductions of the original, but also it combines other positions and, therefore, serves as a metonymy.[36] The mirror reflection helps Andrea to understand her aunt and to redefine her simplistic goals and obstacles, contributing to her growth and maturation in the same way that new metonymic associations altered her original metaphors and showed change.

Another even more significant moment of growth and self-realization occurs for Andrea after she leaves Pons's party early and finally falls into a fitful sleep. The importance of this scene is emphasized by Andrea's narration of it before telling about the experience at the party. Andrea wakes in the night to silence within the house and the "shining of the stars" (213). The stars she de-

scribes recall her first night in Barcelona and the association between them and her aspirations of becoming autonomous. Andrea
relates: "My restlessness made me jump out of bed, for these luminous, impalpable threads that come from the sidereal world were
working within me with a strength impossible to define, but real"
(213). The similarities between the "luminous threads" of the stars
and the "shiny threads of water" in the shower on Andrea's first
night in Barcelona calls the reader's attention not only to Andrea's
original aspirations but also to the night when she was not yet
ready to look at her face in the frightening mirror of the bathroom.

These sidereal forces draw Andrea to the mirror, where she
awakens to her sense of self in the strange reflection that she sees
there. (We have previously noted a metonymic link with this scene
in part three, when Andrea is pulled by "an invisible thread" to
rescue Ena from Román's room and, therefore, symbolically to
rescue herself). The shiny threads of the stars have an inherent
communion with the reflection of the mirror:

> Upon getting up from bed, I saw, in Angustias's mirror, that my whole
> room was full of the color of gray silk, and there in the mirror was a
> long shadow. I approached and the specter approached with me. At
> last I was able to see my own blurred face above the linen camisole.
> An old linen camisole—softened by the rubbing of time—covered with
> heavy lace, that my mother had used a long time ago. It was strange
> to be contemplating myself like that—almost without seeing myself—
> with my eyes open. I lifted my hand to touch my features—which
> seemed to be escaping from me—and some long fingers emerged, paler
> than the face, following the lines of the eyebrows, the nose, the cheeks
> which conformed to the structure of the bones. Anyway, I myself,
> Andrea, was living among the shadows and passions that surrounded
> me. (213–14)

The specter in the mirror is and is not her, revealing again the
metaphoric and metonymic aspects of the speculum. While she
can recognize the reflection as her own, it also reveals aspects of
herself that she has not yet understood and that link her to the
phantasmal world of her family.

The description of the gray silk creates an atmosphere of digni-
fied beauty, while the reference to the heavy lace of the camisole
that her mother had also used and that has been softened by time
implies an acceptance of her own heritage. During most of her time
in Barcelona Andrea has wanted to deny her lineage and isolate

her family from her associations at the university, but now she accepts the legacy bestowed upon her. A scene in a mirror at Pons's house earlier the same day had also reflected gray tones as Andrea glanced into it: "I saw myself in the mirror, white and gray, faded among the bright summer suits that surrounded me" (219). At Pons's house the reflection of gray seemed out of place, and Andrea felt ridiculous and ugly as she judged herself there as she thought others were judging her, again pointing to the positional, metonymic effect of the mirror. However, during her self-contemplation later that night she views herself through her own heritage rather than through the lens of the people at the party and is intrigued to touch her own face in an effort to know and accept herself. Her paleness and the structure of her bones and brow exhibit a unique attractiveness and a haunting beauty that she seems to accept and recognize for the first time, combining family characteristics with a positive view of herself.

Andrea no longer feels the need to see herself as Cinderella or in the gay summer garb of the other women at the party; rather, her self-contemplation shows the value of her own self-identity. The use of the mirror quite often shows a quest for identity in women, while time in front of a mirror is a tool of preparation and a re-affirmation of that identity.[37] The mirror functions as this sort of tool by virtue of its incorporation of the principles of metaphor and metonymy, which demonstrate identification, movement, and growth within the individual. Johnson confirms the temporal metonymic effect of the various scenes with speculums when she points out that after Andrea's original refusal to look at her reflected image, subsequent encounters with mirrors demonstrate her change.[38]

In spite of evidence that Andrea has made headway in establishing her own autonomy, several critics point to the circular structure of the novel and Andrea's seemingly naive and repetitive optimism as she leaves for Madrid as evidence that there is no progression in Andrea's development.[39] Nonetheless, current theories that women's self-identity is a circular process are consistent with the circular structure of the novel and should not be considered as a lack of progress. Moreover, Andrea reiterates that she does not hold the same illusions, confirming her growth and change.

Other arguments in favor of a negative interpretation point to the fact that Andrea the narrator must reevaluate her experience.[40] In fact though, Andrea's written expression of her experiences is another way of looking into a mirror in her process of self-realization. Additionally, her writing is a way of controlling her destiny through self-creation and, ultimately, liberation.[41] In this sense, Andrea's looking back on her year in Barcelona and voicing it creatively through writing would be a very positive step. It would transcend the elusive creative attempts of Román, whose products seem to have disappeared like his painting of Gloria among the lilies.

Therefore, in Andrea's mirror or tool for self-creation (her writing of her experiences), it is fitting that Laforet has relied on so many metaphors, metonymic connections, and mirror reflections to let Andrea write her self. Moreover, those techniques serve to precipitate the dialectical effect of the novel. The subjective quality of metaphoric language as subconscious expression encourages an emotive participation by the reader. Thus, concentration upon Andrea's predominately negative metaphors gives a pessimistic picture, while the presence of a narrator looking back on her past also creates tension. However, systematic examination of the use of metaphor, metonymy, and mirroring as devices to reveal the development of the psyche gives a more optimistic feeling of progression within the guidelines of specifically feminine personality development.

While we are never assured of a propitious outcome for Andrea, the suggested continued self-examination is consistent with feminine development and, therefore, is a constructive sign. The negative mood of *tremendismo,* along with positive feminine development within that ambience, adds to the complex and dynamic effect of the novel. Even in the gloomy and controlled environment of post–civil war Spain, *Nada* provides evidence that some women were striving for personal autonomy.

Laforet's second novel, *La isla y los demonios* (1952, The island and the demons), also presents an adolescent protagonist, Marta Camino, seeking to establish her own independence. Like for Andrea, water images also represent freedom for Marta, since she lives "enclosed" in the Canary Islands near the city of Las Palmas.[42] Because Marta yearns to leave the confining island and begin her independent life, the sea is her route to liberty and personal fulfillment. Marta's father died while she was a child, and her mother suffered an attack that left her trapped in a mindless body, so Marta also is essentially an orphan, living with her brother and his wife. Marta complies with her vagabond nature—a trait considered "against the nature" of a woman—by rejecting a marriage proposal and then leaving the island to begin her independent life.[43]

However, while *Nada* and *La isla y los demonios* appear to demonstrate an advancement toward liberty, Gustavo Pérez Firmat finds that Laforet's later works and the fact that she discontinued her writing show the "inability to elect freely her lot in life" and the "abandonment of artistic vocation."[44] Indeed, in her 1955 novel *La mujer nueva* (The new woman), Laforet seems to succumb to the model of abnegation for women that Franco outlined in "La Sección Feminina" (The Feminine Section), a document that prescribed appropriate behavior for women and limited their liberties.[45]

In *La mujer nueva,* the protagonist Paulina (after leaving her insensitive husband Eulogio) ultimately returns to him, renouncing all her personal desires and feelings so that their lives "would be filled by something more than selfishness itself."[46] Although Paulina gives up her life in the city, quits smoking, and prepares to move to a remote area—all for her husband—Eulogio does not make any self-sacrifices. Paulina reassures herself that God will help her with "each abnegation,"[47] echoing the religious martyrdom that Franco solicited from Spanish people (especially from women) in order to maintain his control.

In *La insolación* (1963, Sunstroke), the first novel of an intended trilogy, Laforet employs a motherless, male protagonist, Martín, who becomes the close comrade of Ana and Carlos Corsi, siblings who spend their summers in Beniteca, Spain. Martínez Cachero calls Ana and Carlos "coprotagonistas" (co-protagonists) and feels that at times Ana "parece más efectivamente protagonista que Martín" (seems to be more effectively the protagonist than Martín).[48] Ana exhibits even more independent characteristics than Andrea and Marta in Laforet's first novels, but it is significant that she has not grown up in Spain.

The people of Beniteca consider the nonconformist Corsi children immoral, and unjustly accuse Martín of being Carlos's homosexual lover. Even Martín's father rejects him, and Martín feels that "the whole world was his enemy,"[49] emphasizing the rigid and confining roles for both men and women demanded by Spanish society. The only remaining support for Martín is the embrace of his maternal grandmother—a traditional, self-sacrificing woman—who reinforces woman's role as nurturer. Laforet's last two novels suggest that she was partially persuaded by Franco's propaganda. All the other Spanish women in *La insolación* are portrayed as mindless, frustrated creatures, controlled by male domination.

Ciplijauskaité suggests that women's novels of self-realization are born of women's repression, and are women's attempt to break from the confinement they feel.[50] The next novel examined, Ana María Matute's *Primera memoria,* illustrates how metaphor, metonymy, and mirrors can convey the feeling of entrapment from which Andrea seems to escape in *Nada,* but which still shackles other women.

2

The Entrapment of the Distorted Mirror in *Primera memoria*

There are numerous similarities between Laforet's *Nada* and Ana María Matute's *Primera memoria* (1960, First memory), which also won the Eugenio Nadal Prize.[1] Both involve a young female protagonist who goes to live with relatives some time after her mother dies. Both are narrated in first person by the protagonist, who reveals her perceptions of a new situation and often interjects observations made well after the experience. The two protagonists also express a great disparity between their ideals and their perceptions of a frightening reality. One difference, however, is that Matia, the protagonist of *Primera memoria,* is several years younger than Andrea in *Nada.* While Andrea is already a young adult seeking self-autonomy, Matia conveys her traumatic transition from the innocence of childhood into the adult world of love, betrayal, and war.

Matia is twelve when she goes to live with her grandmother, but most of the narrative takes place when she is fourteen. However, in *Nada,* Andrea begins her university studies when she arrives in Barcelona, making her approximately seventeen or eighteen. Bergmann notes that, in spite of the age difference, Andrea has "not yet ventured into the labyrinth worlds of love and work."[2] In contrast, Matia's budding sexuality is a significant undertone of *Primera memoria,* and Margaret Jones observes that the children in Matute's works live in a world of harsh reality that causes them to have to grow up very suddenly.[3]

The use of metaphor and metonymy to describe this loss of innocence in *Primera memoria* reveals a more inauspicious outcome for Matia than for Andrea. Matia eventually links nearly all the characters and incidents to the same negative metaphors, instead of adapting her metaphors like Andrea does. The repetition of negative metaphors ultimately conveys Matia's entrapment in her situation. Additionally, mirror images in *Primera memoria* do not reveal the progressive and positive formation of self as do those in *Nada*. Although some of Matia's use of the speculum contributes to her sense of individuality, most of her mirror reflections present a distortion that reinforces her sense of insignificance.

Following her mother's death, twelve-year-old Matia is taken from her father to live with her grandmother, her Aunt Emilia, and her fifteen-year-old male cousin, Borja, in a small town in Mallorca after the outbreak of the Spanish civil war. Matia's portrayal of her manipulative cousin Borja coincides in many respects with that of her dictatorial grandmother, Doña Práxedes.[4] Although Matia and Borja are constant companions, Matia conveys her mistrust of him. When Matia befriends Manuel Taronjí, a youth whose home is located in the middle of Doña Práxedes's property, her grandmother disapproves and Borja becomes jealous. But Matia and Manuel share childhood memories and secrets, and Manuel admits that his real father is Jorge de Son Major, Doña Práxedes's estranged brother. Borja works out a scheme to incriminate Manuel, theatrically confessing that he has stolen money from his grandmother and lying when he says Manuel forced him to do it. Although Matia knows the truth, she feels she cannot help Manuel. Borja also has a plan to discredit her, and she is certain her grandmother will believe him rather than her. The novel ends with a feeling of hopelessness and existential despair for Matia,[5] and Manuel is sent to reform school.

After first arriving at her grandmother's house, Matia attempts to preserve her own private world by imaginatively escaping from her overbearing family with Gorogó, her rag doll. But her grandmother's oppressive intrusion into her life and Borja's attempts to control her demonstrate to her that she must abandon her secure childhood. Similar to Andrea's articulating her fears as a nightmare in *Nada*, Matia metaphorically describes herself as a trapped little animal. She recounts the terror of her first night on the island, when her grandmother brought her to a musty hotel: "The very intricate forged iron bed frightened me like an unfamiliar animal."[6] After awakening at dawn, the strange locale frightens her even more: "Accustoming myself to the darkness, I located, one by one, the missing tiles in the wall, the big stains on the ceiling and, above all, the entangled shadows of the bed, like serpents, dragons, or mysterious figures that I scarcely dared to look at" (14). Matia's nighttime fears intensify in the daylight, and her metaphors express a primordial fear of an animal being pursued and trapped.

While in *Nada* Andrea expanded her original metaphor of the nightmare by employing descriptions that fit metonymically with that idea (like phantoms, skulls, darkness, and death), Matia similarly extends her metaphor of the hunted and snared animal. For example, Matia often characterizes her grandmother as a predatory animal: She describes her grandmother's scrutiny of her and Borja's activities as "like a greyhound" that "sniffed" their footsteps to find them (19). While the greyhound metaphor is an extension of her fear of being pursued, the verb "olfatear" (to sniff) conveys another image associated with an animal tracking its prey. If the grandmother found them, Borja would feign innocence: "Borja, hypocrite, hurriedly put on his shoes, with his leg doubled up like a crane" (19). Although Matia implies that both she and Borja were considered the prey, she indicates that, if caught, Borja would pretend to be victimized to win the sympathy of his grandmother. At other times Matia calls her grandmother "the beast" (20), or compares her eyes with "owl's eyes" (120), as the grandmother scrutinizes Matia's appearance.

Doña Práxedes's constant use of binoculars to survey her property and the surroundings is another extension of the idea that she is a predatory bird or animal with augmented visual powers. Matia combines this metonymic association with other metaphors and metonyms of predatory animals to describe her grandmother peering out the window with binoculars: "Her eyes, like long tentacles, entered into the houses and licked, swept, inside the bedrooms, under the beds and tables. They were eyes that read one's mind, that lifted up the white roofs, and flogged things: intimacy, sleep, fatigue" (60). Although her eyes with binoculars are described metaphorically as an animal with tentacles, the metonymic associations again suggest an animal like the greyhound, tracking and sniffing its prey. Moreover, an animal that pursues and then licks its victim suggests a cruel type of play, instead of a need to fulfill basic hunger.

At other times, instead of using animal metaphors, Matia suggests that her grandmother plays with or intrudes in the lives of others by comparing her to a cruel demigod.[7] The first reference to her with godlike qualities is somewhat puzzling when Matia states: "She seemed like a beaten Buddha" (11). Her grandmother had been about to fall asleep and was complaining of her age and financial problems. Later, however, it appears that she might have been pretending to be weak, much like Borja was inclined to do, to evoke sympathy. Matia's other metaphors of her grandmother as a godlike figure do not demonstrate a beaten figure. For instance, Matia again describes her grandmother with her theater glasses:

There she would be, like a paunchy and peeled god, like an enormous and gluttonous mannequin, moving the strings of her marionettes.

> From her study, the little houses of the colonists with their yellow
> lights, with their women cooking and their shouting children, were like
> a diminutive theater. (60)

As before, Matia conveys the cruelty and selfishness she senses in
her grandmother. It is obvious that she empathizes with the people
Doña Práxedes observes, because she is so often scrutinized herself. Doña Práxedes tries to impose the same control on others
that she uses to menace Matia when she says, "We will tame you"
(13), implying that she—like a god—will mold Matia into the image
she wants.

The similarities that Matia notices between Borja and Doña
Práxedes, including their bravery, the appearance of their knuck-
les, and their manipulative natures, are further reinforced by a
comparable godlike metaphor equating Borja with a puppeteer.
Matia relates a dream she had:

> . . . I was dreaming that Borja held me captive with a chain and that
> he was pulling me toward him, like a fantastic puppeteer. I rebelled
> and wanted to shout—like when I was little, in the country—, but
> Borja held me firmly. (And why? Why? If I hadn't even committed any
> grave fault, why would he imprison me with the secret?) (25)

With Borja's and her grandmother's omnipresent intrusion on her
liberty, it is no wonder that Matia often remembers the iron bars
of the bed (and the sensation of being a trapped animal) from her
first night on the island. Borja's chain that controls and restrains
Matia in the dream also metonymically links the puppet with a
captive animal. Matia's questions within the parentheses indicate
that her feeling of being Borja's prisoner was one that continued
long after her dream, into the time she writes her narrative.

But Matia is not the only person who feels trapped by Borja:
Matia is also puzzled by the control that Borja exhibits over their
tutor, Lauro el Chino. Lauro is the son of the housekeeper Antonia,
and had been expelled from a seminary for a reason unknown to
Matia. Matia's expulsion from her school Nuestra Señora de los
Angeles (Our Lady of the Angels) gives her a commutuality with
Lauro, and perhaps makes her more sympathetic toward him.

However, after visiting Lauro's room with Borja one day, Matia
reveals another animal-like metaphor expressing her apprehensions about Lauro and Borja. As Lauro rubs her and Borja's shoulders, Matia observes in the mirror: "his hand that went up and
down, like the rats along the cornice of the roof, and although I
didn't say anything, I was filled with anxiety" (29). Watching

Lauro's hands creeping over their bare shoulders is exceedingly disturbing for Matia. While the rats seem to symbolize a sexual perversion on the part of Lauro, perhaps Matia formulates that possibility as a metaphor because she cannot consider it rationally at that point. Her metaphors, like Andrea's in *Nada,* communicate subconscious feelings. Because she observes Lauro's caresses reflected in a mirror, she also may experience an intensified perspective of the event, as when Andrea saw the reflection of her aunt Angustias's hand.

However, the metaphor comparing Lauro's hands to rats also incites curiosity about Borja's character, as he seems to guard the secret of Lauro's depravity in order to control him. If Lauro is ratlike, then Borja must be at least equally as menacing, if not worse. Also, despite the negative connotations of rats, they are still rather small animals that are likely to be trapped or killed by larger animals. In this sense one might perceive an element of compassion or empathy in Matia's attitude toward Lauro.

While Matia reveals her perceptions of both Lauro and Borja, that metaphor and the description of Lauro's room become more significant when Matia enters the church of Santa María the morning after she and Borja discover Manuel's father's body near their hidden boat. On entering the church, Matia experiences an uneasiness similar to her sensation in Lauro's room:

> In the enormous palate of Santa María there was something like a solemn fluttering of wings. And I asked myself if perhaps in the darkness of the corners bats were nesting, if there were rats fleeing or chasing each other among the gold of the altarpieces. (79)

Matia's fear of rats in the church recalls not only Lauro's depravity but also his dismissal from the seminary, suggesting that the church of Santa María is a representative of the Catholic Church in general. Thus the Church also seems to enclose perversions.[8] Because the rats may either be running away or pursuing each other, one again senses Matia's enigma about Lauro's character. She identifies him both with herself as a victim and with Borja as a predator. Much later, when Matia accompanies Borja as he makes his fraudulent confession, a bat inside the church flies against the walls and then dies. Matia relates on the same page that Lauro had been killed in the war, suggesting another link between Lauro and small "animals" that are victims of the Church, and resolving some of the ambiguity she feels about Lauro.

Since Matia's original metaphor about the rats also implicated Borja, he, too, becomes linked with the Church. Other metaphors equating Borja with "a little apocryphal monk" (26) and "the little Saint that resembled Borja" (80) reinforce similarities between Borja's attributes and the Church. Like Borja, the church of Santa María (and the Catholic religion it represents) intimates disguised corruption and manipulative power.

In addition to the rats, however, there are other significant descriptions in common between Lauro's room and the Church. While depicting Lauro's room, Matia stresses that the flowers by his window were "de un rojo encendido, con forma de cáliz, y tenían algo violento, como el odio cerrado de Lauro" (a burning red, in the form of a calyx, and they contained something violent, like Lauro's bottled-up hate, 29). The word "cáliz" here (meaning both the botanical term *calyx* and *chalice,* or communion cup) forms a link between the flowers in his room and Catholicism. Because they contain hate and something violent, they suggest the "cup of bitterness" of which Christ speaks, and convey that acrimony is an integral part of the Church.

After noticing Lauro's red flowers, Matia begins to feel similar negative reactions connected to other blossoms on the island. For instance, while Matia is in the church that morning, the smell of flowers there also reminds her of the red gladioluses by the staircase of her grandmother's house. Her thoughts stray to an incident when she was talking with Borja's friend Juan Antonio on that staircase. When Juan Antonio began to caress her leg, she was repelled by his sweaty hand as if it were a toad. She then stood up and pushed him into the flowers beside the stairs, which "exhaled a great perfume" (82). Matia has actually made a subconscious metonymic association between the incident in Lauro's room, the flowers in the church, and the flowers at her grandmother's house where Juan Antonio made a sexual advance that was disturbing, yet intriguing, to her. After that, all her references to flowers on the island contain unsettling erotic undertones that the reader links metonymically to the incidents with Lauro and Juan Antonio. Thus, flowers (especially red ones) come to symbolize sexual anxieties because of the repeated metonymic association between flowers and incidents that have erotic implications.[9]

Matia further connects, by way of more metaphors, the lush floral vegetation on the island with certain misgivings. For example, Matia explains her fear of the wind in storms as being like "the movement of an animal that might be climbing over the wall" (88). She then joins the perturbing feeling of the wind (which is

like an animal) to flowers: "the flowers that sprung forth unexpectedly, from the little gardens and orchards, behind the houses in the
town, inspired a similar fear in me: as if revealing some mystery
beneath the island, some reign, perhaps, beautiful and evil" (88).
Matia mentions that, in contrast to the little delicate flowers where
she used to live, the flowers on the island "dominated everything:
the air, the light, the atmosphere" (89). The flowers have a wild,
barbaric quality that is reminiscent of the savage animal metaphors.
Along with their sensual qualities, these feral blooms express
Matia's apprehension of becoming an adult. This whole process
of subconscious association was precipitated by the incident in
Lauro's room.

In addition to numerous connections stimulated by the visit to
Lauro's room, Matia's description of the church is another key
scene that illustrates her complicated intertwining of metonymic
associations. Not only does Matia link the cathedral to Lauro and
Borja, her first visit there is also the axis for a multitude of other
correlations. For example, Santa María's green cupula that shines
cruelly, "like a shout" (77), can also be linked to Matia's grandmother. Before entering the church, Matia stops to look at Jorge
de Son Major's white rooster, which is perched in the top of the
fig tree. Trying to hurry Matia, Doña Práxedes calls sharply to
her three different times: "Matia! Matia!" (76). The effect of her
grandmother's cry is like the cruel green "shout" of the cupula of
the church, as it produces in her a "rare sensation of confusion, of
fear" (76). Then, inside the church, the dark corners where Matia
imagines rats remind her of Doña Práxedes's house: "Grandmother's house was also gloomy and dirty" (79). The odor of the
church is also similar to that of her grandmother's house, including
the smell of flowers—like the gladioluses where she pushed Juan
Antonio.

Analogous words and descriptions also link the rooster in the
tree outside the church to Matia's grandmother and to the ideas of
the Catholic Church. For instance, Matia describes the rooster in
this way: "And there was the mysterious rooster that had escaped
from Son Major, white and shining. His choleric eyes, elevated
over the branches, looked at us defiantly" (76). When her grandmother begins to call, Matia looks at her: "Grandmother was looking at me with her smoke-rimmed eyes, beneath her white wave
of hair that shined in the sun" (76). The radiant white of the rooster
forms a link with the grandmother's snowy hair shining in the sun,
while the emphasis on their eyes also connects them. Doña Práxedes's impatient attitude suggests that her eyes would also be

angry and defiant. Later, in Matia's description of the coping of the church, she employs a metaphor that compares it with the rooster: "It was white, with borders and flecks of gold, and shone in the darkness (like the open and majestic wings of Son Major's rooster, still soaked from the storm, over the velvety leaves)" (81). The characteristics in common between the grandmother, the rooster, and the church form metonymic connections that increase Matia's apprehension as she enters Santa María Church.

In addition to the physical characteristics linking her grandmother and the aforementioned items, there are several connections between all these and the Crucifixion. For instance, Doña Práxedes's three shouts to Matia while she is watching the rooster in the fig tree foreshadow Matia's betrayal of Manuel; the incident is reminiscent of Christ's warning that Peter would deny Him three times before the cock crowed.[10] When Matia describes her grandmother as "a round, black mass, like a stone about to roll" (76), one is reminded of the stone rolled in front of the door to Christ's tomb. All the metonymic connections suggest negative aspects of the Crucifixion, while nothing recalls the promise of the Resurrection.

Matia reinforces the Church's ominous presence with more metaphors of animals pursuing and devouring prey. She likens walking beneath the arches inside Santa María to being "inside the whale, with its enormous ribs" (81), while she similarly portrays Doña Práxedes in her corset as "trapped like a whale" (75). Thomas feels these metaphors indicate that Matia is "figuratively being 'swallowed' by her grandmother."[11] Matia repeatedly expresses her feeling of being trapped and pursued by Borja, her grandmother, and even the Church, while metonymic connections tie more and more of her life to those original fearful metaphors of entrapment, suggesting a complicated web from which she cannot escape.

Another important allusion to confinement occurs in Matia's many references to wells.[12] She describes the atmosphere of the church as having "greenish-black humidity, like a well's" (79), and also remembers the well close to her grandmother's house:

(. . . At the end of the slope was the well, next to the stone staircase where I pushed Juan Antonio that afternoon. The well had a great dragon's head with its mouth open, covered with moss. And there was a very deep echo whenever something fell to the bottom. Even the movement of the chain made a horrifying echo. And I used to hang my head over the darkness of the well, toward the water. It was like smelling the dark heart of the earth.) (107)

Matia's references to the stairs where she pushed Juan Antonio, the dragon with the open mouth, and even the chain, metonymically link the well to the symbolism of the flowers and to her metaphors of being pursued. Like the flowers, the well attains a status of symbolism that expresses her apprehensions about growing up. The well is also where she first confides with Manuel: A dead dog had been thrown into his well, contaminating the water and suggesting death and entrapment. In this sense, the well (mentioned as a metaphor inside the church) functions metonymically, by connecting other situations and places, and metaphorically, by transmitting strong existential connotations.

All the metaphors and metonymic connections mentioned so far have illustrated Matia's negative and fearful perceptions of her situation on the island, like Andrea's exaggerated metaphor comparing her life to a nightmare in *Nada*. After Matia begins her friendship with Manuel, however, she establishes a camaraderie that offers her support: Manuel is "a little lost animal, just like me" (142). Matia's metaphoric description of a dove that flies over as she talks with Manuel is reminiscent of Andrea's timid expressions of hope: "We lifted our heads. A dove, one of the ones Grandmother raised, was crossing over the slope. Its flight seemed to rub against the roof of the air. Its shadow crossed over the ground, and something in it trembled, like a blue and fugitive star" (137). The dove here seems to acquire the characteristics of Andrea's positive metaphor in *Nada* comparing the stars to her liberty, but with religious intimations—somewhat like the dove that appeared to Noah after the flood.

Later, when Manuel, Matia, and Borja go to visit Jorge de Son Major, an association between the previously mentioned rooster and the doves transfers some positive characteristics to the rooster. Doña Práxedes's doves fly over the garden of Son Major while the young people are there, and he explains: "The doves come to my house, and my white rooster, according to what Sanamo says, prefers the fig tree in your garden (193). The exchange of the birds seems to indicate the possibility of a truce between the estranged siblings and, therefore, gives the rooster a positive aspect. The reader, at this point, might expect a softening in Matia's negative portrayal of her environment, much as Andrea experiences after her perspective of Angustias changes.

In a similar manner, after the visit to Jorge de Son Major's garden, Matia perceives a more positive connotation (for a time) to the church's stained-glass window of "San Jorge y el Dragón" (Saint George and the Dragon). Es Mariné (who owns a cafe at the port) suggests the connection between Son Major and the window: "Have you seen the stained glass window of Saint George? . . . That's what Jorge de Son Major was like" (107). Matia had formerly noticed the blood-red reflections on the church floor as sunlight entered through that stained-glass window (echoing the color of the flowers). The filtered light cast shadows that looked like the terrifying dragons she imagined her first night on the island. Until she talked with Son Major, the church's window had presented only negative connotations.

Thus Matia's friendship with Son Major and Manuel helps to reduce some of her fears. For instance, Matia scares away a lizard that "resembled Saint George's terrible dragon in the stained-glass window of Santa María" (147–48), simply by standing up after a conversation with Manuel.[13] Even the religious elements negatively linked to Borja, Doña Práxedes, and Lauro are more positive when associated with Manuel: "She knew that Manuel had been with the monks, and there was something monastic in him, perhaps in his voice, in his eyes" (137). Matia gains personal strength from her affiliation with Manuel and begins to overcome her feeling of being a little animal in a cage, neutralizing the overwhelming negative atmosphere she has expressed.

Nonetheless, after Borja's threat that Matia will go to reform school and his farcical confession to the priest Mosén Mayol and to Doña Práxedes, the negative connotations of the Church and the rooster—and of everything linked to them—return. In the last paragraph of the novel Matia again describes the rooster: "There was Son Major's rooster, with its choleric eyes, like two buttons of fire. Elevated and shining like a fistful of lime, and shouting . . . his horrible and strident song" (245). Once again, because of the link between the rooster and Matia's grandmother, the reader is reminded of Doña Práxedes's cruel animal-like qualities. But also inherent in that association is Judas's betrayal of Christ and Matia's complicity in the injustice done to Manuel. The rooster is no longer the sign of a truce but, rather, of enmity and coercion.

Moreover, Matia's embrace of Borja as she looks out at the rooster places her squarely in the domain of her nemesis: ". . . we went toward each other, as if pushed, and embraced each other" (244). Although Matia cannot cry about what has happened, Borja, oddly, begins to cry: "I felt his tears falling down my neck, entering into my pajamas" (244). Borja's tears metonymically echo the incidents when Matia compared Lauro's hand caressing her shoulder to a creepy rat and Juan Antonio's hand on her knee to a slimy toad. All three occasions contain implicit lecherous advances, but in the other two cases Matia, even though subconsciously, rejects or condemns the action with her metaphor. With Borja, however, she submits to his libidinousness, even justifies it, because of his tears. Despite having observed numerous times that Borja acts hypocritically in order to control others, she does not repel his embrace. She submits to his control and to all the lecherousness she had formerly condemned.[14]

Matia had previously been linked to Manuel because they both owned toy puppet theaters and because they were both "animalitos" (little animals). Likewise, there was a connection between Matia and Lauro because they were both dismissed from religious institutions. Therefore, their destruction means her downfall, too. Moreover, she contributed to Manuel's ruin, echoing the actions of Borja and her grandmother. In a similar manner Lauro was linked to Borja by his perversion and by the metaphor of the rats, and Manuel to Borja by the possibility that they were brothers.[15] The metonymic web linking Matia, Manuel, Lauro, Borja, the grandmother, the Church leaders, the antagonists in the war, and even the persecutors of the Jews centuries before,[16] suggests the circular shape and depth of the well that Matia mentions so frequently. The negative aspects eventually submerge and drown all positive images, suggesting a very pessimistic outcome for Matia and, ultimately, for all of Spain.

The way that Matute uses metaphor and metonymy throughout *Primera memoria* to suggest this very gloomy future can be explained further by examining the references to childhood stories as metaphoric mirrors and models.[17] One fairy tale in particular— Andersen's "The Snow Queen," with its main characters Kay and Gerda—illustrates the principle of negative imagery in *Primera memoria*. In "The Snow Queen," a mirror is invented by a demon that has the following characteristics: ". . . every good and pretty thing reflected in it shrank away to almost nothing. On the other hand, every bad and good-for-nothing thing stood out and looked its worst."[18] Likewise, the metaphors Matia utilizes reflect the negative, animalistic, and greedy aspects of her relatives, minimizing any good qualities. It is as if Matia were forced to look at the world reflected in the distorted mirror invented by the demon.[19]

Perhaps more significant, though, is the metonymic chaining of these negative metaphors to things that otherwise might be considered positive, like the adverse associations with flowers, the color white, and the Church, and the linking between characters in the novel. This metonymic chaining again echoes an idea from "The Snow Queen" when the distorted mirror breaks "into hundreds of millions and billions of bits."[20] The fairy tale relates that these bits did even more harm than the original mirror as each fragment had all the power of the whole. Often these fragments entered people's eyes or hearts and "distorted everything they looked at, or made them see that every thing was amiss."[21] The negative metaphors and the subsequent metonymic chaining likewise multiply and reveal Matia's subjective—even distorted—perspective. This analogy between the demon's distorted mirror and the use of metaphor and metonymy in *Primera memoria* also demonstrates the intrinsic parity between these tropes. Their combined effect in Matute's novel is an extremely adverse one, negating the positive aspects of Matia's childhood illusions, the positive associations of her relationship with Manuel and Son Major, and all the optimistic characteristics of fairy tales and religion.

Matia's references to fairy tales and biblical stories serve to underline the contrast between her ideal childhood and the unscrupulous adult world she must enter. As Bergmann points out, Matute "uses them consciously and skeptically to demonstrate the hypocrisy of the world Matia is beginning to understand."[22] Therefore, the seemingly positive and idealistic role models of "The Little Mermaid" (who aspires to attain an immortal soul through her love) and of Gerda (whose undying love for Kay gives her powers stronger than magic) are negated by inimical metonymic applications. While in *Nada* Andrea rejects patriarchal fairy-tale models that do not fit her aspirations, Matia finds the idealism in fairy tales to be dysfunctional as metaphorical role models in the adult world.

However, while she rejects the idealism of fairy tales, Matia does not completely reject the negative elements. Bergmann notes that Matia "forgets the last-minute transformation of the mermaid into a 'Daughter of the Air'; she recalls only the failure of love to save her life."[23] Likewise, she ignores the successful transition that Kay and Gerda make into adulthood while remaining "children at heart."[24] Instead, she remembers the effects of the distorted mirror, causing her to be distrustful and suspicious. Therefore, Matia remains bound to the effects of fairy tales, transferring their fatalistic elements, but not their idealism and positive lessons, to her perspective on life.

Another element from her childhood that Matia takes with her to Doña Práxedes's house is her black rag doll Gorogó, Deshollinador (De-sooter). Losing Gorogó at the end of the novel mirrors her loss of childhood and innocence.[25] Gorogó is also significant in that he seems to be based on the character of another of Andersen's fairy tales, "The Shepherdess and the Sweep."[26] Matia is similar to the Shepherdess in the story, with her love and dedication to her rag doll Gorogó, Deshollinador. In turn, Manuel (with his dedicated love for his family and his tenderness toward Matia) seems analogous to the Sweep and is, therefore, associated with Gorogó. Matia further extends the comparison by communicating intimately with Manuel: "And because of that I told him so many things. In a low voice, as if it were only for me or Gorogó" (142). Manuel, in a sense, begins to fulfill the role that Gorogó held during Matia's childhood. After Borja incriminates Manuel, Matia cannot find her doll Gorogó, strengthening the connection between Manuel and Gorogó: Manuel's future will be lost when he goes to reform school, and Matia will probably never see him again. Indeed, Gorogó seems to be a complicated metaphor, suggesting the chimney sweep in Andersen's tale, who, in turn, suggests Manuel.

However, in several respects, Gorogó is more than just a metaphor, because he also embodies metonymic characteristics (much like the mirror that includes both metaphoric and metonymic aspects in *Nada*). First of all, Gorogó represents an aspect of Matia's life taken with her from her childhood home to the girl's school—from which she was expelled—and then to the island, where she is undergoing a transition to adulthood. Much as the successive scenes of Andrea in the mirror recorded a temporal progression and maturation, Matia's communication with Gorogó records her change and development.

Additionally, Gorogó represents a difference in positional contiguity, like a mirror that reflects others' as well as Matia's viewpoint:[27]

> There, in the lodge, I would hold onto my little Black Gorogó, that I kept ever since I can remember. The one that I brought with me to Our Lady of the Angels, that the Subdirector tried to make me throw into the trash, whom I kicked, causing my expulsion. The one who sometimes was called Gorogó—the one for whom I drew little cities in the corners and margins of books, invented with the tip of a pen, with winding staircases, slender turrets, bell towers, and asymmetric nights—and other times was called simply Black, and was an unfortunate boy who cleaned chimneys in a very remote city of Andersen's. (116)

Because Gorogó sometimes is worthy of palatial cities created in Matia's imagination and other times has to clean chimneys—almost as if he were being punished—he represents the judgments that others have proffered about Matia, or that she has sensed from others. Therefore, Gorogó is a type of mirror, reflecting Matia's self-concept, as well as the judgment of others about how worthy she is or how disgraced when reproved. Matia stresses that Gorogó is not just an ordinary doll but, rather, "for traveling and to tell him injustices" (127). Since Gorogó is a vestige of Matia's self-concept that functions principally before she reaches puberty, Gorogó functions almost as "pre-mirror" in Matia's construction of her identity. Matia reveals that she out-grows Gorogó, although she still needs what he fulfilled: "I pulled out . . . my little Black, looked at his little face and asked myself why I couldn't love him anymore" (115).

The notion of Gorogó as Matia's "pre-mirror" fits with her expulsion from the school Nuestra Señora de los Angeles. The subdirector (most certainly a nun) tried to throw Gorogó into the trash and precipitated the kick that caused Matia to be expelled. Since mirrors are used for looking at one's self (considered by many to be an act of vanity) and for aiding women in their creation of an autonomous self, both actions might be considered sinful by a conservative nun. Kicking the subdirector of the convent demonstrates Matia's attempt to preserve her self-identity and her failure to conform to the rules set forth by the nuns of the convent, who typically would be striving toward selflessness and a certain homogeneity.

Gorogó also serves as a "pre-mirror" several times when his appearance is followed by relationships with other characters who function like mirrors for Matia. The first such encounter occurs in her aunt's room after Emilia discovers Gorogó hidden inside Matia's dress. This discovery inspires Emilia to attempt to communicate with and befriend her niece, an effort that is not entirely accepted by Matia (who finds her aunt's otherwise passive nature repulsive). After her aunt drifts off to sleep, however, Matia finds herself intrigued by Emilia:

> I sat up little by little, leaning over to look at her. It was like leaning over a well. As if suddenly Aunt Emilia had begun to tell me all her adult secrets, and as if I didn't know where to hide my face, full of fright and embarrassment. (128)

The allusion to looking down into a well suggests that Matia could at least partially see her own reflection, but since it would have been distant, dark, and frightening, she hid her face to avoid seeing herself that way. The well here functions like a mirror into the future and also contains the portentous symbolic implications seen in Matia's other references to wells.

The idea of reflection is further reinforced by Matia's curiosity about Emilia's polished nails and the surprising decision that she, too, would polish hers some day, acknowledging that she would emulate her aunt. But Matia concedes that the day she would polish her nails "would be in another life, almost in another world" (129). She can hardly visualize herself as the flabby, passive Emilia, trapped in her bedroom and waiting for her husband. This negative future reflection of herself is brought about directly because of her aunt's discovery of Gorogó. It should be remembered that Matia did not want to reveal him, suggesting that she did not want to look into the "mirror" her aunt provided. This reflection also suggests an element of inevitability of the future, another sort of entrapment for Matia.[28]

The negative future reflection seen in her aunt draws Matia to Emilia's dressing-table mirror to attempt to refute it:

I looked at my thin shoulders in the mirror, browned by the sun, where my white straps and locks of hair stood out, escaping from the braids that Aunt Emilia poorly fastened, with the glow from the sun like a halo. The reddish locks made me think: "With the light behind me I look like a redhead like Manuel, and everybody thinks I'm a brunette . . . I'm not a woman. Oh, no, I'm not a woman," and I felt as if a weight were lifted from me, but my knees were trembling. (129)

Matia's bronze shoulders and the coppery tints of her hair seem to belie her similarity to her aunt and to the image that others hold of her. Her elusive hair color suggests that she is more like Manuel and his red-headed mother, Sa Malene, whom Matia finds especially attractive because of her bravery and independence. Matia is relieved to find she is not yet a woman—she is not yet like her aunt—but the trembling of her knees foretells the probability of that fate.

At first, it appears that a more positive mirroring begins to occur for Matia shortly after she quietly escapes from her sleeping aunt's room and has her first significant conversation with Manuel. Because Matia voluntarily shows Gorogó to Manuel, it is evident that she wants to reveal her innermost thoughts. Matia openly states her disgust with the injustices that her family and the others in the town have committed against Manuel and his family, distancing herself from the established control that she detests. She speaks to Manuel as if she were confiding with Gorogó: "I told him so many things, as if it were only for me or Gorogó" (142). But in her relationship with Manuel, Matia sees herself as some sort of monster:

> It was me, only me, who was betraying myself all the time. It was me, myself, and nobody else who betrayed Gorogó and Never-Ever Land. I thought: "What kind of monster am I now? . . . What kind of monster, now that I am no longer a child and I'm not, by any means, a woman? (148)

Reflected off Manuel's goodness, Matia sees herself as sinful: "(I imagined myself as the Devil in Paradise)" (148). She knows that, in the same way that her grandmother and Borja are manipulative, she can also manipulate Manuel. For example, she orders: "Come with me, dummy" (149). Although Manuel is a replacement for Gorogó, the element of control that Matia exercises over Manuel also suggests that he becomes a puppet for her.

Matia's ambiguous control over (and dependence on) Manuel can be seen later when Borja demands that Manuel go with him to see Jorge de Son Major. Although Matia feels very uncomfortable about permitting Borja to exploit Manuel in order to visit Son Major, she ignores her feelings and says nothing. But during their meeting with Jorge, Matia clings to Manuel's hand much in the same way that she had clung to Gorogó in her first conversation with Manuel.

Just as Manuel served as a mirror for Matia earlier, Jorge does now—echoing only the positive aspects she saw in her aunt's dressing table mirror. After discerning a feeling of trust and love for Jorge, Matia reveals the reflection he provides for her:

> I lifted my head toward Jorge, kneeling next to him. But how could his gaze hurt so much? He untied my braid, my hair slipped out over the nape of my neck, and for a moment I felt his fingers brush my skin. He tried to fasten the braid again, but didn't know how. As it separated, I saw the spark of light in my hair and I heard him say:
> —How odd! It's not black, it's reddish. (199)

Jorge's comments about her hair assure her that she is not like her aunt; she again resembles Sa Malene, Manuel's mother. However, this positive reflection is also rescinded (much as her shaking knees belied her relief after gazing into her aunt's dressing-table mirror) when Matia seeks Jorge's help after Borja's "confession" incriminating Manuel. As Matia calls to Jorge, his balcony remains closed—even though Sanamo assures Matia that he is there: "It was as if there had never been anybody in that house, as if it had never even existed, as if we had made it all up" (243). Therefore, any positive reinforcement Jorge gives Matia also disappears, as if it had not existed.

All of Matia's mirror reflections ultimately confirm the uneasiness that she expressed upon first looking into the mysterious, steam covered mirror in her grandmother's bathroom:

> "Alice in the looking glass," I thought, more than once, contemplating myself in it, nude and desolate, with a great desire to cross its seemingly gelatinous surface. That very sad face—mine—with startled eyes was, perhaps, the very face of loneliness. (73)

Her lonely, sad reflection tempts her to escape from the frightening world of her grandmother's house by entering into a childhood story through her imagination, by fleeing reality, and even perhaps by abandoning her sanity.

In this instance, as well as in the other reflections noted, Matia does not have a positive identification within the mirror that would allow her to create her self-image in a normative manner. La Belle explains that almost any crisis can cause a separation between a woman's identity and her ocular presence. This separation is indicated by a difference in what a woman has become (what she sees in a mirror) and what she has perceived herself to be.[29] Normally, use of a mirror helps reconcile this difference, but for disturbed personalities the mirror continues to reflect an image that is not recognizable as self.[30] Matia does not identify with the image she sees, and escapes with distorted perspectives of prepuberty, fairy-tale models rather than progressing in her identity.

Matia's final act of mirroring—her written inspection of self—also reflects a disapproving image. Although for Andrea in *Nada* (and for many women) writing is a part of their continual self-discovery and ultimately their liberation, for Matia it reveals her acceptance of the "antinarcissism" that Cixous sees in male dominated society.[31] Whereas at first Matia condemns Borja's domineering and hypocritical nature, her later reflections tend to accept those qualities as normal: "He feigned innocence and purity, bravery, in front of our grandmother, when in truth—oh, Borja, perhaps now I'm beginning to love you—he was an impious, weak, and arrogant piece of man" (12). Her defense of Borja as she looks back demonstrates submission to him, just as embracing him after he incriminated Manuel made her an accomplice. It is indeed as if she has been "tamed" and "broken" as her grandmother vowed when she said "We will tame you" (13).

While Matia defends Borja, she denounces her own life as she looks back upon it in her writing:

(Here I am now, in front of this glass so green, and with a very heavy heart. Can it be true that life uproots scenes like that one? Can it be true that as children we live our whole lives, in one gulp, in order to repeat ourselves later, stupidly, blindly, without any sense whatever?) (20)

The green glass parallels Emilia's afternoon glass of cognac and hints that Matia has become like the aunt she despised. Thus Matia finds her adult life absurd and grotesque, while she reminisces longingly about the time when she still held herself in esteem. She attempts to relive her childhood by constantly referring to fairy tales and childhood stories as an adult: "(Never-Ever Land didn't exist and the Little Mermaid never got an immortal soul, because men and women don't love each other, and she was left with a pair of useless legs, and she turned into foam)" (243). As she repeatedly looks back on them, the fairy tales are distorted and stripped of their positive details. Thus Matia's reflection through writing is not a circular motion, but a downward, limiting spiral—a boring movement that creates the entrapping well, echoed by her gaze into the green glass as she writes.[32]

In *Nada*, Andrea's use of the mirror conforms to normal and progressive self-development, echoing La Belle's observations about women's use of the speculum: Andrea uses her reflection to contribute to her maturation. However, Matute's utilization of the same device conveys a bizarre distortion that traps Matia in the very reflection that she wishes to avoid. All of Matia's semblances reveal a negative image that she is forced to accept.

Matia's self-reflections reveal the same ominous, ensnaring qualities as the negative metaphors that were linked metonymically to all facets of her life. This duplicated fatalism evident from the examination of metaphor, metonymy, and mirror images in *Primera memoria* can be contrasted with the use of these tropes to reveal Andrea's progress in *Nada*. In *Primera memoria* that type of growth is not seen. Even though metaphoric expression similarly reveals Matia's emotive reactions while living with her relatives during a year of adolescent transition, metonymic extensions do not change Matia's perception of her situation. Instead, the original negative metaphors are extended metonymically to encompass everything, resulting in a pervasively ominous description that encloses her entire world. These metaphors function like the demon's distorted mirror that, broken and dispersed, causes problems everywhere. This diffused negativity multiplies to include the society and history of Spain, as well as Matia's individual aberrant development. The "monster" of Matia's story grows to dynamic proportions, condemning her to a life of self-hatred and reversing the autonomy seen at the end of *Nada*. Matia's distorted "mirror" traps her in a heinous and savage world from which she cannot escape.

But while Matia's inner development is thwarted, María del Carmen Riddel points out that Matia is a survivor.[33] She does reach adulthood and look back on what happened in her adolescence to attempt to make sense of it. This cyclical look backward to the incidents that inhibit the freedom felt in childhood is potentially indicative of the "process of rebirth" in midlife or later. Matia's reevaluation of her life holds the possibility of renewed liberation, and disperses fragments of experience and resistance to female readers. In feminine narrative, even texts that appear to submit to societal control over women reveal aspirations that inspire others. By the mere act of writing, Matia and other women writers empower themselves and others.[34]

Before writing *Primera memoria,* censors prohibited publication of Matute's novel *Las luciérnagas* (Fireflies), which she rewrote and published two years later in 1955 as *En esta tierra* (In This Land). She reveals that this censorship conditioned her toward the gravely serious "habit of self-censure" causing her to reveal many things in *Primera memoria* and *Los hijos muertos* (Dead children) "in a pedantic form, nearly absurd, so that . . . they could 'pass' the censorship. . . ."[35] This elaborated style that includes metaphoric expression and indirect mirroring continues into the next two novels of the *Los mercaderes* (The merchants) trilogy.[36]

Los soldados lloran de noche (1964, *Soldiers Cry by Night*) continues the animal imagery of *Primera memoria,* describing the sea as "quiet, tame, like a sleeping animal" when Manuel Taronjí is released from reform school.[37] Although this second novel of the trilogy concentrates on Manuel, the main protagonist is Marta, the young widow of a political friend of José Taronjí (Manuel's murdered father). A calloused and numbed Manuel seeks Marta to discover the meaning behind José's murder, and to avenge his family. As Marta voices her thoughts to Manuel—using him as a mirror to reflect the meaning her dead husband brought to her hard, empty life—Manuel, too, begins to soften. But before he has a chance to contemplate his own image, they are massacred by Spanish soldiers, nullifying any growth through mirroring.

La trampa (1969, *The Trap*), the last novel of the trilogy—like *Primera memoria*—reveals that Matia is trapped by her own warped reflection in the mirror. When Matia and her son Bear return to the island home to celebrate Doña Práxedes's centennial birthday, both mother and son become ensnared in a plan that results in Bear's murdering a man in a fatuous act of vengeance. Matia finds Bear's friend Mario (the instigator of a plan to avenge Mario's murdered father) hidden in one of the unoccupied rooms of her grandmother's house. With the first glance into Mario's eyes, Matia has the uncanny feeling of looking into a mirror: "Then I thought I saw myself . . . reflected in another mirror, and another, and another."[38] Mario's and Matia's fate—as well as Bear's—are magnetized and molded by their heritage.

Mario experiences three days of self-discovery—via a physical and emotional relationship with Matia—that tardily convince him not to involve Bear in his meaningless revenge. But as Mario and Matia revel in their lovemaking, Bear slays Mario's father's murderer single-handedly. Just as Matia's body formed Bear like "a repugnant lump of tapioca," Mario "formed [his] little, particular, and obscene vengeance."[39] Matia's and Mario's union traps Bear in a tragic providence that ensnares and ravages all three of them, echoing the proliferating evil power of the fairy tale's broken mirror mentioned in *Primera memoria*. *La trampa*'s focus on four people's lives, instead of only Matia's, emphasizes the dispersal of corruption in society and manifests a more complicated novelistic structure than *Primera memoria*'s. But Matia's pensive writing as she gazes into the green glass in *Primera memoria* suggests the cyclical look back (and possibility of rebirth) occurred after the devastating events of *La trampa,* giving a more optimistic influence to the trilogy.

Although *Primera memoria* and *Nada* relay the development of young women who are somewhat precocious and independent at the outset, the next novel examined—Mercè Rodoreda's *La plaça del Diamant* (1962, Diamond Plaza)—traces the maturation of a relatively uneducated woman, whose childhood has already "tamed" her to espouse society's patriarchal norms. Indeed, Natàlia (Rodoreda's protagonist) might be seen as a more typical female from the era of the Spanish civil war, who has accepted her role as woman in a male-dominated society.[40] Rodoreda reveals a more subtle, long-term development of her protagonist, while her use of metaphor and metonymy in *La plaça del Diamant* creates an aesthetically fulfilling work.

3

Metaphor and Metonymy: A Bridge Between the Gaps in *La plaça del Diamant*

La plaça del Diamant (1962, Diamond Plaza) by Mercè Rodoreda has been translated into at least thirteen languages and published throughout the world.[1] Like *Nada* and *Primera memoria,* the protagonist of *La plaça del Diamant,* Natàlia, is an adolescent female whose mother has died. However, instead of expressing aspirations of liberty and autonomy, Natàlia seems confused about her role and tends to accept the advice of others. While Andrea and Matia are well educated, atypical, and nonconforming as young girls, Natàlia is more compliant and passive and never refers to anything she has read. Unlike the other two novels, where the fictional events occur within about a year, Natàlia's quest for self-identity transpires over more than two decades of her life. Between her courtship and the marriage of her daughter, Natàlia complies with the role of submissive female prescribed by the norms of Spanish society, feeling guilty about the confusion she senses. Finally, after her daughter's wedding, Natàlia perceptively sees her life in retrospect and emerges from her disorientation and subjugation.[2]

While Andrea's and Matia's retelling of their stories seems to be a written narration, Natàlia's relation has informal, oral qualities and is directed to an equally unpretentious listener, supporting the notion that she is relatively uneducated. She tells her story as if she were speaking to a close friend of the same social class.[3] But through Natàlia's unaffected monologue, readers detect a rich and intellectually fulfilling work that suggests Rodoreda's protagonist suffers from a lack of confidence and experience rather than from inadequate acumen.

Rodoreda utilizes a variety of techniques to successfully intice readers into believing Natàlia's story is so guileless while it creates such a profound impact on them.[4] One technique that Glenn observes is the use of "gaps and blanks" that stimulates readers to interact with the text.[5] Readers must creatively fill the gaps left by

Natàlia's unvoiced emotions and unspoken criticisms, and clearly must particpate in the mental state of the presumably unquestioning narrator/protagonist.[6]

The possibility of a breach between Natàlia and her more literate readers is negated by critics who have noted the presence of mythic, allegoric, and symbolic elements that are ultimately very fulfilling.[7] However, Rodoreda's use of metaphor and metonymy is essential in the creation of Natàlia's naivety as she conveys her symbolically rich story and in bridging any gap between the protagonist and the readers. Indeed, while defining metaphor, Terence Hawkes notes, "the reader is forced to make an imaginative 'completion' from within his own experience of what the metaphor figuratively suggests." By its very nature, metaphor accounts for at least part of the gap to be filled by readers, and Hawkes's quote hints at a point in common between a narrator's use of metaphor and the readers' role.[8]

In contrast to Andrea's metaphors in *Nada* and Matia's in *Primera memoria* that express apprehension about their situation and their desire for liberty, most of the metaphors Natàlia employs are initially simple, almost trivial ones, often suggested to her by others to explain basic functions of life. These uncomplicated metaphors are then expanded throughout the novel by their metonymic association to diverse incidents that occur in Natàlia's life, giving the original metaphors added complexity and meaning and illustrating Natàlia's sensitive consciousness. The expanded metaphors become replete with meaning that readers must interpret and unravel.

Natàlia's self-scrutiny by directly gazing into a mirror is very limited, demonstrating her lack of confidence and obscured self-identity. But she eventually begins to consider herself in a new way. Indeed, her narration of her life demonstrates the same positive "mirroring" as Andrea's written account in *Nada*. Thus the importance of the metaphor and metonymy in the work again comes to the forefront, as many of Natàlia's attempts to look at and define herself are deflected through metaphoric mediums, such as mother-daughter "mirroring" and the "mirror-effect" as she retells her story.

Natàlia's story begins when she is a teenager and meets Quimet, a young self-employed carpenter, at a dance in the Plaça del Diamant in prewar Barcelona. While dancing, Quimet renames Natàlia "Colometa"[9] and affirms that she will marry him within a year. After marrying, their children, Antoni and Rita, are born within several years. The appearance of a wounded *colom* at their flat initiates Quimet's dreams of an ideal life raising and selling *co-loms*.[10] When Quimet's carpentry business falters, Natàlia seeks employment as a housekeeper in addition to caring for her own home, children, and the rapidly multiplying *coloms*. Exhausted and inundated with the noises and smells of the birds overtaking their home, Natàlia begins to destroy the eggs to save her own sanity. After Quimet leaves for the war and is killed, Natàlia and the children are starving to death when she decides to kill them and herself.[11] When she attempts to obtain nitric acid to carry out her resolution, the store owner, Antoni, senses her despair, offers her a job, and gives her some food. After several months, Antoni asks her to marry him, and although her children adjust well to the marriage, Natàlia is filled with guilt. Not until her daughter's wedding can Natàlia free herself from the memory of Quimet and start to accept herself and her new life with Antoni.

From the outset of her story, Natàlia's naïveté is apparent in her use of metaphoric clichés that help her to understand the circumstances in her life. For example, when Natàlia relates the story of her wedding night she relates a metaphoric expression that the readers recognize as an "old wives's tale":

I had always been afraid of that moment. They said that you got to it by a path of flowers and that you left by a path of tears. And that they deceived you with happiness... Because when I was little I had always heard that they split you open. And I had always been afraid of dying split open. (63)[12]

Her fear about her first sexual intercourse—that she will be split in half by it—and, therefore, be led down the road of tears, causes her literally to burst into tears and confess her terror to Quimet. In contrast, this metaphoric cliché that reveals Natàlia's innocence and fear is probably initially humorous to the readers.

However, a comparable metaphoric expression, rooted in a similar superstitious and uneducated belief, develops a meaning that is much more imaginative and satisfying. After the birth of her first child, Antoni, Natàlia expresses wonder and dismay about her newborn child and her frustrations while trying to care for him:

I moved him, and he cried. I bathed him, and he cried. He was nervous. . . . When he was naked he cried harder than when he was dressed and he moved his toes as if they were fingers and I was afraid he would pop. That he would split open at the navel. Because the umbilical cord hadn't fallen off yet and you could see that it was about to fall off. The first day I saw him as he had been made, when the midwife taught me

how I had to hold onto it to bathe him, she told me as she put him in
the washbasin:

—Before we're born we're like pears: we've all been hanging by
this cord.

. . . And they've always told me that the navel is the most important
part of the person. (79)

The metaphor comparing people to pears again may cause readers
to chuckle and feel superior to Natàlia's credulous acceptance of
this explanation. This metaphor seems to fit into Umberto Eco's
classification of the "merely 'acceptable'" in terms of metaphorical
expression.[13] It is "acceptable" because the two things being compared—a child attached to its mother by the umbilical cord, and a
pear hanging from a tree—can be easily linked together.

In this case readers can effortlessly trace what Eco calls "the
metonymic chain" behind the metaphor in order to see what makes
the metaphor between the umbilical cord and the pear possible.[14]
Both a mother and a pear tree are elements in nature capable of
reproduction. The baby is attached to the mother and nourished
through the umbilical cord, while the pear is nourished through
the stem attached to the tree. This metaphor, although somewhat
appealing, is too obvious and missing the tension that would make
it more fulfilling. It does, however, reinforce Natàlia's innocent and
sensitive personality. To Natàlia, the idea is important and helps
explain a perplexing matter in a simple and natural way.

The metonymic chain involving the umbilical cord becomes
more complicated, however, as references to it are repeated and
associated with other ideas throughout the novel. Later, when Natàlia begins to destroy the eggs of their *coloms,* she has a recurring
nightmare that involves the idea of the umbilical cord. The metaphorical connotations have become much more complex and the
metonymic chain is more obscure:

> And I would wake up at midnight, as if they were pulling from inside
> with a cord, as if I still had an umbilical cord and they were pulling me
> out whole through the navel and with that big tug all of me went out:
> eyes and hands and fingernails and feet and my heart with a channel
> in the middle with a big, black clot of dark blood, and my toes lived
> as if they were dead; it was the same. Everything was sucked out of
> nothing again, through the umbilical cord that had dried out attached
> to it. And all around that tug that pulled me there was a cloud of pigeon
> feathers, spongy, so that nobody would realize anything. (140)

The umbilical cord here is linked not only to the birth of children
but to the obstructed incubation of the *coloms* and to Natàlia's

guilt. The unraveling of the metonymic chain behind this dream cannot be completely accomplished, however, without examining the progression of the *coloms* as the key metaphor within the chain.

Although the metaphoric meaning of the *coloms* is the most important and fully developed of the work, it, too, begins as a simple metaphor that Eco might call "merely acceptable." The chain begins in the first chapter when Quimet renames Natàlia "Colometa."[15] Quimet creates the metaphor of Natàlia as *coloma* shortly after meeting her at the dance in the Plaça del Diamant:

> . . . and he said . . . you and I will dance a waltz in the Diamond plaza ... whirl and whirl... Colometa. I looked at him very uncomfortably and told him that my name was Natàlia and when I told him that my name was Natàlia he laughed again and said I could only have one name: Colometa. (22)

It is easy to see the metonymic process Quimet follows to name Natàlia "Colometa" as she twirls in her white dress with the starched petticoats while they dance in the plaza, where there was—quite possibly—an abundance of *coloms*. The immediate physical attraction that the two felt while dancing is suggestive of the mating dances of birds.

In addition to the facile reconstruction of the metonymic chain, the metaphor naming Natàlia after a bird is a fundamental type of metaphor that Leví-Strauss recognizes in the most primitive societies.[16] Quimet is comparing the life of birds to his own world, in a very basic and rudimentary manner. Moreover, the introduction of a wounded *colom* into their home allows them to continue making metaphorical associations between the bird world and their own lives.

Whereas at first there was only the connection Natàlia = *coloma*, the adoption of the *colom* as a pet permits Quimet to associate it with his personal idealized dream of life, of which Natàlia naturally plays an important part. They construct an elaborate *colomar*, introduce other *coloms*, and Quimet begins to expound his plans for the future:

> Quimet was so happy... He said that we could have eighty pigeons and with the chicks that the eighty would have we could already begin to think about closing the store, and even buying some land soon, and Mateu would make him a house with the profits. (124)

Although Quimet's view of the *coloms* reveals his dreams and goals, Natàlia's perspective is more practical. She is the one who has to feed and water the birds, and she cleans up their messes. Therefore, another metonymic divergence is expressed by her feelings: *coloms* = work, problems. She explains: "I could only hear pigeons cooing. I killed myself cleaning up pigeon messes. I smelled like pigeons all over. Pigeons on the terrace, pigeons in the apartment; I dreamed about them. The pigeon girl" (124). While exhausting herself with so much work, Natàlia finds out Quimet is giving the birds away, adding to their financial difficulties. But whenever she complains to Quimet about this situation he seems to develop another mysterious pain in his leg.[17]

When Natàlia begins to destroy the eggs, it is not only because of her dislike of caring for the birds. Since Quimet has constructed an entry between the *colomar* and one of their bedrooms, giving the *coloms* more space, Natàlia finds them all through the house when anyone leaves the door open. They spill over into the house, constantly entering and leaving "like in a lunatic's game" (126). The birds intrude into the flat and into Natàlia's own essence:

> . . . I felt the cooing of pigeons and my nose was filled with the odor of pigeon fever. It seemed to me that everything about me, my hair, my skin and clothes, smelled like pigeons. When nobody was looking I smelled my arms and I smelled my hair when I fixed it and I didn't understand how I could have that odor near my nose, the odor of pigeons and baby pigeons nearly choked me. (126)

The quiet destruction of the eggs represents a basic struggle to preserve the inner space of her being—her own sanity—and becomes an absolute necessity for her self-preservation.

But destroying the birds's eggs is not an easy task for Natàlia. Although they symbolically represent the conflict between Quimet's dream and her necessity to preserve her own psyche, they also have become metonymically associated with her own children. She says of the *coloms* at one point: "They seemed like people" (127), echoing Leví-Strauss's idea about the tendency to associate human lives with the lives of animals.[18] Once, when she returns from the house where she has been working, she finds that the children have let the *coloms* inside and they are all playing together. She later expresses her association between the birds and her children to their friend Mateu: "I explained to him that the children and the pigeons were like a family... that the pigeons and children were all one" (135).

Therefore, the guilt Natàlia feels as she destroys the eggs (reflected in the previously mentioned dream involving the umbilical cord) is caused in part by the metonymic association between the birds and her children. The children were attached to her by the umbilical cord, the *coloms* = children, and the destruction of the eggs = tugging at the umbilical cord (cutting off the life sustenance). Natàlia does not express all these associations, rather, it is ultimately up to the readers to form the connections. Obviously there are also associations of herself as *coloma* and Quimet's dreams represented by the birds; obliterating the eggs is both necessary and detrimental.

Thus the introduction of the *coloms* into the flat begins a process whereby the original cliché-like metaphor of Natàlia as *coloma* begins to acquire new meaning. While it once expressed a novel idea to Natàlia and Quimet, readers may be tempted to consider such a trite metaphor as "my little pigeon" ironically, or as a parody of a metaphor.[19] But the original metaphor acquires a new literal level with the adoption of the *coloms* as part of the family and with the new associations that develop when Natàlia constantly hears their cooing ringing in her ears, and her skin and hair smell of them. The name Colometa and metaphors involving the *coloms* mean much more than when they were first introduced: They include a cliché along with a new literalness. Likewise, saying "These birds are like my family" would seem banal if the *coloms* did not actually play with the children and did not become nearly as significant in Natàlia's and Quimet's lives. Therefore, these metaphors become recharged with meaning, and the readers no longer consider them as clichés.[20]

The parallel between literal and poetic expression is continued when Natàlia's destruction of the *coloms* coincides with the beginning of the civil war in Spain, allowing more metonymic linking. Natàlia says: "And meanwhile I dedicated myself to the great revolution with the pigeons, come what may, as a thing that had to be very short" (141). After speaking about her "revolution," Natàlia continues by describing Quimet's participation in the war, allowing the two ideas to be connected. Later, when she learns that Quimet has been killed, she goes out to the terrace for a breath of air and to think. The nearly simultaneous discovery there of the last, and original, *colom* suggests another metonymic divergence involving *coloms*:

And inside, at the back, with its feet up, was a pigeon, the one with the spots. Its neck feathers were wet with the sweat of death and its little eyes rheumy. Bones and feathers. I touched its feet, I only ran my finger over them, doubled back, with the little toes hooked over.

It was already cold. And I left it there, in what had been its house. And I closed the door. And I returned to the apartment. (171)

Readers are left to make their own metaphor comparing Quimet and the initial bird that inspired his dreams (Quimet = *colom*), and to feel the emotion that Natàlia's words only suggest.

By this point in the novel, readers are enticed to make other new metaphors on their own. Often these metaphors are not obvious without reconstruction of the metonymic chain. For instance, readers can convert a simple statement about the papers and trash blowing in the streets at the end of the war into a metaphorically rich image because of the foregrounding of simple metaphors enhanced by metonymic linking.[21] Natàlia observes:

> And they began to go away. The shopkeeper below said: look, look, so many newspapers and so many posters... hey... hey... to cross the world. And the last day it was windy and cold and the wind made the ripped papers fly and they filled the streets with white spots. (176)

The papers flying through the streets remind readers of skeletal or ghostly birds, like the last *colom* that was only bones and feathers, of Quimet's death (and the deaths of so many others) caused by the war, of the starving and nearly skeletal children waiting in the apartment for food, and of the death of dreams and hopes. The image of the *colom* is no longer only one that lives in an elaborate blue *colomar,* it is also depicted by trash blowing in the street, reflecting the economic depravity of the people of Spain and their lack of hope after the war.

The hopelessness and utter despair that Natàlia feels at this time result in her plan to kill her children and herself to hasten their imminent death by starvation. The figurative language in the novel after her decision tends to echo previous metaphors and to tie them all together, resulting in a complicated interweaving. This fusion of metaphors (previously observed with the *coloms* and the umbilical cord) continues and increases. Natàlia relates another dream after her decision to kill the children, linking her children to the eggs she destroyed:

> . . . they were no longer children. They were eggs. And the hands seized the children, all made of shell and with the yolk inside, and lifted them very high and began to shake them: at first unhurriedly and then furiously, as if all the anger about the pigeons and the war and about having lost had been put in those hands that were shaking my children. (182)

Natàlia's guilt after her earlier dream about the *coloms* and the umbilical cord is echoed here, and readers are reminded of her need to destroy the birds' eggs. She feels a similar exigency and guilt about killing her children and herself.

Natàlia's decision to use a funnel to pour nitric acid down the throats of her starving children while they sleep metonymically cements two images previously linked, seemingly, only by coincidence. Early in the novel Natàlia relates: "I remember the pigeon and the funnel, because Quimet bought the funnel before the pigeon had come" (82). The *colom* associated with the funnel is the original wounded one, the one that inspired Quimet to build the *colomar* and to dream of raising numerous birds. The arrival of the wounded *colom* and Quimet's purchase of a funnel, associated simply because they occurred on the same day, seems like an unimportant detail at the beginning of the novel.

But planning to use that funnel to kill her children results in a chain that leads from the children back to the *coloms* and the eggs she destroyed. Readers recall that *coloms* = children and think about the associations of the umbilical cord and of the funnel with both children and *coloms*. The repetition and mixing of the various images come together in a dizzying sort of complexity and help to create the feeling of enclosure and confinement that Wyers describes in the novel. The association of these images reflects Natàlia's confusion and guilt as she unconsciously associates images representing love and murder, rebellion and entrapment, destruction and creation. At this point, Natàlia's funnel seems to represent the same limiting, downward circular movement as Matia's fascination with the well in *Primera memoria*.[22]

Natàlia's dizzy spells in the second half of the novel parallel the whirling feeling readers perceive as the various metaphorical images intertwine and twirl together. After Natàlia wanders into a church, desperate and weak from hunger, her hallucinations climatically confirm her decision to kill her children using the funnel. The raindrops she describes outside the church are converted into little balls "that spilled over the altar" (186), like the *coloms* that spilled through her house. The following quotation illustrates the convergence of the various images:

> Those little balls were like fish eggs, like the eggs that fish have inside in that little sack, that's like a child's house when it's born, and those little balls were born in the church as if the church were the womb of a big fish. (186)

The memories of the birth of her own children and of the *coloms* and eggs reappear. Images from her dream of the destruction of the eggs surface as the little balls acquire the color and odor of blood. The voices of the people singing in the church also enter into her hallucination:

> . . . the singing of angels rose up, but it was the song of furious angels that scolded the people and told them that they were facing the souls of all the dead soldiers in the war and the song said that they should look at the evil that God was spilling over the altar; that God was showing them the evil that had been done so that all of them would pray to end the evil. (186–87)

The evil of war spills across the altar, echoing the previous images. Birth, death, war, children, and *coloms* are mixed together with other images showing the effects of hunger, grief, guilt, and madness on Natàlia.

With the intervention of Antoni, the shopkeeper who provides some material stability for Natàlia and her children, she no longer is compelled to carry out her desperate plan. When Natàlia abandons that undertaking, she also seems to reject the constricted view of life that the funnel represents. As Natàlia's situation changes, her metaphors (including the association with the funnel) also begin to be modified by their association with different items, reflecting her altered reality and mental state after her marriage to Antoni.[23] For example, Natàlia's perspective of the *coloms* becomes more like Quimet's former idealized picture of them and represents her idealization of her earlier life with him. She describes her repeated vision of the *coloms* in the same blue *colomar* as before:

> Everything was the same, but everything was beautiful. They were pigeons that didn't make messes, that didn't have vermin, that only flew through the air above like God's angels. They escaped like a shout of light and wings above the terraces... (222)

The metonymic chaining is continued, now including the idea of God and the angels from her hallucination in the church, but her perspective has changed, reflecting the transformation in her life. But the repetition of the image of the *coloms* forces readers to include the old associations as well as the new—just as Natàlia's own memories affect her perception of her life at any given moment.

Other images change as well to reflect the transformation in her life. For instance, the eggs of the *coloms* that once overflowed into her house, and that changed to little balls crowding and multiplying in the church, are echoed by a string of pearls that breaks and spills over the dance floor after she dances with her son at her daughter's wedding. The pearls, too, gain human characteristics— like the eggs and the balls: "I took the pearls out of the coin purse and put them in a little box and I kept one and later I dropped it into a seashell so that it could keep the sea company" (244). She again unifies her past and present, inducing readers to synthesize these elements in the consideration of her present state, when she continues her thoughts about the pearl: "I thought that the seashell was a church and that the pearl inside was pastor Joan and the hummm... hummm... a song of angels who only knew how to sing that song" (244). Readers are reminded of Natàlia's wedding to Quimet by mossèn Joan, her hallucinations in the church when she thought she heard enraged angels singing, and perhaps some moments in between. The juxtaposition of these varied experiences suggests that Natàlia is synthesizing a new—and somewhat paradoxical—meaning of her life.

Likewise, the associations are cumulative when Natàlia ventures out in the early morning after her daughter Rita's wedding and returns to the Plaça del Diamant with a knife. She draws the readers though scenes of the past by using a metaphor comparing the plaza to a funnel and mentioning small flying shadows, which once again recall the *coloms:*

> And I turned my face to the door again and with the point of the knife in block letters I wrote Colometa, fairly deep, and, without knowing what I was doing, I began to walk and the walls were carrying me, not my steps, and I entered Diamond Plaza: an empty box made of old houses and the sky for a lid. And in the middle of that lid, I saw some little shadows fly and all the houses began to swing as if everything were submerged in water and someone began to slowly agitate the water and the walls of the houses stretched up and began to grow together and the hole in the lid was stretching and beginning to form a funnel. (249)

Natàlia begins to scream into the imaginary funnel, much as she screamed when Antoni, her first child, was born. Readers remember all the past associations of the plaza, the *coloms,* and the funnel; but at the same time they are taken beyond all the old meanings to a new and still undefined expression of Natàlia's life. There is a feeling of termination and death when Natàlia carves "Colometa" into the door of her old home, as if for a tombstone. But, at the same time, a suggestion of change and birth appears, as if Natàlia were emerging from the fluid of a womb with her scream. The image of the funnel is converted into a birth canal, altering its former constrictive meaning and delivering Natàlia from her restricted confinement and guilt.

The ambiguous synthesis of old and new meanings continues until the last sentence of the novel with a simple but poetic and symbolically charged repetition of old images mixed with new feelings. Natàlia climbs back into bed with Antoni after her experience in the plaza and embraces him (probably for the first time) to warm him: "as I ran my hand over his belly, I found his navel and I put my finger inside to close it, so that all of him wouldn't empty out through there... All of us, when we are born, are like pears..." (252). Although the images are old and already filled with quantities of previous metonymical associations for Natàlia and for the readers, Natàlia applies them to a new feeling of tenderness toward Antoni, encompassing both the old and the new, but revealing a new sense of liberation for her. For the first time she feels free enough from her past to return some of the affection that Antoni has cautiously tried to express toward her during the years of their marriage.

A new feeling of peace emerges from Natàlia's description of some birds in the last few lines of the novels, linking her sentiments with theirs in a different way:

> ... some shrieking birds that came down from the leaves like lightening, got into the puddle, bathed in it with their feathers bristled and mixed the sky with mud and with beaks and with wings. Happy... (253)

The birds are happy mixing the perfect reflection of the sky with the mud in the puddle; a combination, perhaps, of the ideal with reality. For Natàlia, at any rate, it is a synthesis of the past with the present that reveals a new state of peace and contentment with her life. Also indicative of her growth and change is her reference to "birds" instead of more *coloms*. She no longer sees her life as controlled by ideals imposed upon her but, rather, has begun to define her own philosophy in life, seeing happiness in situations that do not conform with what Quimet and patriarchal society have prescribed for her.

Just as Natàlia's metaphors connect diverse elements—birth and death, past and present, ideal and reality, old and new—the use of metaphor and metonymy by Mercè Rodoreda in *La plaça del Diamant* serves to bridge the gap between her unpretentious narrator and more sophisticated readers. Even though readers at first may note the simplicity of Natàlia's expressions, they later find her metaphorical expressions challenging, as they acquire depth by added metonymical associations, revitalization by integration with literal meaning, complexity from interweaving with other images, ambiguity, and finally change—reflecting Natàlia's growth. Readers are pulled along with Natàlia, via her metaphors and ensuing metonymic associations, to empathize with her guilt and enclosure and then to feel her sense of freedom from confinement.

While at first the readers sense a gap between their position and Natàlia's and a disparity between what she says and what they understand, they can also detect a void in Natàlia's perception of her own identity. The lack of mirror scenes or other reflective devices that would reveal what Natàlia thinks of herself creates more of the "empty spaces" that Glenn finds so significant in the novel.[24] Just as Andrea's refusal to look at her face in the mirror at the beginning of *Nada* demonstrated her lack of positive identity, Natàlia's exclusion of comments about herself, how she looks, and what she thinks about herself demonstrates an even weaker self-identity.

Natàlia does comment several times about her lack of self-identity and her confused self-image, saying: "but what was happening to me was that I didn't know very well why I was in the world" (47). She even reveals that this poorly formed self-concept is frightening to her: "At home we lived without words and the things that I carried around inside me scared me because I didn't know if they were mine..." (34). Natàlia attributes the stifled communication in her family first to her parents' repeated arguments followed by silence and then to the death of her mother. Although her father remarried, his new wife never established a close relationship with Natàlia, and she describes herself going through life like a cat "with its tail down" (34), a metaphor which conveys her lack of self-pride.

It is apparent that Natàlia never experienced the positive mother/daughter mirroring that Ena and her mother enjoy in *Nada,* and in which Andrea is able to participate after becoming the "adoptive" daughter of Ena's parents. Natàlia and her mother seem to suffer from the "antinarcissism" Cixous describes,[25] and their deflated self-image results in their silence. Natàlia, like Andrea in the beginning of her narration, and like Matia in *Primera memoria,* does not have a positive female role model from which she can "mirror" her identity.

Because of her doubts about her own identity, it is easy for Natàlia to accept the passive role of dutiful wife and mother imposed upon her by a patriarchal society. Quimet further complicates her self-identification by imposing the name "Colometa" on her, thereby denying her identity as Natàlia. It is not surprising, therefore, that Natàlia becomes fascinated with a display of dolls in a department-store window. The dolls typify what Quimet wants her to be: attractive, docile, submissive, quiet—an entity for whom he can create an identity and a name. Metaphorically, the dolls serve as a mirror for her as she tries to fulfill the role that her husband wants her to play.

For example, one day when Natàlia runs into Pere (the boyfriend she broke off with to marry Quimet), he tells her he hardly recognized her, causing her to think about her own identity and her role as Quimet's wife. Natàlia's reaction is to go to look at the doll display. Although she tells Quimet about seeing Pere, she does not tell him about the dolls: "And I didn't tell him that when I had got off the streetcar I had gone to look at the dolls in the display window of the oilcloth store and because of that, dinner was late" (70). Looking at the dolls in the window is a private act for her; it is an attempt to define her own identity, even though she unconsciously is trying to find herself within the norms her husband has established.

After the birth of her son Antoni, she continues to visit the dolls in the window. She sees their situation as more ideal than her own, as she tries to cope with the responsibilities of raising a baby, and her temperamental, but alluring, husband:

Many afternoons I went to look at the dolls with my son in my arms: They were there with their round, chubby cheeks, with their sunken glass eyes, and the little nose lower and the mouth, half open; always laughing and charming. . . . Always there, so pretty inside the display window, waiting to be bought and carried away. (82)

The dolls appear to be content and sure of themselves, qualities that Natàlia cannot identify in her own personality. They also have the fairy tale-like hope of being purchased—then they would be even happier. The dolls serve as a "model and a mirror" for Natàlia, emulating the effect of fairy tales on women and demonstrating (Natàlia believes) that her role in life is to be passive, patient, and expectant in spite of any feelings of discontentment.[26]

Natàlia's repeated interest in the dolls has the same metaphoric quality of rebirth and escape as that of the fairy tales in *Nada* and *Primera memoria,* while the passive model the dolls present remains within the norms of patriarchal society. The person who buys them would fulfill the role of the prince, a function that Natàlia unconsciously finds slightly discordant in the relationship with her own "prince," Quimet. Despite Quimet's magnetism—"he was very well made" (63)—he often abuses Natàlia's sense of self, causing her to envy the dolls' position.

But Natàlia becomes disenchanted with the dolls as a model for her life when their friend Mateu's wife, Griselda, leaves him. Natàlia's earlier description of Griselda conveys the same fascination she feels toward the dolls in the window:

> Griselda can't be described: She was pale, with a handful of freckles on the upper part of her cheeks. And tranquil eyes of mint green. Thin at the waist. All of silk. . . . A doll. She didn't talk much. (94–95)

Mateu is even more fascinated with Griselda. But Griselda's departure with another man leaves Natàlia confused about emulating a doll-like model, and Mateu openly wishes Griselda were more like Natàlia. Her rejection of that model is reinforced by another friend, Cintet, when he confirms that "Griselda was a doll and Mateu was too much of a man for a doll" (156). Like Andrea's rejection of the Cinderella role in *Nada,* Natàlia, too, begins to spurn the fairy tale-like "mirror" of the dolls.

Yet after Natàlia learns of Quimet's death, she stops again at the shop window with the dolls that had comforted her. But this time she is not so much attracted by the dolls as by a teddy bear with a blue ribbon around its neck: "It was seated at the feet of a very rich doll . . . and with its arms open" (181). The description of the bear suggests a metonymic link to Mateu, with his blue eyes, his devotion to Griselda (seated at the doll's feet), and his admiration of Natàlia (echoed by the bear's open arms). Not only does Natàlia's new interest in the bear demonstrate rejection of the dolls as her "mirror," it also shows that she now must look at herself as someone other that Quimet's wife.

The subsequent disappearance of the bear from the store window is exceedingly disturbing to Natàlia, because it represents her only remaining optimistic possibility after Quimet's death:

> Things were still put in front of me, they all stopped in front of my eyes as if before dying they wanted to live in them forever. And the

crystal of my eyes caught it all. The bear wasn't in the oilcloth store anymore, and when I saw that it wasn't there I realized that I really felt like seeing it. (191)

The bear's disappearance serves to confirm her decision to end her life and that of her children. All hope of finding a place for herself in the barren, postwar world disappears: The dolls no longer reflect her hopes, and the bear and its inherent possibilities are gone. Natàlia no longer recognizes any vestiges of herself in the store window she has used as a mirror since the beginning of her marriage to Quimet.

Ironically, it is because of a mirror that Natàlia is saved from her self-destruction. Antoni, the owner of the store where she goes to obtain nitric acid, later reveals to her that he has a mirror in his store, placed so that he can observe people in front while he is in the back room. The day she came for nitric acid, he saw the desperation in her face reflected in that mirror and ran after her to see if she wanted a job. Because of his concern for Natàlia, Antoni, in a sense, makes her more aware of herself and impels her to look at herself.

It is relevant then, that while describing Antoni's house, Natàlia mentions "the mirror with wood decoration on the top part" (197) above the console in the living room. Also, when Antoni asks her to come and see him on a Sunday afternoon, Natàlia self-consciously looks at her own reflection in the store windows along the way:

. . . I walked unenthusiasically and wasted time looking at myself in the reflection of the display windows, where everything was darker and shinier. My hair bothered me. I had cut it myself and I had washed it and it was going wherever it wanted. (203–4)

Antoni's unusual request to see her on a Sunday (her day off) makes her nervous, even though she does not know he will ask to marry her. His attention prompts Natàlia to think about herself and to look at herself. Although she is not entirely pleased with her self-reflection, looking directly at herself in the store window demonstrates her increasing self-awareness. Rather than absorbing the estimation of others, or avoiding self-reflection by aspiring to be a doll, Natàlia actually considers her own attributes and debilities as she peers into the glass.

The mirrorlike store windows bring to mind the temporal contiguity illustrated by Andrea's successive use of the mirror in *Nada*. As with Andrea, one can follow Natàlia's progressive autonomy by examining these scenes. At first Natàlia sees the dolls as a reflection of her self, but later she rejects the dolls and focuses on the bear, and lastly she actually looks at her own reflection as she becomes more self-confident. The store window and its contents serve as a metaphoric mirror for Natàlia, and the successive images demonstrate the metonymic progression of self. She finally focuses on her own reflection, illustrating her new concept of self.

After accepting Antoni's proposal, Natàlia shows as much autonomy and consciousness of self as she ever has, demanding certain concessions from Antoni: clothes for herself and the children, new iron-frame beds for them, and wallpaper in the kitchen of Antoni's home. She no longer is passive, as she was in her marriage to Quimet, but knows what she wants and does not hesitate to ask for it. The dissimilarity between Antoni and Quimet contributes to her change. Unlike Quimet, Antoni encourages Natàlia to express her desires, and respects them by complying. While Quimet is physically magnetic and strong, Antoni has a scarred face, an apricot-shaped body, and—because of an injury in the war—is impotent.[27] But Antoni's compassionate and unthreatening qualities allow Natàlia to form her own sense of identity.

Despite her new sense of self-worth and power at the beginning of her marriage with Antoni, Natàlia (like Andrea in *Nada*) experiences a setback in her process of self-realization. Just as Andrea experienced debilitating guilt after her uncle Román's suicide, Natàlia, too, begins to feel guilty about her marriage to Antoni and her new, more assertive self. After her daughter Rita's First Communion, Rita asks if Quimet might still be alive. Natàlia is then filled with self-reproach about her decision to marry Antoni, imagining what would happen if Quimet were to come back: "And if he were alive like Rita's friend's father, and came back sick and found me married to the shopkeeper that sells vetch? I only thought about that" (218). Natàlia, feeling trapped in her marriage, relives her life with Quimet in her imagination. She forgets all the unpleasant details, even of caring for the *coloms,* and seems less and less in touch with reality. Sometimes she is afraid to leave the house, and other days she spends hours sitting on a park bench dreaming about her former life. Her state is reminiscent of Andrea's empathetic, nearly catatonic sleep after Román's suicide, but Natàlia's condition of compulsion and self-condemnation lasts for years.

The end of Natàlia's culpability occurs only at the prospect of Rita's marriage to Vicenç. Her daughter's forthcoming nuptials initiate the recall of her own marriage to Quimet. As she watches

Rita in a pensive mood before the wedding, Natàlia reveals the sudden perception of looking at herself in the past:

> . . . and suddenly I realized that I was on top of the shadow of Rita's head; more clearly, the shadow of Rita's head was climbing over my feet, but in spite of everything it seemed to me that Rita's shadow on the floor was like a lever, and that at any moment I could rise through the air because the sun and Rita on the outside weighed more than the shadow and me inside. And I intensely felt the passage of time . . . the time inside of me. (234)

Natàlia, like Ena's mother in *Nada,* begins to comprehend the sense of her own existence through her daughter: Rita—like many daughters—is her mother's mirror. By beginning to understand her own role, Natàlia is lifted, as if by a lever, from her guilt and depression.

Rita's marriage provides a reflective medium for Natàlia that continues during the ceremony, the festivities, and into the early hours of the next morning. The decorations in Vicenç's restaurant (where they celebrate the wedding party) are like the ones that decorated the Plaça del Diamant at the dance where Natàlia first met Quimet. When she dances with her son Antoni, dressed in his soldier's uniform, Natàlia feels "as if the column of the bed were breaking" (243), echoing the moment when he was born. His buttons then snag her strand of pearls, breaking them, just as she broke the bed column while giving birth to him. This incident serves as another link to her past.

After the festivities are over, Natàlia mentions: "In the mirror of the console I was looking at the top of my head, only a few of the hairs" (243). Even though she takes a very brief and partial look at herself, Natàlia does not seem displeased. Her new identity at the wedding as "la senyora Natàlia" is one with which she is beginning to be comfortable.

Natàlia's return to the Plaça del Diamant before dawn the day after the ceremony intensifies the mirroring effect of her past life that Rita's wedding initiated. She explains: "It seemed to me that everything that I did I had already done, without being able to know where or when, as if everything were planted and rooted in a time without memory..." (248). She describes the knife that she pulls from the table drawer to take with her as "made very well" (246), duplicating her words about Quimet on their wedding night.[28] With this knife she carves the name "Colometa," and then continues on to the Plaça del Diamant.

The scream she emits in the middle of the plaza echoes the one that she released while giving birth to Antoni, but this time she delivers her own freed self:

> . . . I gave a scream from hell. A scream that I must have carried inside myself for many years and with that scream, so huge that it was hard for it to pass through my throat, a little piece of emptiness left me through my mouth, like a little beetle of saliva... and . . . that piece of emptiness that had lived so long shut up inside me was my youth that escaped with a scream that didn't know very well what it was... (249–50)

Natàlia is then freed from the remorse and confusion about her identity she felt throughout her youth, and undergoes a metaphoric rebirth of self.[29] This new life is a circular movement in her development which at first might seem regressive, but which actually illustrates the progressive circular development that critics describe in women's development. Natàlia's rebirth delivers her from the compulsive behavior and guilt that restrict her.[30]

Although Natàlia's use of the mirror is much more refracted and tentative than that of either Matia in *Primera memoria* or Andrea in *Nada,* Natàlia's hesitancy to look at herself shows she has unconsciously internalized the goals of patriarchal subjugation for women. While Natàlia rarely appraises herself directly during her marriage to Quimet, his death and her subsequent marriage to Antoni cause her to contemplate herself and her own needs. Even though the guilt that many women feel after tasting liberty engulfs Natàlia for many years, the re-creation of her own existence through her daughter helps her overcome that guilt and focus on her own identity again.

The circularity inherent in Natàlia's retelling of her life is very similar to the progress toward autonomy that Andrea demonstrates by writing the story of her year in Barcelona.[31] Natàlia exhibits growth by voicing ideas she has not expressed before—breaking her fairy tale-like silence—and by making judgments that were not apparent to her earlier.[32] For instance, Natàlia tells her listener that although her friend "la senyora Enriqueta" asked her to describe her wedding night with Quimet, "I didn't dare because we didn't have a wedding night. We had a week of wedding nights" (62). Although Enriqueta serves as a mirror/mother, Natàlia cannot divulge to her how much she enjoyed Quimet's sexuality. But Natàlia's retelling of her story goes beyond the degree of confidentiality she shares with Enriqueta and expresses her true feelings. Therefore, the circular movement demonstrated by "mirroring" her life—retelling her story—shows expansion and growth, and not the limitation and reduction seen in Matia's repeated looking back in *Primera memoria.*

Thus, not only do metaphor and metonymy serve to bridge the gap between the narrator and the reader, they also help Natàlia cross the void of her poorly formed self-image. Since Natàlia's "mirrors" are often metaphoric substitutions for actually looking at herself, and since they are modified as her life progresses, the role of metaphor and metonymy as a bridge in Natàlia's identity formation is fundamental. Even though Natàlia initially laments the loss of her mother as a mirror or role model, she is finally able to define her own identity and achieve a sense of contentment and self-assurance.

La plaça del Diamant depicts a protagonist that is initially much more passive than the young women in the previous two novels. However, the protagonists in other novels by Rodoreda—Aloma in *Aloma,* Cecília in *El carrer de les camèlies* (Camellia Street), and Teresa of *Mirall trencat* (Broken mirror)—demonstrate a willfulness that is similar to that of Andrea in *Nada* and Matia in *Primera memoria.* Aloma and Cecília share with Andrea, Matia, and Natàlia the experience of reaching adolescence without the guidance of their mothers.

Aloma's rebelliousness is symbolized in the first chapter of *Aloma* when she empathizes with a dirty, stray, white cat that repeatedly comes to the garden of the family home where Aloma lives.[33] Over time, the resigned, tired cat bears litter after litter of kittens before a watchman clubs her to death one night while she is giving birth. Aloma's story mirrors the oppression of the female sex demonstrated by the cat. Aloma lives with her brother Joan and his wife, Anna, and cares for their son Dani. Joan consistently asserts his control over Aloma and even burns the books bequeathed to her by their brother Daniel before his suicide. When Anna's brother Robert comes from Argentina to live with them, Robert and Aloma become lovers, but he abandons her before discovering she is pregnant. A somber aspect of marriage is highlighted when Joan mortgages the family home to get money to seduce an attractive neighbor. The subsequent loss of the house and his child Dani's death cap the negative events in her brother's married life.

While Aloma's attitude throughout the novel defies patriarchial norms suppressing women, Randolph Pope points out that the published version from 1968 is notably toned down from Rodoreda's original version. Rodoreda and her lover of many years, Armand

Obiols, edited the original text, and there were significant changes that "silenced . . . the repression against women that Rodoreda had denounced masterfully in 1936."[34] Rodoreda's censorship of her own text is similar to Carmen Laforet's lessening of feminist causes in her later novels.

The protagonist Cecília Ce's situation in *El carrer de les camèlies* (1966) also echoes that of the stray cat in *Aloma*. A night watchman discovers the abandoned infant Cecília after she is left at the garden gate at a house on Camellia Street. Although the owners of the house take care of Cecília, she leaves her adopted family at the age of fifteen to live with Eusebi in a shantytown. She then becomes the mistress of a series of men and the victim of repeated physical and emotional abuse. Even after two attempts at suicide she emerges as a survivor, much like Natàlia in *La plaça del Diamant*. Also like Natàlia, Cecília is an innocent who seems to communicate orally and leaves glaring omissions in her story, partly because of her modest education and her insecurity.

The omissions and gaps in *El carrer de les camèlies* are also bridged by metaphoric tropes and mirror images that suggest explanations for things the protagonist leaves unexplained. For instance, the beautiful blossom on a cactus plant in the garden of the home where Cecília was abandoned seems to symbolize her positive qualities. Every year on the anniversary of the date she appeared the cactus blooms, but its blossom is so ephemeral that everyone must run to see it before it closes. The owners interpret it as a sign that God was pleased by their care of the orphan. In contrast to this positive symbol, a dark stain resembling blood remains in the street on the very spot where she was found, inciting questions about the nature of her origin. The doubts about her heritage, like the stain in the street, mark her life. In a later scene, Cecília regards herself in a mirror, metonymically linking the stain to her future as a passionate woman: "I was falling in love with myself. The blood came, and I listened to the sometimes sleeping blood, red down the silk of my thighs."[35] Cecília's mysterious and marginal origin—without a proper mother—defile her destiny and identity in a culture where passion and sexuality are negative attributes for a respected woman.

Although Teresa in Rodoreda's *Mirall trencat* grows up with her own mother, she eventually disputes with her, as does Teresa's daughter Sofia with Teresa. The novel reveals Teresa's life through more than three generations, mirroring the rise and decadence of her family. The prevailing theme of the novel, however, indicates that various members of the family are "disparate fragments of mirror," and that each fragment helps to cross some of the "folds of memory" before one can "become a presence."[36] Thus the function of the mirror in *Mirall trencat* is similar to that of the other novels examined here, helping the protagonist to discern her subjugated identity.

While in *Mirall trencat* Teresa and her daughter—although they have living mothers—must struggle to define themselves, the majority of the novels have exhibited motherless daughters. *Nada, Primera memoria,* and *La plaça del Diamant* all demonstrate the lack of a positive female role model in the protagonist's search for identity in a patriarchal society. Despite this absence, Andrea in *Nada* and eventually Natàlia appear to make progress toward autonomy. However, Matia in *Primera memoria* seems unable to avoid the passive and self-denigrating model that her aunt Emilia provides. In the next novel, *Julia,* another negative role model, Julia's mother, contributes to Julia's complete loss of identity. While both Matia and Natàlia at times show signs of personality disorders, Julia's narration reveals a severe split in her identity and a debilitating regression to her childhood.

4

The Reflection of Dangerous Division
in *Julia*

Born in 1947, more than twenty years after Laforet, Matute, and Rodoreda, Ana María Moix belongs in the second generation of writers after the Spanish civil war. But Moix published her first novel, *Julia,* in 1969—just nine years after the publication of Matute's *Primera memoria.*[1] Several critics regard *Julia* as a transitional novel between those by the previously mentioned authors, and later novels by Carme Riera, Monserrat Roig, and Esther Tusquets.[2]

Like *Nada, Primera memoria,* and *La plaça del Diamant,* the protagonist of *Julia* is a young female in search of her identity. In contrast with those earlier novels, where loss of autonomy is associated with initiation into adulthood, Julia's banishment of innocence is a childhood rape that violates her self-worth. While the other protagonists lamented the lack of a mother figure as a model, Julia's mother reinforces a split in Julia's personality by alternately lavishing her with affection, then completely ignoring her. Additionally, *Julia* is noticeably different from the previously examined novels because of its third person narration. Although the voice is third person, the view is through the protagonist's eyes and, in this sense, similar to the other three novels.

Julia begins with the unnerving sensation of another's presence, as twenty-year-old Julia awakes terrified from a recurring nightmare. She feels as if someone is in her room, and is unable to calm herself enough to go back to sleep. Instead, childhood memories flood through her mind, revealing Julia's attempts to gain her mother's favor, jealousy of her two brothers, her brother Rafael's death, and her parents' marital difficulties. Much of Julia's need for attention and her fears arise after being raped by her brother Ernesto's friend when she is six. She never reveals what has happened, never even admits it to herself. Feeling trapped and worthless, Julia finally attempts suicide. After recovering consciousness, she has the personality of Julita, her childhood nickname. The presence that Julia felt during her nightmares was Julita haunting her.

Critics have explored the various techniques that contribute to the sense of "doubling" and division in *Julia*.[3] Although the "doubling" of self appears similar to the effect of looking in a mirror to form one's identity, there is an ominous difference when a reflection is completely distinct from the self: "to exist in multiplicity is, in a sense, not to exist at all because self-conception requires some conviction in the singularity of one's being."[4] Julia's "doubling," in effect, reflects disintegration—instead of creation—of self. When Julia actually looks at her reflection in the mirror, the same loss of self-identity is apparent.

While *Nada* and *Primera memoria* rely heavily on the use of metaphor and metonymy to reveal the subconscious desires and fears of the protagonists and their progressive maturation (or lack of it), the metaphorical expression in *Julia* often describes an unknown or vague element. A key metaphor describing Julia's life as a "partially cut film" transmits the idea that part of Julia's memory is obstructed from her.[5] Another metaphor relays Julia's difficulty in interpreting her feelings: "those moments of insomnia were like pulling an endless thread that gradually became snarled up so that it ended in a tangle from which only sleep could free her" (27). These metaphors expressing Julia's confusion invite readers to make metonymic connections about Julia's life in order to untie the knot that Julia cannot.

Similar to the metaphor of Julia's memory as an edited film, another metaphor—comparing her memory to "a vehicle . . . driven by a crazy, suicidal person" (54)—reveals that she has little control of her past thoughts. The car's driver transports Julia to places she does not want to go and converts her reality into a horrifying fiction. Because Julia's subconscious will not allow her to remember certain things, readers must fill the gaps in the narration by metonymically connecting the memories and images Julia does recall. Julia cannot progress by changing metaphoric conceptions through subsequent metonymic associations (as do Andrea in *Nada* and Natàlia in *La plaça del Diamant*) because of her repressed memories. Instead, part of her is arrested at a certain stage of which she cannot remember the details. Although these metaphors make direct comparisons that reveal Julia's incomplete memories, they evade a clear expression of her emotions.

Moreover, instead of the lack of development that Matia demonstrates in *Primera memoria* by her static metaphorical expression, metaphors in *Julia* often describe characteristics that R. D. Laing identifies as schizophrenia. Laing explains that schizoid personalities are disjoint in their ability to relate to others and to themselves and, thus, experience despairing aloneness and isolation. Moreover, a schizophrenic often feels incomplete and "'split' in various ways . . . as a mind . . . tenuously linked to a body, as two or more selves, and so on."[6] Julia experiences separation of her personality into two parts referred to as "Julia" and "Julita," as well as suffering inability to form close ties with others. Frequently "Julita" is enigmatically alluded to as another person hiding in the same room to harm her, hinting at the dangerous division in Julia's thought processes. Other more direct metaphors depict her life with terms that Laing has heard repeatedly from schizophrenics.

Often, however, the expression in *Julia* is more subtle, reflecting Benjamin Hrushovski's observation that metaphor need not be a direct comparison involving only a few words, but that it may begin with a connotation and form an "open-ended" and "dynamic" meaning.[7] The description of Julia's waking from her nightmare at the beginning of the novel, for example, is so exaggerated that it has metaphorical implications. The first sentence describes Julia covering her head with the sheet and crouching under the covers with her knees pressed to her chest "until she was curled up into a ball" (9). Since the frightened dreamer is even beyond adolescence, this fetal position suggests that Julia would like to return to the security of the womb. Julia's fear upon waking—a fear that causes her heart to beat in her throat, makes her mouth dry, and nearly stops her breathing—is so emotive that it has metaphoric significance. She also senses that she is not alone in her room:

> She had the impression that she needed more air, that she was going to suffocate. When she held her breath for a few seconds, it caused an intolerable pain in her chest, and when she let it escape, bit by bit, she thought she heard the howls of another body that wasn't hers, and they were going to wake the whole house. (9)

Her fright is reminiscent of Matia's metaphors in *Primera memoria* when she feels like a trapped animal and of Andrea's perception in *Nada* that her grandmother's house is filled with ghosts. But the realization that Julia's reaction transpires when she is twenty, that it has occurred repeatedly since she was a small child, and that it produces real physical symptoms, makes her terror more than a metaphoric expression of her subconscious. Julia's "phantoms in her bedroom" (10) depict an abnormal fear that becomes a psychotic reality for her.[8]

Memories flood Julia's consciousness during this fearful state, but—in contrast with the other novels examined—there are few direct comparisons describing her fright. Metaphorical qualities emerge from the exaggerated emotions that Julia expresses, and the vocabulary is reminiscent of the metaphors in earlier novels. But Julia's memories suggest that her thought process is on a metonymic level of associations and has not evolved enough for her to convert it into metaphoric expression.

Julia makes many metonymic associations between the things that have happened in her life, but often she is unable to make the connections that would enable her to arrive at an ultimate conclusion or to interpret her emotions. For example, after the death of her paternal grandmother when she was quite small, Julia mentions that "every time she was cold, heard the word river, or was scared at night" (19) her thoughts returned to the night her grandmother died. She remembers her brother Rafael singing to her, and her aunt Elena crying (although she thought it was her mother crying at the time). Because there was an *armario* (wardrobe) in the room where she stayed, an *armario* reminds her of a coffin, and a coffin of seeing her mother dead. Likewise, her mind links many different thoughts that all lead to the image of her mother in a coffin. This image, however, does not have a logical interpretation for her: One thought leads to another until it becomes a "circle of images" (27) that is impossible for her to decipher. It is as if she has formed a metaphorical comparison with one element hidden: "mother in coffin" = ?

Readers might conclude that the image of "mother in coffin" expresses Julia's fear that her mother (to whom she is so attached at the time of her grandmother's death) will also die. Another passage, however, reveals a change in Julia's sentiments toward her mother:

> It was absurd to pretend to search for one day in her memory, one unforgettable incident, to determine the cause of that loss. It had been a slow process, unconscious then, a long and slow process that appeared in her mind like a partially cut film, but with an indisputable continuity in spite of long, obscured, veiled, forgotten segments. (53)

Although it does not seem strange that Julia no longer reveres her mother the way she did as a child, nor that she does not remember the exact reasons for that change, her feelings show an abrupt reversal: "I couldn't stand Mamá . . ." (32), "Then I hated her" (13). This evolution suggests that the image of her mother in the coffin might also have an opposite meaning: "mother in coffin" = "hope that she will die." The anxiety produced by this perception would be closer to guilt than fear. Yet the blank sequences in Julia's memory prevent her from interpreting the "mother in the coffin" image.

The dreams that Julia remembers also serve as a metaphoric expression of her unconscious. Laing calls dreams the "royal road to the unconscious . . . to becoming conscious,"[9] expressing that dreams communicate from the unconscious in the same manner that Lacan has described of the metaphor. Julia's recurring dream as a little girl intimates that there is yet another meaning to the vision of her mother in the coffin. In the dream everyone escapes by boat from a huge fire except Mamá, who does not arrive in time. Julia fears that her mother will burn up in the fire and equates herself with Bambi "after his mama died in the fire" (25). Mamá, however, stands calmly waving good-bye as she is about to be engulfed by flames, thereby implying that it is Julia who suffers most—not her mother:

At the end of time they would separate the good ones from the bad ones. They would alienate her from Mamá, that was sure. She, Julia, was bad: everyone assured her of it. And she would contemplate Mamá's face telling her goodbye, while she, Julia, would be dragged away toward hell. (15)

Being dragged into hell indicates that Julia subconsciously feels her own fate is the same as her mother's in the dream: She is also swallowed up by fire.

This similarity suggests that Julia's relationship with her mother shows signs of the "permeable ego boundaries" that can occur between mothers and daughters,[10] causing difficulty in distinguishing one's own identity. Laing explains that a "firm sense of one's own autonomous identity" is necessary in relationships with others: "Otherwise, any and every relationship threatens the individual with loss of identity."[11] Julia's art as a child shows that her whole world is identified through her mother—almost everything she draws is of her mother: "Mamá in the sea, Mamá and the moon, Mamá and the gypsies . . . Mamá, Switzerland, and the train" (21). She titles the one sketch not including her mother "Mamá isn't here" (21). Instead of having a clear sense of her own identity, Julia confuses her own existence with her mother's.

Julia's sense of self is so closely tied to her mother that she fuses fears for her mother with her own fright. Moreover, she feels guilty even attempting to exist when her dream eradicated her mother. Julia's dream about the fire includes the concept that she was "bad" (15), revealing her guilt as, what Laing calls, an "inclusive sense of badness or worthlessness" attacking her "very right to *be*." Moreover, Laing mentions fire as one of the images schizophrenics repeatedly use to describe that their identity is being threatened by "engulfment" or "absorption into" another person. Other images of this threat are "being buried, being drowned, being caught and dragged down into quicksand."[12] Julia not only dreams of fire but imagines her father drowning and speaks of herself suffocating and unable to breathe in many instances. Being dragged down into hell also would fit into the same category.

Julia's nightmare is, in effect, a metaphoric expression of the fear she feels for herself, projecting the engulfment she unconsciously feels onto her mother.[13] Although she may be on the "road" to "becoming conscious" of her feeling of engulfment, Julia never becomes fully aware of what is happening to her. The imaginary vision of her father drowning—and the guilt she feels for imagining it—are similar expressions of her unconscious. Thus the image "mother in coffin" is equivalent to destruction of self for Julia, as well as the seemingly opposite concepts of fear and hope of her mother's death. The resulting implied metaphor of "mother in coffin" = "self in coffin"—which Julia never voices—leads back to the confusing "circle of images" from which Julia cannot escape.

Thinking of her brother Rafael also gives Julia a feeling of circularity and vertigo, as well as guilt for hating him as a child: " . . . and Julia asked herself sometimes if Rafael died, precisely, because of that hate" (16). Memories of Rafael also initiate the metaphoric expression of her lack of control:

> She found out that then, in that exact moment, the time was ending that she could restart that singular vehicle that was her memory, a vehicle that was sometimes a sports car, driven by a crazy suicidal person, that raced ahead at full speed, crashing against the arboreal shadows in the road and running over all the obstacles that appeared in its path, and other times, was a funeral car, black, driven by a ghost and attended by four cadaver valets. The appearance of that singular vehicle, her memory, had converted reality into fiction. A thousand things had remained behind, in the past, and she, Julia, was there, also forgotten, suffocating, struggling with herself among shadows in hopes that they would open up the path to her so that she could reach the real moment where the other Julia, older, unknown, lived. (54)

While the trope of the car explicitly reveals lapses in her memory, the passage also conveys open-ended suggestions to the division within her identity.

It is not she, the twenty-year-old, "older" and "unknown" Julia who is in control of her memory, but rather another facet of herself:

> . . . it was Julita, little, thin, fast, and slippery, who always got ahead of her in taking control of the motor of her memory to guide her along crooked, confusing roads, abruptly changing directions as if she wanted to play in a labyrinth with no exit and at the same time amuse herself by tricking Julia. (55)

The areas to which Julita (the faction of Julia that existed as a little child) wants to direct the memory are "dark tunnels, dilapidated bridges" where "repugnant reptiles" hide waiting for a "prey" (55). They are parts of the "film" excised from Julia's memory and suggest an ugly, confusing, and traumatic occurrence that she repressed as a child.[14] The idea that Julita is now "reproaching her for having abandoned her in her childhood" (55) suggests that there is a segment of Julia that wants to expose these hidden parts and wants revenge. Again the idea surfaces of a dangerous division in Julia's personality. There is a part of her that knows something that another part does not and, even worse, one faction of her personality wants to harm the other—exposing her to the troll-like creature under the bridge.

The novel later reinforces this idea of revenge and vindication of one part of Julia against the other with a metaphoric description: "Julita had converted herself into a martyrized god for Julia, a god that demanded continuous sacrifices in order to calm his old pain" (63).[15] After Julia's attempted suicide she conveys that it is only "Julita . . . little, thin, barefoot, uncombed braids, shorts and a navy blue T-shirt with an anchor on the front" (220) who survives. This description of herself as a six-year-old is the one that Julia repeatedly uses to describe the other, arrested facet of herself that demands a sacrifice. "Julita" also is described as "seated in that doorway" (63, 220), waiting:

> Julita never forgave her for having abandoned her there, in an immobile universe, without time, in whose shadows she struggled against herself, and from where Julia could never, never rescue her. Julita reproached her for the great weakness, the immense cowardice that impeded her from freeing her forever. Because of that Julita kept returning. (63)

Like a ghost, Julita returns (often during the night) to haunt Julia and beg to be liberated.

Precisely what happened to "Julita" is what Julia cannot remember and does not want to relive. However, the thought of her childhood self always evokes a certain memory:

> The presence of Julita in her mind, pulled Julia toward a memory that appeared clearly at first, complete, with an uncontrollable force and whose clarity vanished then with the same abruptness with which it had been born again in her memory, leaving her in pain, full of resentment. (60)

Julia clearly remembers traveling in a paddleboat with her brothers and two of their friends (perhaps the "four valets" of the motor car metaphor). Tired of paddling, Julia jumps in the water to swim, with one friend—Víctor—following her. After she and Víctor swim to the shore to rest and he warns her of the sea urchins, her memory becomes clouded.

Not surprisingly, the description of what follows in that memory is an ambiguous, evasive representation of what actually happened. Readers must make their own metonymic associations and metaphoric conclusions in order to realize that Víctor did more than knock Julia down and prick her with a sea urchin. Julia describes that Víctor "got a hold of a sea urchin" (61), while her thoughts diverge to the times that her brothers caught sea urchins and put them in buckets with lye to remove the quills. Julia's thoughts about removing the quills of sea urchins can be considered a metaphoric expression of how she might protect herself.[16] The metonymic association of similar qualities between the sharp quills of the sea urchin and the threat of the painful rape of a six-year-old permits the "sliding into metaphor" that the Shapiros describe.[17] Thus while six-year-old Julia probably does not completely understand what is happening to her, and the older Julia does not want to remember, Moix's description provides the readers with material to make their own metonymic associations that result in metaphoric interpretation of the incident. During Franco's rule, an indirect metaphor of this type would be important to avert the censorship of such a taboo theme.[18]

Julia once again tries to protect herself from Víctor—this time with actions instead of thoughts—when she grabs the sea urchin from his hand "smashing it against Víctor's shoulder, who was breathing very heavily" (62). Despite her resistance, Víctor overpowers her, although the text—like Julia's memory—does not offer a clear description:

> Julia remembered the bad breath in her nostrils, Víctor's shout, and the continued blows received. Víctor, upon feeling the spines of the

sea urchin against his skin, had jumped, and she laid down on her stomach. The rocks thrust into her flesh, and her whole body ached. (62)

Instead of a literal account of an incomprehensible experience that Julia wanted to erase from her memory, the text offers a metaphoric description of her reaction: "She was hot, very hot, as if the sun had hidden itself inside her body" (62). Readers can associate the invasive heat of the sun, whose shape and rays are similar to the sea urchin, with the consummation of Julia's violation.

Through language that invites metonymic extension, *Julia* describes a violent sexual impropriety against a young girl that is much more vile than those described in the earlier novels studied. While Andrea fears that Román might rape or harm Ena in *Nada*, and Borja blackmails Matia with lies about her sexual conduct in *Primera memoria*, the debilitating force of patriarchal power over females is most vividly expressed in *Julia*. In contrast to Natàlia in *La plaça del Diamant*, who as a young girl passively accepts the role imposed upon her by patriarchal society, Julia emerges from her conflict with male superiority "dizzy, bathed in sweat, unable to understand what was asked . . . unable to answer" (62), "doubled over herself in pain" (62), and even incapable of walking. To describe this horrifying invasion of personal liberty without censorship, Moix relies on reader participation. Readers continue metaphoric and metonymic processes in order to reconstruct the memory Julia has already censored.

Julia's vanquished state after being raped contrasts greatly with her thoughts of removing the quills of the sea urchin and her brave retaliatory attack against Víctor. The description following the rape shows its effect on Julia's sense of self:

She drew in her legs, sat down on her heels, and bent over, resting her forehead on her knees. She didn't remember how long she stayed like that. The sea seemed very far away, so far that she would never be able to reach it. (62)

Like the "ovillo" (ball) she forms when she wakes from her nightmare, her humbled, bowed position is a sign of regression. The sea—a force indicative of positive feminine development and of nature's "green-world" refuge from patriarchal oppression—seems infinitely distant.[19] While in Laforet's *Nada* Andrea desires to be a "drop in the current" as an expression of her liberty, this is a futile goal for Julia. Unlike Andrea, Julia's hopes and fears are often not as metaphorically explicit. As with the description of the rape itself, the metaphoric values of the language used must be reconstructed to make metonymic connections and form metaphoric conclusions.

Even though the rape is a tremendous assault on Julia's sense of self, the final blow comes from her family when she returns home—especially from her mother:

> When they arrived at where the others were and Aurelia began to yell at her and Mamá to slap her, releasing in that way the impatience they felt (I don't want you all to walk alone along the rocks, someday you'll give us a real scare.) (62)[20]

Her mother's reaction not only fails to address the trauma Julia has just suffered, but actually intensifies it. Despite having adored her mother, Julia expresses ideas that metonymically link her mother with Víctor.

Julia's mother affirms that Víctor is "a fine young man, well-mannered, kind, and distinguished" (60), but Julia's father does not like him and even tells Ernesto not to associate with Víctor. Probably to incite jealousy, her mother alludes that Víctor is attractive and "an attentive man, elegant and sensitive" (60). It is Julia's mother who permits Víctor to visit the garden in the evenings after dinner while she chats with her friends. During those evenings, Víctor often demonstrates to Julia how bears kill their victims:

> While he was explaining, he hugged Julita tightly. Julita felt uncomfortable with Víctor. She was suffocating with heat, it anguished her to be on Víctor's lap and that he was hugging her to show her how bears devoured their victims. Let me go, shouted Julita. Víctor would laugh, but he wouldn't release her. He would say: Yummm, now I'm eating you (and he'd open his mouth really wide), I'm a bear, a terrible bear. With her face buried in Víctor's chest, she saw only darkness, noticed the annoying contact of his burning and sweaty skin and heard the conversation of Mamá and her friends like a distant murmur, as if they weren't in the garden. (59–60)

Víctor's pretense foreshadows the rape that occurs later, and Mamá's indifference to Julia's situation in the garden again makes her Víctor's accomplice.

The close contact of Víctor's skin brings to mind the sweaty odor that Julia describes during the rape. Julia's olfactory perception of Víctor is another factor that links him with her mother, as Julia also notices her mother's aroma. Mamá complains—"you sniff me like a dog" (21)—as little Julia follows her scent. At that time her mother's smell is pleasant to her, but later Julia finds it displeasing—just as Víctor's is offensive: "the many objects of the bedroom smelled of Mamá's perfume. It was an acidic smell, as of lemon" (32–33).

Moreover, Víctor's charade echoes Mamá's games with Julia at age four or five, during the times she liked to play with her. Julia would climb in bed with her mother, who tickled her until she could not stop laughing. Mamá then would hold very still, pretending she was asleep and not answering Julia:

> Wake up, wake up. It was when Julita felt discouraged, seated on her knees, that Mamá suddenly got up and shouted: Uhhhhh, where is my ugly one? and again began the rain of kisses, nibbling, tickles, and Julia's uncontrollable laughter. (20)

Although Julia waited with anticipation for the days her mother would call her into bed to play, the game was often so intense that Julia feared her mother might be dead ("mother in coffin") as she pretended to sleep. And usually, in the deluge of kisses, tickles, and nibbles, "Julita would suffocate, she couldn't stop laughing" (17–18).

The tickling game with her mother resembles Víctor's imitation of a bear—which foreshadows Julia's rape—and all the aforementioned incidents leave Julia breathless, out of control, and suffocating. This choking feeling is also the same one that Julia describes on waking from her nightmare when "she felt like she needed air, that she was going to asphyxiate" (9), and echoes Laing's descriptions of incidents that "engulf" a personality and threaten one's identity. Therefore, readers can easily link the "invisible weight" (64)—and the breathlessness after Julia's nightmare—with the rape that she cannot remember clearly and even with the idea that her mother is an accessory to that incident.

Since no one (except Rafael) actually comforts her after the rape or protects her when Víctor teases her, Julia transfers some of her anger and hate to other members of her family, as well as to her mother. One night in her childhood, when Julia's parents have a fight, Mamá pretends to faint to scare Papá. All the children are frightened and think she is dead. Julia is especially terrified, again confusing her feelings with those of her mother: "She was scared. If Mamá had died, she would die too" (67). After waking in the middle of the night, Julia wanders down into the dining room in the darkness. There she hears someone breathing and sees a shadow moving:

> She shut her eyes. She wanted to scream. She couldn't. She opened them. Someone was there, in the dining room, a big body, very big, like a bear . . . She screamed . . . until the light of dining room was turned on and Papá appeared with his hand on the switch, dressed and with a sleepy face. (68)

Because Mamá is sleeping, Papá will not permit Julia to see her, and Julia continues to feel that her father has hurt her mother. Julia transfers some of her animosity toward Víctor to her father—he too is a "bear"—and again confuses her experience with her mother's: "Julia remember the appearance of a confused and dark feeling toward Papá" (68).

At times, however, Julia's father appears to have the potential to help her by recognizing her good qualities. A positive relationship with him would also help to neutralize some of her subconscious negative feelings toward males after being raped. But like the relationship that Chodorow notes between many fathers and their children, Julia's father remains emotionally distant. His noncommittal relationship aggravates her feelings of "non-being" and increases her hostility toward him. Therefore, when Julia experiences "the incomprehensible but real desire to see him sink into the sea" (71) and the desire to push him into the well in the garden, she senses an element of power over him if he should quarrel with her mother again.

Later, however, Julia is confused about her thoughts and overcome with guilt. To punish herself for wishing her father would die, Julia expresses an idea that complicates her feelings even more: "she felt for the first time the need to think about something that would fill her with pain, with fear, with anguish. She imagined Mamá dead." (76). The idea of "mother in coffin," and the unfinished metaphor that it suggests, again comes to mind. Once more readers perceive the "circle of images" that Julia complains of in her thought processes. Like Matia's limiting, downward spiraling of metaphors that results in the image of the well in *Primera memoria,* Julia's inability to complete and then modify the metaphors expressing sentiments about her rape and her treatment by her family suggests a lack of growth and a cycle of guilt, self-punishment, and self-destruction.

Julia begins to identify too much with what Laing would describe as her "unembodied" self of six when she was raped:

> She, Julita, little, thin, barefoot, and braids undone, erased everything with her presence. She avenged herself by reappearing now, after such

a long time. Julia, at last, understood the trap set by Julita, her revenge. Nearly physically she felt Julita's fingers ripping the mask off her face, the mask of her twenty years. (217)

Since "unembodied" people experience themselves as being "divorced or detached" from their real bodies,[21] Julia is "unembodied" when she feels she is Julita: Although Julia is actually twenty, Julita is only six. The "unembodied" Julita becomes more real than Julia's actual self when Julita rips the "mask" off her twenty-year-old self. The trap that results when Julita takes her vengeance of Julia marks the beginning of Julia's state of psychosis. Laing explains that psychosis occurs when "the individual begins to identify himself too exclusively with that part of him which feels *unembodied.*" Another danger of strong identification with the "unembodied" self is that the true self becomes even more isolated, remote, and fragile, making life for the psychotic schizophrenic like "a state of death-in-life."[22]

Julia defines her "death-in-life" state metaphorically after Julita takes control. She describes Julita leading her "toward a corner of a solitary beach" with "the summer sun sliding into her flesh and an old pain inserted in her body" (217), echoing the situation of her rape. The metaphoric description of her feeling reveals she is punished by being forced to stay in an isolated house on the beach, while everyone else is "enjoying a beautiful and crazy party that had ended for her. . . . A party for the others, celebrated in an immense garden . . . from which Julita had been excluded without knowing why" (217). Julia feels excluded from all the joy of life, as if she were being punished for her guilt, and her life takes on qualities of death.

Julia's attempt at suicide occurs after she tries to obtain reassurance and support from her professor Eva following harsh criticism from her mother and grandmother Lucía. When Eva says goodbye on the phone, it is a rejection for Julia by the only person who values her. Like Matia in *Primera memoria,* Julia feels the inescapable lure of the entrapping well that represents death and decay: "The living room ceiling retreated more and more from her, Julia was falling slowly into a deep and dark well whose walls covered with filth and grease were squeezing together more and more" (212). Instead of the open sea that receded from her after the rape, the grimy, trapping well reaches out to suffocate her. Unlike the time when she attempted to fight back with the sea urchin, her body is now "lead" (213), and the "metallic cloth that separated her from the world" (217) becomes more pronounced.

The number of metaphors describing her state of mind increases as she attempts to communicate her complete despair and the sensation that her life is unreal. In the last paragraph of the novel Julia conveys that she is beginning "a monotonous, boring, unreal day" and that she exists in "an immobile universe, without time" (220). These images describe the vacuum surrounding the identity of a schizophrenic—a vacuum that Laing says eventually collapses and traps the identity it is supposed to protect.[23]

But even her suicide attempt might be considered a desperate effort to fight and regain the last shred of her identity and control. Her hatred of the family that has suffocated her identity causes her to want revenge even as she sinks into "the emptiness and darkness. . . . She would avenge herself, she needed to make them suffer" (212). Julia had contemplated killing herself, but had not dared to before. Moreover, after her effort fails, she reveals: "She had intended to kill Julita, but only she remained" (218). Laing explains that one's identity becomes extremely fragile after it is isolated from the world in the way schizophrenics do. On the other hand, the false and "disembodied" selves that schizophrenic personalities develop to protect their real selves are hard to eliminate: "A ghost cannot be killed."[24] Thus, although her suicide is an attempt to save herself, Julia dies while "Julita" remains in control.

While much of the novel avoids direct metaphoric comparisons of Julia's feelings because of her unconscious desire to suppress the memory of her rape, metaphors show that Julia has blocked these areas from her memory. Equating the memory to a "partially cut film" (53) and a vehicle with the driver out of control invites readers to discover what Julia has repressed. The pattern of metonymic connections that Julia sees as a "circle of images" and a "tangle of threads" demonstrates the process of linking that Julia cannot complete, and eventually leads back to her rape. Readers can extend these metonymic links farther to see that Julia's family continues the violation of her sense of self. Julia seeks to protect herself by withdrawing from society, further illustrating Laing's observations of schizophrenic personalities. The profusion of metaphorical description at the end of the novel demonstrates how Julia increasingly perceives her world as an unreality when she enters into a psychotic stage of schizophrenia.

Various critics have inferred that Julia's confined, hopeless, and pawnlike situation within her family is metaphoric of the individual's situation during Franco's dictatorship.[25] Indeed, Julia compares her family's actions to "an unending card game" in which the children are the cards (117). Similar to Matia's metaphor of her grandmother as a cruel puppeteer in *Primera memoria,* Julia's individual situation takes on a more universal connotation. Likewise, Julia's schizophrenia fits into Rigney's hypothesis that female madness in literature is a metaphoric expression of an "alienated female consciousness in opposition to a male society or to individual male authority figures."[26] While it is Víctor who rapes Julia, Julia's family—a metaphoric microcosm of the patriarchal and fascist attitudes prevalent in Spain at that time—ignores and even continues the violation. Julia's maladjusted parents are the first descendants of Franco's rule (represented by Julia's dictatorial grandmother Lucía and Don Julio), and the effect on Julia is even more intolerable, forcing her to employ a schizophrenic solution to her "unlivable situation" in society.[27]

While the protagonists of the other novels examined lamented the lack of a mother, Julia's neurotic and insecure mother—still dependent on her own dictatorial mother—confuses Julia's exploration of identity. Hirsch helps to clarify this enigmatic situation when she states: "Dead mothers do elicit a certain nostalgia; nevertheless their absence invariably furthers the heroines' development." Even though females yearn for a mother figure as a model, the intense mirroring between mother and daughter complicates autonomy and, in Julia's case, leads to schizophrenia. At the same time Rigney sees insanity in women as "a search for the metaphoric mother."[28] Because Julia's mother ignores her daughter's development, Julia seeks another model in counterparts of her own mother.

Julia then attempts to mold her identity in the reflection of these substitute mothers—as in a mirror. Bellver calls Julia's relationship with her aunt Elena, her school director Miss Mabel, and her college professor Eva "duplications" of her relationship with her mother:

> Julia's surrogate mothers . . . while they constitute idealized, understanding and loving mothers in contrast to her immature, self-centered, and inattentive mother, . . . also multiply Julia's unified concept of her mother as a person who gives and then withdraws love.[29]

In her relationship with all of them Julia perceives rejection, or a negative reflection of herself, just as she has with her mother.

In each of her associations with the "doubles" of her mother, Julia expresses a physical attraction toward them that critics have seen as lesbianism.[30] But Julia's tendency toward homosexuality is a further indication of the trauma forced on her by society and her family. Julia's need to affirm her identity is so strong that it becomes physical in its character—like an infant that needs tactile, human contact. Karen Horney identifies homosexual tendencies as one of the four main symptoms of character disturbances in adolescent females and explains that these young women are usually not aware of the sexual nature of their feelings.[31] In spite of Julia's longing for affection from her aunt Elena and her teachers Miss Mabel and Eva, her homosexuality still exists on an idealistic level—evidenced by her reaction to the physical advances of her schoolmate Lidia. Julia uses a metaphor of "ants that were fleeing from a fire" (174)—fear of engulfment—to express her terror of the situation and is so distressed that she must see the doctor because of stomach pains.

Instead of a conscious physical desire, Julia's thoughts of these mother/mirror-substitutes are on a metaphoric, subconscious level. When Julia describes working with Eva as "the continuation of a party abruptly interrupted many years ago" (206), she further connects Eva with a need not met by her mother. Julia noted that her mother had created "a festive atmosphere, a childhood carnival of wild laughter" (37) in her early childhood, but that happiness had changed forever. Eva (and Elena and Mabel before her) represents the model and mirror of the "desires . . . illusions . . . dreams" (206) that Julia's mother could not fulfill and that protagonists in earlier novels looked for in fairy-tale ideals.

In contrast, Julia's thoughts about the men she knows are mainly negative. She feels detached from Andrés as he escorts her to and from her classes at the university, and her possibility of becoming involved with a male is scarred by her repressed rape and her relationship with her family. After being kissed by Rafael's friend Carlos, Julia has a nightmare about that kiss in which she links Carlos with her father. After waking, she is convinced that Carlos was really her dead brother Rafael, and she feels that further contact with Carlos would be illicit. Also the image of "a beach, rocks, a sea urchin, the paddle boat floating on the sea" (209) enters her mind, making her feel so dirty that she must shower at three in the morning. One of her only positive relationships with males is with her brother Rafael, and his death leaves her feeling responsible and guilty.[32] It is no wonder that physical contact with the females from whom she hopes to receive positive affirmation seems more appealing to her.

Another apparently positive relationship for Julia is with her grandfather Don Julio, who seems to function as a more beneficial mirror for Julia than her mother does. Bellver calls Don Julio "the mirror in which Julia saw her image reversed into what she might have become" and her "alter ego or male counterpart."[33] Indeed, Julia seems to be happier and stronger than at any other time while she is living in the mountains with her grandfather. After returning home, however, Julia discovers that she cannot reveal her true feelings and situation to her grandfather, but must write "without complaints, telling him lies" (130) to maintain his favor. She writes, lying to him: "Everyone is afraid of me and respects me. They say I'm a living portrait of you" (131).

Thus, instead of Don Julio providing a positive mirror for Julia, she cultivates an alternate self in his image to win his affection. A false self, moldable to the will of another, ultimately isolates and harms the true self.[34] Don Julio's domineering relationship with his own children (Julia's father and aunt Elena) hints at the negative influence he might have on Julia. Her grandfather precipitates another split—similar to the one between Julia and Julita. She seems well adjusted while she is living with him, but ultimately she has estranged her own identity.[35]

Just as Julia's relationships with other people weaken her identity by echoing her mother's rejection, reminding her of her rape, or further fragmenting her self-concept, the instances when Julia actually looks at herself in the mirror demonstrate negative development as well. At first, Julia recognizes and evaluates herself: "She looked pale, with her eyes too wide open to maintain the hope of being able to fall asleep soon. She had dark circles under her eyes. She pushed her hair aside, long and dark—not too unruly—from her face" (45). Although Julia's reaction is not especially positive, it is obvious she has spent time regarding herself in mirrors: "from time to time she stayed a long time contemplating herself in them" (45). According to La Belle, and from what has been observed in the other novels examined, this time in front of the mirror would be a positive step in her formation of identity.

Julia feels her eyes and hair are her strong points and prefers looking at these two features. Although she perceives a key to her identity in her eyes, Julia does not like others to look at them because they are "too expressive" (45): "when she felt happy, mad, anguished, sad, or any emotion, it was obvious in her eyes and others knew it. She believed that everyone could find out what was happening inside her merely by looking at her eyes" (45). She is fearful that others will ascertain her character before she does, so she has developed techniques to avert her eyes. This fear illustrates that she is far from affirming her identity, and any self-disclosure through her eyes would threaten her self-control even more.

Her hair, on the other hand, is the feature with which she can demonstrate the most control and individuality. In contrast with her mother's blond hair, Julia's hair is "black, long, and fine" (46) and is a point of contention where she can assert her own will against her mother's and grandmother's:

> Mamá and her grandma Lucía often advised her: you should do something with your hair. Julia meditated what she could do with her hair. In the end, she opted for doing nothing, that is: to leave it straight and comb it in the direction it took on it's own, falling in a natural way on both sides of her face. (46)

Although Mamá wants Julia to go to the beauty shop, Julia defiantly coerces the maid into cutting her hair. The mirror reveals that her hair is one aspect that distinguishes her, and she fights to maintain that distinction.

Later gazes into the mirror, however, do not reveal the individuality that Julia had noted in her eyes and hair. Instead, she observes that her reflection is horrifying after Rafael's death: "Upon looking at herself in the mirrors she told herself that she looked like a ghost and the dead one was her" (152). This ghostly image is even more pronounced just before her attempted suicide: "Passing in front of a mirror she saw herself pale, uncombed. She seemed like a ghost. She had the sensation of being asleep and living a nightmare" (213). The unreality of her reflection is emphasized by her sense of being in a nightmare, echoing the "death-in-life" state that Laing notes in schizophrenic psychosis. The autonomy and dominion of self that Julia had begun to notice because of her hair is eradicated by her disheveled appearance, and her sense of identity has faded. The mirror reveals an otherness indicative of a dangerous division of self, previously noted in metaphors and metonymic connections. Suicide seems like a logical method to eliminate the ghostly "other" in the mirror.

Just as the instances of mirroring confirm Julia's self-division in the novel, *Julia*'s third-person narration reflects the same disturbing detachment. While Andrea in *Nada* and Matia in *Primera memoria* write their stories, and Natàlia in *La plaça del Diamant* relates hers orally, Julia's story is apparently a memory going through her mind. Julia's thoughts about her life after waking from her nightmare, as well as the lack of punctuation in the novel, suggest Julia is rethinking her own story—or mirroring it in her mind. However, Julia's mirroring does not indicate progress toward autonomy but, rather, more division. The use of a third-person narrator with a first-person perspective suggests that the Julia thinking of her life does not see that life as her own. She narrates as if she were talking about another person by not using the pronoun *I*. Thus Julia's recollection of her life reveals the continuation of self-division that becomes more pronounced throughout the novel.

The metaphors and metonymy that revealed progress toward autonomy in *Nada* and *La plaça del diamant* and constricted to show negative development in *Primera memoria* are manipulated to reveal degeneration into schizophrenic division in *Julia*. Moix also employs metaphor and metonymy to convey problematic conditions in society that women authors had not dared to explore before, conveying, for instance, the details of Julia's rape with these tropes. Julia's schizophrenic condition can be attributed to the loss of identity and control she suffers after being raped, symbolizing patriarchal dominion over women. Her family, as a representation of society in general, increases her sense of having been violated and forces her to deal with her unlivable situation in a manner that Laing describes as schizophrenia. Julia's condition echoes Phyllis Chesler's idea that women's insanity is "an intense experience of female biological, sexual, and cultural castration, and a doomed search for potency."[36]

Mirror images in the novel also reflect increasing bifurcation of Julia's personality. That dangerous and increasing division fragments Julia's strength and reduces her to the dependent condition of a small child—but a child who is the "monster" that ultimately destroys her. While the previously analyzed novels by Laforet and Rodoreda intimate some hope for female autonomy, Moix's *Julia* conveys an aberrancy that is even more heinous than that described by Matute in *Primera memoria:* It describes a primitive sacrifice demanded by society that eventually turns woman on herself. But like the effect of *Primera memoria,* readers again perceive the need to improve societal conditions for women.

Moix's second novel, *Walter ¿por qué te fuiste?* (1973, Walter, Why Did You Go Away?), also intimates that society views women as monstrosities. Although *Walter*'s protagonist Ismael is a male cousin of Julia's, Levine calls him the "male alter ego of Julia herself."[37] Like *Julia, Walter* begins with an older protagonist (Ismael is about thirty-four) in a dreamlike state, recollecting childhood in an attempt to fathom the present. For seven years, Ismael has been searching for Lea (a cousin whom both Ismael and Julia adored) to give her some letters Julia wrote before committing suicide. Ismael's job as circus cowboy and his alcohol dependency are indications of his depraved and depressed condition. His sexual relationship with Albina, the circus' "half woman, half horse,"[38] is a metaphorical manifestation of the fear (instilled in young men by their religious education) that women are diabolical, monstrous sirens: "Girls are a weapon in the power of the devil, who uses them to make you sin, to pull you away from God, to brutalize your soul that is still white and to take it to hell."[39]

The ingrained cultural notion that women are dirty, mutant creatures is metonymically expressed by another female cousin pondering about her menstrual period: "Why did they call it that? I never liked menstruation, the word sounded like monster, monstrosity, monstruation, menstruation."[40] The perceived aberrancy of females affects the relationships of all of Julia's and Walter's cousins as they explore their personal and sexual identities during adolescence. Despite the many cuts made by censors, criticism of Spanish society and elaboration of sexual matters are much more direct in *Walter* than in *Julia*.

If the ambiguously expressed themes of rape and female homosexuality in Moix's *Julia* help make it a transitional novel, the next work—*El amor es un juego solitario* (1979, *Love Is a Solitary Game*) by Esther Tusquets—openly voices concerns of the newer generation by exploring a woman's *ménage à trois* and her fulfillment of explicit sexual fantasies.[41] While the novels previously analyzed focus principally on an adolescent female's search for identity and autonomy, *El amor es un juego solitario* features a married adult woman. Tusquets's novel hypothesizes a situation where a young woman—similar to Julia—befriends an older woman—like the professor Eva in *Julia*. In *El amor es un juego solitario,* however, the older woman's identity is even more fractured than the younger one's, continuing the dialogue about the emotional crises that can occur for women.[42] Like Julia, Tusquets's protagonist Elia cannot grow up and lives in "a world of adult children who have never learned to grow up."[43]

5

El amor es un juego solitario: Loss of Truth through Baroque Metaphors and Provocative Mirrors

After having examined Julia's personality disorders in Moix's novel *Julia,* it is easier to understand the negative female development in Esther Tusquets's prizewinning novel *El amor es un juego solitario* (1979, *Love Is a Solitary Game*).[1] While *Julia* relates the story of a young woman whose insecurity stems from her childhood rape, *El amor es un juego solitario* recounts the experiences of Elia, a middle-aged married woman with children, whose crisis centers on the aging process. Whereas Julia masks her true personality behind her childhood self, Elia attempts to cover her poorly developed self-image by playing out roles that she has encountered in literature or in other people's perceptions of her. The disparity represented by Julia's first-person perspective in a third-person narration is exaggerated even more by a third-person multiple focalization in *El amor es un juego solitario.* In addition to providing Elia's view of the action, the narration reveals the perspectives of Clara and Ricardo, the other players in the love game that distracts Elia from her concealed and isolated self. Critics recognize the erotic expression in Tusquets's work as a distinct change from novels written by women before Franco's death.[2]

In Elia's literary and theatrical simulations of life and love, metaphors help to create the exotic atmosphere for her contrived adventures. But within those simulated roles readers also encounter metaphors that express Elia's desire to be rescued and to save her own weakened identity.[3] Elia fleetingly and timidly expresses her own subconscious desires, putting them aside and hiding behind staged roles when she confronts resistance from others. Even though Elia associates these adopted metaphoric guises with her own life, the metaphors usually signify a contiguous and parallel association for her—like a metonymy—rather than a personal expression of equivalence of her feelings.[4]

In this instance, where metaphors function in a metonymic sense, the distinction between metaphor and metonymy becomes even less distinct—like the Shapiros's description of the circular qualities of metaphor and metonymy working together. One might also consider Elia's use of secondhand metaphors from other texts as diluted or "weak" metaphors of her own condition. Like the "weak" metaphors that David Lodge defines, these metaphors are more related to metonymy because "they depend on contiguity and context" rather than expressing an equivalence of Elia's personal subconscious.[5] Although Lodge's description of a "weak" metaphor is actually one in which the "terms of comparison are not widely separated,"[6] Elia's adopted metaphors are also "weak" and related to metonymy because they are a diversion from, and a mask over, her own personal expression.

Because the metaphors are somewhat ambiguous and are also metonymically linked to the roles Elia plays, they point more to these roles than to the basic truth about Elia's character. Indeed, the metaphors seem to serve as baroque ornamentation designed to distract attention from herself.[7] The metaphors do not evolve so as to suggest a growing sense of identity, as in the case of Andrea in *Nada,* or an increasing awareness of self, as in the circumstance of Natàlia in *La plaça del Diamant.* Instead, Elia's metaphorical expression intimates the creation of a camouflage designed to shield Elia from her own reality. This evasion of reality results in a "story of anti-development."[8]

Just as metaphorical expression reveals Elia's inclination toward the theatrical instead of the real, her use of mirrors also demonstrates how she contrives to alter reality. Elia establishes relationships with Clara (a college-age woman whom she has befriended) and Ricardo (a former schoolmate of Clara) because they mirror an image of her that she considers favorable. Decorative mirrors also serve to reflect the roles Elia plays and to bolster a false image of youth. Yet when Elia unexpectedly catches a glimpse of her face in a looking glass, she feels distressed and lost upon seeing her real self.

Elia's erotic game begins when her friend Clara relays a message from Ricardo, who desperately wants to meet Elia. Instead of being repulsed by the neophyte Ricardo, as Clara is, Elia associates Ricardo's longing with an erotic segment of an adventure novel she read as a young girl. Elia perceives Ricardo both as a passionate animal—young and uncorrupted by society—and a creator of a literary world. Elia and Ricardo finally establish a rendezvous in a hotel room decorated with mirrors, where Elia instructs Ricardo in the art of making love to her. During the course of their relationship, Clara continues to serve as a liaison between Elia and Ricardo and finally becomes an unwilling participant in their staged passion.

The paragraph of the adventure book Elia remembers describes the carnal attraction of primates in the jungle and is full of metaphors and metonymic suggestion. In that story, the hormonal scent secreted by the female apes attracts male primates from remote parts of the jungle, but the text depicts this biological phenomenon in emotive terms:

> An obscure call. In the spring a strange perfume invades the jungle, and the superior simians restlessly prowl around the lairs of their mates. There is most likely a taste of dust . . . and a curious laxity or lethargy that imposes an unusual rhythm on their movements, a special timing, like slow motion (the simians sniff the air with their nostrils dilated and wander among the trees with the heavy clumsiness of a pantomime).[9]

The words *call, perfume,* and *taste* intimate that the hero lost in the jungle is associating human sexual attraction with the seasonal mating of primates. The narration then further conceptualizes these metonymic connections into metaphoric expression, suggesting that the apes' biological urge is like a pantomime of human passion, with a more relaxed, clumsy, and unpressured atmosphere—as if one were filming human activity in slow motion.

While the adventure text already contains metonymic and metaphoric expression, Elia continues that process in her thoughts about Ricardo:[10]

> . . . she thinks that now it is also spring—spring again—and that the big simians, the gorillas perhaps or the orangutans, are doubtlessly sniffing the air in remote jungles, restlessly ready to initiate the same ritual dance around the lairs of their females, among the mixed aromas of sex, of decay, of flowers. It is an intense call, an obscure call, Elia remembers, and she laughs. (11)

She associates Ricardo's interest with the "male and female" located in "very distant points of the jungles" (11). The male (Ricardo)—because of "the unique aroma, unmistakable" (11) of the female in heat—patiently seeks her, knowing she will submit to her instinctive urging. Thus Elia decides, before meeting Ricardo, what the nature of their relationship will be. The jungle metaphors create a lush, erotic setting with which Elia artfully embellishes her newest diversion.

But while the narrator of *El amor es un juego solitario* continues to create metonymic and metaphoric links between Elia's situation and the jungle adventure book, other metaphoric intertexts surface as well.[11] Before meeting Ricardo, Elia imagines herself as the mythical and seductive Danae, caressed by the golden light of a transformed Zeus.[12] She metaphorically envisions Ricardo as her creation "as if he had been born of her, with the first and incorporeal covering of light" (17): He is "born" because of her sensuality. Elia also posits herself as a "nymph," while Ricardo is the "uninitiated faun" (21), and sees herself as a female Pygmalion who will create a loving image in her likeness. Ricardo is the mirror image of her own desire, reflecting not so much her need to love another as a need to love her own self.[13]

The metaphors communicate that Elia wants to create a male who will respond to her, and that she also wants him to re-create her. The imagined Ricardo is not only the "uninitiated faun" and the male born of her, but he is the golden light that enters her window and transforms her into the creative Danae:

> . . . before the persistence of the man's gaze or the caress of light and gold, Danae finally emerged sweet and purring, emerged slowly as if parting tides of tepid water or very thin purplish veils with her passage, she emerged alienating, rejecting with her passing, imposing distances, provoking and finding smoothness, toward the more corporal covering of the hands, the mouth, the thighs of the man, this masculine figure that some mid-days superimposed himself and blended, as if he had been born of her, with the first and incorporeal covering of light. (17)

In order to fulfill her, Ricardo must be a "simian" that awakens and arouses her, as well as "imaginative and poetic" (15), "the adolescent simian, the hairy gorilla, the chimpanzee poet" (16). She fantasizes that he "reconstructs her" and "creates her" (16). In other words, she is looking for a young and innocent male whom she can mold to her own liking, so that he, in turn, can help her to reconstruct and find her own self. These seemingly contradictory qualities of being malleable and formative intimate that Elia would like to help Ricardo, as well as have him improve her.

While Elia's mental foreplay before meeting Ricardo suggests that she may be on the verge of self-expression and self-discovery, she can never quite reach inside herself to rescue the "lost child" (35) whom both Ricardo and Clara notice in fleeting moments. As

Ricardo proceeds with the "scholarly discourse" (26) about his life, Elia tremblingly notices that he has the look of an "abandoned dog" (28). Ricardo's lost and unloved appearance triggers a hesitant and watchful revelation of Elia's confidences:

> . . . the woman speaks to him with hesitation, looking at his eyes, as if she were testing the ground before her in order to assure herself if she can or cannot continue with her truth . . . without both of them sinking, her truth and she herself, in the deep, boggy swamp through which they fearfully advance . . . on account of the hope that if they succeed in reaching the bank perhaps he . . . can extend his hand to them, and pull them out of their hell and redeem them. (34)

Elia is cautiously revealing her personal truth, hoping that Ricardo will respond favorably to her situation. She feels trapped and afraid and wants him to rescue her—which also would help him to feel loved and wanted.

Readers can metonymically link the "lost child" emerging from the swamp with Danae's transformation that enables her to arise, seductively and creatively, from her watery confinement. But the "lost child" is also a metonymic extension of the lost hero in the original jungle story. The metaphoric rescue from the "swamp" indicates that Elia would like to convert Ricardo into a hero. Like Danae, Elia would beget a hero because he had revived and rescued her. These similarities allow the reader to metonymically connect the metaphors and decipher Elia's essential and subconscious desire to be rescued—saving her hero at the same time. She does not want to be indebted to her hero but, rather, to exist on an equal level with him. Her subconscious revelation is "her truth" (34), a truth that Elia fears will be reengulfed, along with her, in the "deep, boggy swamp" (34). This fear, as well as Elia's reluctance to reveal too much about herself, brings to mind Julia's anxiety in Moix's novel that others will perceive too much about her by looking into her eyes. These misgivings also recall R. D. Laing's observation about the dread of "engulfment" by others in schizophrenic personalities who are not ontologically secure.[14]

Even though Ricardo tries to listen attentively and to make intelligent observations about Elia's disclosure, "the truth is that she has scared him profoundly" (35). Ricardo indicates that his sense of autonomous identity is at least as fragile as Elia's: "his fear was even greater than Elia's" (35). As Laing explains, a meaningful relationship with another person is not possible without a firm sense of one's own identity, as giving part of one's self to another can be threatening.[15] Thus, when Elia tries to convert Ricardo into a person who can help "a lost child, a disoriented little girl that is looking for some support and is going to break into tears" (35), Ricardo shrinks, terrified, from her plea. Even though the "lost child" in the swamp conveys Elia's essential expression of self, this self-revealing metaphor must be abandoned when Ricardo becomes frightened of the responsibility of saving her. His identity is too weak to aid Elia in a search for hers.

Elia, therefore, discards her "lost child" metaphor, and adopts a disguise:

> . . . and then Ricardo has stopped her there, in the bank itself, in order to make her abandon the whole burden behind them, and, while this burden sinks heavily and without noise into the dirty water, to see her emerge one more time at last like a nymph, and in the eyes of the nymph—that don't look anything like the eyes of a little girl—there is a dark flash, that nevertheless lasts less than an instant, and then Elia laughs, and presses his hand with tenderness, and begins to speak about Rimbaud. (35)

Much as schizophrenics adopt alternate selves that are moldable to the will of others,[16] Elia uses her imagination to convert herself into a nymph, feeling that she must mask her real identity to give Ricardo what he wants to see. The change is quite elusive in some respects, as the nymph that rapidly surfaces can be metonymically connected with Danae and her seductive sensuality. In spite of the subtlety of the hasty disguise, it betrays Elia's "truth." Coinciding with Laing's observations about schizophrenia, Elia's real self—revealed by the shadowy flash of her emotions—is again isolated and withdrawn into the "swamp" that weakens and suffocates it.

The "deep, boggy swamp" that traps Elia like an "inferno" (34) is also reminiscent of the metaphoric description in *Julia* of the isolated house on the sun-ravaged beach where "Julita" is confined while others are enjoying a continual party. Julia's metaphor evokes the "death-in-life" state that Laing describes of schizophrenics who become psychotic after having isolated and weakened their true self.[17] Like Julia, Elia also experiences periods when her life seems more like death. Clara has often observed Elia in such a deathlike condition:

> Because Clara has seen Elia seated for hours and hours, sometimes for whole days, barely dressed and disheveled . . . without hearing or really attending to anything any more. . . . And Clara has seen her crouched naked on one edge of her enormous bed, with her face to the wall, with a bottle of sleeping pills on the nightstand—without ever

knowing or being able to find our how many she has taken—. . . deafly chewing her disillusionment and her rancor like a fatal drug. (53)

Elia's abhorrence of the self that others do not care to see—the self she does not really even know—acts like a venom, further damaging her chances to become an autonomous being.

Elia's life, like that of the young Natàlia in *La plaça del Diamant,* demonstrates a lack of pride in and a disenchantment with herself. Elia, too, accepted the passive role of wife and mother imposed upon her by a society that saw her as "that different girl" (10) and that disapproved of her indulgent parents. But in her later attempt to escape from her unhappy marriage and submissive role, she becomes ensnared in another trap: the ruse that sexual latitude is equal to liberation. Both men and women often consider women's autonomy or liberation in terms of sexual behavior.[18] While Franco's code of conduct for women in Spain required that women be chaste,[19] women's later attempts to express their sensuality often became a misguided end instead of a complement to an autonomous self. Thus Elia's "role—the vocation, the art, the vice—unique and obsessive of loving" (52) is often "a mere pretext to escape for a few hours from the emptiness that is devouring her . . . to escape the swamp that will have to devour her and gobble her down finally perhaps in its bottomless whirlpools" (52). The sensual jungle of the primates, through which Elia tries to escape, also contains the entrapping swamp where she feels like a lost little girl.

When one considers becoming enslaved to "liberated" sexual behavior, the metonymic connections between the seemingly disparate metaphors of the mating apes and the lost girl in the swamp become more apparent. Although the sexuality inherent in the metaphor of the primates disguises the vulnerability of the "lost child," the two ideas essentially derive from the metaphoric hero lost in the jungle. Thus the metaphors that might lead to Elia's self-discovery also contain ambiguous and diverse elements, hinting at the potential for misinterpretation within a metaphor. Stacey Dolgin believes that in "the Tusquetsian world view, ostensible opposites are, in fact, synonyms,"[20] highlighting ambiguous polarities in Tusquets's work. Tusquets's metaphors also encompass this diametrically combined worldview. For instance, Elia's characterization as both "child" and adult in the metaphor comparing her to a nymph and her concurrent experience of "thirst and intoxication" (67) illustrate the coalescence of appositions. Loss of truth occurs

when one side or another of the expression is favored and the
"precarious equilibrium" (67) that Elia feels is disturbed.

Jacques Derrida's description of the intrinsic fragility of metaphors illustrates the potential danger of misinterpreting Elia's
metaphoric expression: "Metaphor is the moment of possible sense
as a possibility of non-truth. It is the moment of detour in which
truth can still be lost."[21] While La Belle explains that the mirror
can either trap or liberate women, depending upon its use,[22] each
metaphor also retains the possibility of misconception. Thus metaphors comprise the capability to cast Elia into either a positive
or negative role. Since metaphors are indicative of the personal
subconscious, they can be misinterpreted not only by readers but
also by the subject and the people with whom the subject tries to
communicate.

For instance, the metaphor of the primate in the jungle (indicative of female sensuality and freedom from antiquated sexual
norms) also can connote brutality and subjugation to physical urges
that can leave the female enslaved—or trapped and lost in the
jungle swamp. One version could be liberating for Elia, while the
other would compound her negative self-image. Likewise, the
metaphoric adaptation of the myth of Danae (suggesting an awakening of sensuality and creation) also conveys the invasive power
of a male who entraps the female, permeates her being, and causes
her to propagate more patriarchal lineage. The father and son are
indistinguishable at times, as if the mother had no role in the creation. In Elia's quest to be "reinvented," an equitable interpretation
of her metaphors is essential to others understanding her and in
her own definition of self.

Elia's lack of autonomous strength, however, allows others to
obfuscate her essential expression and leads her to an erroneous
characterization of her self. When Elia notices Ricardo's fear and
hesitation to save the "lost child," she abandons her attempt to
define herself and assumes a role she thinks he wants her to play.
Her adoption of the nymph role—the role that disgüises her metaphor of wanting to be rescued and to rescue another—limits her
ability to save herself. Elia camouflages herself as a seductive
nymph in order to protect herself from Ricardo's disapproval.
Elia's subconscious metaphors based on literary texts, when influenced by Ricardo's interpretation and desires, become twisted
to the point that Elia no longer recognizes them as expressions of
her self but only as roles that she performs.

The metaphors projecting Elia's ambivalent balance between an
adult woman and a child reflect Franco's attempt to confine women

to what Martín Gaite describes as a dependent, childlike role. These opposing descriptions of adult and child illustrate a component of what La Belle calls "the alternations between the poles of oxymoronic identity."[23] Elia's masklike roles eventually obscure the balance between the paradoxical poles of her identity: "the possibility for evolution or change doesn't exist in Elia, the possibility to overcome anything does not fit within her, because in a certain sense, only in a certain sense, she will never be an adult woman" (66). Instead, there is only the "eternal child or eternal adolescent that is searching, in a precarious equilibrium on the loose cord where she balances herself over anguish, always dual and ambivalent in her expressions" (67). The preceding metaphor describes the tenuous balance between truth and falsehood; it conveys Elia's anguish about heading in the wrong direction, but she is confused, trapped, and unable to go the other way.

A sense of Elia's entrapment is apparent when Ricardo speaks "in a thorough and exact way, in interminable, progressive, maniacal precision" (90) of including Clara in their love game. Elia vaguely notices the dangerous trap that entices her further away from the truth:

> At some point there must be a mistake, a trap must be hidden, but she forces herself in vain to discover where the trap is located, where the error begins, or, in case neither an error or trap exists, to discover the reason that Ricardo's argument . . . disarms her and crushes her. (90)

Ricardo's twisted reasoning leads Elia far from the "lost child" with whom she identified before she entered their love "game." The "truth" of the "lost child" is misplaced in the erotic jungle swamp, and that essential metaphor becomes just another role for Elia.

Later metonymic connections between the lost little girl and the seductress express Elia's desire to deny that she is lost and seeking help. The "lost child" becomes a role employed by the seductress to further ensnare her victims. Concealment of the verity in the "lost child" makes the entire novel appear an artifice.[24] Elia and the other characters lose the delicate moment of metaphorical truth that Derrida describes and become trapped in an artificial void. Readers, however, can uncover the elements of character truth in the novel by retracing the metaphors and metonymic connections revealing Elia's essential expression.

Since Clara's admiration of Elia has been tarnished because of the affair with Ricardo, Elia must act out a special part to entice

Clara into the game. Elia senses that Clara is repulsed by the seductive role she has employed with Ricardo and her many former lovers. Therefore, in her relationship with Clara, she decides to discard that guise and use another she believes will be more pleasing to Clara:

> . . . it is not the goddess of easy laughter, it is not the woman of the brazen and lewd world, it is not the triumphant and initiative nymph ready for expert caresses and perverse disguises, it is not this one who is cradling her: it is an infinitely sad and desolate little girl. (104)

A shift to Clara as focalizer reveals that Elia was right. Clara perceives Elia as "a little girl . . . a poor woman who struggles in vain to escape with her dreams from the swamp, and who cradles in herself, as she cradles her, all the loneliness and fears" (104). Elia performs the role in which Clara likes to imagine her, as the innocent, magnificent, and imaginative "Queen of the Cats" (104), who comforts all the poor, stray, and wounded—like Clara. To Clara, Elia becomes both innocent and motherly, replacing Clara's own unloving mother and remaining pure as she satisfies Clara's sexual desires.[25] Clara is unaware of, or disavows, the sexual character of her love for Elia and rationalizes their physical contact by equating it to the good feeling she had while sleeping at a friend's house as a little girl. To continue denying the sexual aspect of her relationship with Elia, Clara must see Elia as young and innocent—like Clara's childhood friend with whom she shared secrets during the night. Therefore, the role of the "lost child" is the perfect ruse for Elia to captivate Clara.

But Elia merely executes the role of the "lost child" in order to retain Clara's admiration, instead of truly revealing herself to Clara. Elia turns away from Clara to sleep and says farewell the next day with a smile "a little uncomfortable, perhaps feeling somewhat guilty" (116), revealing Elia's deception of Clara. Elia uses a former truth to ensnare Clara into a situation in which she will become "the public . . . one spectator . . . someone distinct" who "can appreciate and immortalize perhaps this exquisite scene" (78)—the reenactment of the love scene between Elia and Ricardo.

Like the ghostly reappearances of "Julita" in Moix's novel, the "lost child" acquires ambiguous and even sinister qualities when Elia uses that role to lure Clara into the love game. But while "Julita" becomes the "monster" who destroys herself, Elia is also destructive to others. In her seductive siren guise with Ricardo, and in the equally false role of the "lost child" used to captivate

Clara, Elia sacrifices her friends as well as herself. Her game functions as a "drug" (70) in her empty, boring life, and Elia numbs herself to the consequences for others: "everything and everyone would cease to exist and Elia would advance over their cadavers, scarcely noticing them beneath the souls of her naked feet" (70). Elia's bed becomes "an altar" and she is "covered with the nudity of the supreme priestess" (72), as she immolates Ricardo and Clara, drawing them into her game of "chess with the devil" (130). Ricardo is initiated into a role of sexual "dominion and . . . power" (123), "a complicated game against the devil" (129) that can only hurt others, while Clara becomes more "inert" (128) and "too sad" (132) to rebel against the usurpation of her will. They sink deeper and deeper into "the bottomless trap" (44), reminiscent of Matia's well in *Primera memoria*.

Although there is an abundance of metaphoric expression and metonymic extension in *El amor es un juego solitario,* the metaphors do not indicate that Elia is confronting her own reality: Instead, she is attempting to escape from it. The metaphors of the "lost child" and Danae—that once conveyed Elia's subconscious desire to be rescued and to save others—become metonymically linked with the metaphorical roles that protect and insulate Elia's identity. Just as the Shapiros describe metonymy that slides into metaphor, Elia's metaphors—after losing their balance of truth—slide into a condition that is similar to metonymy. While they still intimate Elia's personal qualities, they no longer express an equivalency for her. Metaphors attributed to her view of reality indicate that she is trying to obscure her subconscious by means of ornamental roles she employs. Although these roles seem designed to hide and protect her fragile identity, eventually they camouflage it for so long that even she does not recognize it. Just as incomplete but repetitive metaphors suggest Julia's repression of her rape in Moix's novel, Elia's continued use of guises makes it impossible for her to disentangle her true feelings from her adopted literary roles.

In many respects, the roles that Elia acts out function like the fairy tales that serve as mirrors and models in *Nada* and *Primera memoria*.[26] Elia imagines myths and models that appear quite different from traditional fairy tales, but they still suggest she is trapped in repressive and compulsive patterns that prohibit her from becoming an autonomous being. Although the myths of Danae and the nymph depict a metaphoric rebirth of a more sensual woman, they also point at a new type of compulsion—the compulsion to fulfill a sensual role. Elia's new role, like Kolbenschlag's

description of fairy tales, is "emblematic of predisposing conditions of a particular social milieu."[27] That milieu, in Elia's case, is
the Spain of the late Seventies that offered more sexual freedom
for women, but their "freedom" was also a new way to subjugate
them.[28]

Despite the changed character of the "liberated" and passionate
myths Elia imagines, the texts are still steeped in patriarchal conventions. For example, the male hero lost in the jungle envisions
female apes as sexually uninhibited women. The position of the
female primate in the text, however, is not very liberated. She is
a slave to her biological drives and to the persistent males who
track her down by way of a scent. Likewise, in the myth of Danae,
female sensuality is aroused while the heroine is trapped in a tower
and raped by Zeus. Even though Elia may think she is sexually
liberated in her love games, free from the confines of marital conventions, these imagined episodes suggest that she senses her lack
of autonomy. Ultimately, her roles of Danae, female ape, and "lost
child" are not an improvement over Andrea's aspiration in *Nada*
to look into the mirror and see herself transformed into Cinderella:
All the models involve submission of the self to patriarchal texts.

While Elia's imagined "fairy tales" reflect her subconscious in a
deflected manner—similar to Julia's dreams in Moix's novel—the
existence of other mirrorlike reflections in Elia's love games is
underlined early in her relationship with Ricardo. Elia and Ricardo
both use the other to reflect the image that they want to see of
themselves:

> . . . this precious image that they chisel and sketch of themselves, that
> they tirelessly reflect and multiply one against the other, in a game of
> mirrors that reproduces and projects them toward infinitude, the two
> of them so ingenious. (35)

However, Ricardo and Elia not only use each other to infinitely
reflect false images of themselves, Molinaro illustrates how all
three of the participants in the *ménage à trois* use the others to
find favorable self reflections. According to Molinaro, this empty
mirroring "disguise[s] and thus protect[s] their simulacra" and results in a circular vacuum of endless reflections.[29] Molinaro's words
"disguise" and "protect," and the subsequent "vacuum" that sub-
stitutes for life, are again reminiscent of Laing's descriptions of
schizophrenic personalities and the "death-in-life" state.[30]

The suggestion that all three participants in the love game live
in varied states of "death-in-life" also implies the pervasiveness of

potentially schizophrenic "ontological insecurity" in society. Not
only are Clara, Elia, and Ricardo so insecure in their own identities
that they base their lives on unrealities, their immediate families
also reflect signs of unhealthy orientation.[31] Elia's husband ignores
her identity, leaving her alone, lonely, and seeking gratification
from scores of other men. Clara's parents withhold their love to
the point that Clara participates in a lesbian relationship with Elia.
And Ricardo's mother raises a child who is so insecure that he
attempts to overpower Elia and Clara—and the elements of society
that they represent—so he can feel more significant. Ricardo exemplifies the culturally problematic male whose overpresent mother
precipitates fear and resentment of women, as well as an insecure
sense of masculinity.[32] In his relationship with Elia and Clara, Ricardo reveals resentment of his mother and his desire to get revenge against society.

The "contagious disease" (84) that Clara perceives in all of their
lives supports the theory that individual schizophrenic behavior is
a mirror of disturbed behavior in society, and that this aberrant
behavior is self-perpetuating.[33] All three characters reflect and
magnify their infirmities in the others, causing the insecurities to
grow and spread. The third-person multiple focalization in *El amor
es un juego solitario*—revealing the troubled perspectives of Clara
and Ricardo, as well as Elia's—supports the notion of proliferative
personality disorders.

In turn, Elia's personal ontological insecurity can be detected
by her use of mirrors. While mirrors can help to form a sense of
self (especially for adolescent females who are beginning to define
their identity), middle-aged women often turn to the mirror again
for reaffirmation of their identity. La Belle speaks of the "temporal
dimension" of the looking glass, that not only visually records the
past and present but intimates the decay and death inherent in the
future.[34] As women age they often do not want to associate the
image they see in the mirror with their concept of self. An aging
face in the mirror is even more frightening when a woman has
never clearly established her own identity.

Elia, too, is a victim of the temporal aspect of self-reflection;
she experiences a sense of "panic toward aging and death" (148).
The narrator describes her fear of aging and her search for something to postpone the inevitable:

. . . something that postpones the instant that she must confront her
unrecognizable image in her mirrors again, in the eyes of her husband,
her sons, her lovers, an implacable image that now seems magically

displaced and abolished, substituted by another image, although precarious, distinct, that she herself has perhaps made up, but that she
finds magnified, solid, nearly believable, in the eyes of these two adoles-
cents who invent her. (148)

Just as Elia subverts and ultimately destroys the concept of a helpless girl by using it as a seductive strategy, she attempts to refute
the image of her own aging through her roles and pretense with
Clara and Ricardo.[35] The mirror—and the eyes of the men in her
life—reflect that she is less acceptable as she ages. This multiple
negative reflection complicates Elia's attempts to express her true
identity and causes her to hide behind the roles she plays.

Although at times Elia seems to enjoy looking at herself in the
mirror, this pleasure occurs only when she is playing a role that
masks her true self. For instance, when Elia selects a hotel room
for her first sexual encounter with Ricardo, she purposefully
chooses one with mirrors. The room's "phony decor . . . with
perhaps more mirrors than the chambers of a harem" (72) reminds
her of literary scenes and appears to be the perfect setting for her
guise as nymph. The gigantic mirrored surface "will reflect . . . the
nude and embraced bodies of both of them" (72) and will increase
their pleasure, as if they were watching a staged performance of
pornographic literature.

Again, Elia is the recipient of images even as she tries to be the
creator, hinting at a negative effect of dependence upon the mirror.
La Belle points out the importance of woman defining her ego in
creative ways that are not related to her body—especially as she
grows older—in order to free herself from "male / mirror tyr-
anny."[36] Elia's attempts to fill literary roles are based on her sexuality and physical appearance, tying her to the mirror and further
oppressing and frightening her when she unexpectedly confronts
her own reflection. Elia's "delicate and flexible body like that of a
girl or of an adolescent" (61–62) with "the long and fine thighs of
a woman" (62) is a prop or artifice that she employs to seduce
Ricardo and to captivate Clara. Her still youthful body masks her
true age and identity, and the gaudy mirror—baroquely bordered
by "four stucco cupids" (78)—aids in projecting her artificial and
provocative role.

In contrast, whenever Elia unexpectedly sees herself in a mirror
without the disguise of a role, she is frightened by what she sees.
Elia equates the "displeasure that her own unexpected reflection
in a mirror produces in her" (66–67) with "a threat, an occult
danger" (66). The "eternal child" Elia confronts in the mirror re-

minds her of the jungle swamp representing her personal "death-in-life" existence. Suddenly seeing herself reflected in a mirror "often causes an uncomfortable fright in her" (63), as the image it reflects "doesn't coincide very well with the image that she fantasizes of herself" (63). As with La Belle's observations about women in literature who do not recognize their own reflection, and like the division of self that Julia's non-recognition reveals, Elia's reaction to her image in the mirror shows an alarming psychological imbalance.

Further, as Elia's physical characteristics change with age, the mirror will become even more threatening to her. Although she can still use her body as a disguise from the aging she fears, the inevitable degeneration of her physical attributes will make it more difficult to attract lovers. Without the diversion of her love games, Elia sinks into the "emptiness" (52) that Clara has observed, when Elia stares unseeingly at the television for hours and numbs herself with sleeping pills and sedatives. With fewer lovers to distract her from life, Elia's catatonic states will increase—again evoking the idea of the "death-in-life" trap.

La Belle advises that women can employ other, more creative "mirrors"—such as writing—to express their identity. While Clara suggests that Elia might liberate herself by writing, Elia's story is not a positive expression of self. The relation of Elia's *ménage à trois* does not increase her self-knowledge or autonomy the way that Andrea's writing of her experience does in *Nada*, or Natàlia's oral presentation does in *La plaça del Diamant*. In contrast, Elia's story shows even more division and outside control than *Julia*'s third-person narrative with its first-person perspective. Molinaro illustrates the complete lack of autonomy that Elia demonstrates in her own story when she states: "The narrator appropriates her [Elia's] voice and filters it through the narrator's control, just as Ricardo appropriates her body and filters it through his physical control."[37] In spite of Elia's imaginative attempts to be author and creator, the creations imply that she is hiding her identity behind prescribed roles that others assign and dominate.

The original truth about Elia's identity, that metaphors might have helped her express and that the mirror could have helped her define, is circumvented when society forces her to conceal aspects of herself. Elia first protects herself by playing the accepted role of wife and mother, but the repression caused by covering over her own personality eventually causes her to rebel with lovers who temporarily increase her self-esteem. Changes in Spanish society after Franco's death gave women more liberty, and Tusquets's novel is indicative of the literature of the Seventies in Spain that breaks through the taboo against women's expression of their sensuality. However, the sexual "rebirth" implicit in the metaphors of Danae, the female primate, and the nymph do not suggest autonomy for Elia, nor (by extension) for other Spanish women. In her affair with Ricardo, Elia still performs the roles that Ricardo expects of her and masks over her own identity.

Additionally, the fragile, ambiguous moment of truth of Elia's metaphors of identity is lost when the desires of others influence her expression. Readers can metonymically trace this loss of truth to the metaphor of the "lost child" that expresses Elia's desire to save her individuality. But this essential metaphor eventually evolves into just another role that she feels forced to play. The "lost child" becomes as false to her as the provocative mirrors she uses to dramatize the feigned characters in her love game. The truth of her identity has disintegrated to the point that it seems irretrievable, and she can only pull others with her into the choking, inescapable quagmire. Elia loses in her labyrinthine game "with the devil," as does everyone else whom she entices to play.

El amor es un juego solitario is the second novel in a trilogy written by Tusquets.[38] The first, *El mismo mar de todos los veranos* (1978, *The Same Sea as Every Summer*), also features a lesbian relationship between a middle-aged protagonist and an adolescent Clara. Servodidio points out that the protagonist's identity formation was hampered by the lack of positive mirroring between the protagonist and her domineering mother.[39] The unnamed protagonist, E., narrates her own story, communicating to the reader that her sense of identity is more intact than that of Elia in *El amor*. Since E. is a professor, there is an even more obvious dialogue with Julia's professor Eva in Moix's novel.

The predominance of literary metaphorical references, mirror images, fairy-tale models, and the mother-daughter relationship in the protagonist's search to affirm her identity closely link *El mismo mar* with the other novels we have examined. For example, as E. enters her childhood house by the sea, she focuses on a nude male statue put there by her mother. E. defines her mother as a "Greek goddess" in whom "maternity . . . doesn't fit within the possibilities of her magnificent essence."[40] The mother, like Julia's mother in Moix's novel, complicates E.'s identity formation, as do her ineffectual father and her husband Jorge.

E. seeks a positive reflection in Clara, whom she first meets in front of the huge mirror of an ice-cream parlor. Commenting on the list of ice-cream dishes painted on the mirror—"And it's a pity that the mirror . . . only offers predictable and orthodox combinations, and that one can't scandalize . . . soliciting sinfully incompatible and prohibited mixtures"—E. foreshadows the lesbian relationship that develops.[41] The sea serves as the literal and metaphoric backdrop for their affair, in which Clara is described as an "Aztec goddess," the doll Angélica, Rapunzel, Ariadne, a cat, Guinevere, and other mythical, imaginative, and fairy tale characters.[42] Mary Vásquez sees the love between women in Tusquets's novels as metaphoric of love free from entrapment and power plays.[43]

The third novel of the trilogy, *Varada tras el último naufragio* (1980, Beaching after the last shipwreck), intimates a more positive identity resolution for its middle-aged Elia.[44] The timid writer Elia in *Varada* has a friend and alter ego named Eva—again reminiscent of Moix's Eva. Elia's husband abruptly leaves her before she goes to spend the summer vacation with Eva (a self-confident lawyer) and Eva's husband, Pablo. During the summer Pablo has an affair with a younger woman, forcing both Eva and Elia to reconsider their lives and identities. Eva's friendship with the young woman Clara, and Clara's passion for Eva tie *Varada* even more closely with the fist two novels. The switch from a third-person to first-person narrative voice at the conclusion of the novel marks a metaphoric recovery of Elia's identity.

In *Para no volver* (1985, In order not to return), the fifty-year-old protagonist Elena (an unpublished writer) is depressed even before her film-director husband, Julio, leaves her for another woman. Like the other protagonists, Elena uses sex and drugs to cover over her loneliness and depression. Although she attempts to work through her despair with a psychoanalyst—whom she calls "the Magician"—the superior attitude of the psychiatrist precludes the possibility of dialogic interchange: "Elena spent her life waiting to hear some words from the lips of the Magician that . . . would have infinite value and power."[45] Therefore, Elena must search for her identity essentially unguided. The potentiality of the psychiatrist as interlocutor and Elena as a writer link *Para no volver* to the two novels that follow, Carmen Martín Gaite's *El cuarto de atrás* and Carme Riera's *Qüestió d'amor propi*.

Barbara Ichiishi notes that within all of Tusquets's novels a circular structure exists, as well as "a clear pattern of repetition linking each work to the ones that came before,"[46] supporting the notion of cyclical development of women that Pratt, Gardiner, and Ferguson describe. Just as Matia in *Primera memoria* advances societal awareness of women's condition despite her lack of development, Ichiishi feels that development is achieved in Tusquets's novels by the "therapeutic repetition . . . of the central emotional issue in the protagonist's (and behind her the author's) life."[47] In this sense, even negative development, when presented in written form, aids progress. In addition to the textual and personal dialogue between Tusquets and Moix that Ichiishi documents, Elizabeth Ordóñez also notes the bonds of aesthetic concerns, feminism, and friendship between the work of Tusquets, Moix, and Concha Alós.[48]

Although Elia in *El amor es un juego solitario* presents the most negative perspective of what happens to a woman who cannot define her identity, Carmen in *El cuarto de atrás (The Back Room)* gives more hope to women in their creative expression of an autonomous self. Carmen is also an older woman, but she finds and fulfills ways to define herself beyond her physical reflection in the mirror and provides a positive model for other women. Her metaphors and the metonymic links they present also reflect that she no longer fears the subversive power of patriarchal oppression, but that she has come to terms with that frightening intrusion into her life.

6

Metonymy and Mirrors as Process of Identity in *El cuarto de atrás*

Metaphors in *El amor es un juego solitario* convey a loss of truth and meaning in Elia's life. The convergence of metonymic systems in Carmen Martín Gaite's novel *El cuarto de atrás* (1878, *The Back Room*), however, transmits a process of productive change and development for its protagonist, Carmen.[1] Although Carmen appears to be slightly older than Elia, she has found a more constructive outlet for her imaginative identity through writing.[2] Carmen's reminiscing about her childhood illustrates that she has recognized the constraints patriarchal society has imposed upon her and is attempting to regain the freedom she felt as a child.[3] Instead of the labyrinthine cycle of meaningless repetition that Elia's story transmits, Carmen's cyclical reevaluation of her past conveys part of a positive process of self-development and self-creation.[4] The written pages of the novel that appear as Carmen talks with her mysterious interlocutor serve as proof of Carmen's unfolding self-expression.

Just as baroque and repeated metaphors in Tusquets's novel create the scenario for the meaningless games that are an escape from Elia's life, the metaphors in *El cuarto de atrás* also posit the protagonist in a game-playing situation. But while Elia becomes entrapped in her games, the metaphors in Martín Gaite's novel merely suggest the playing field for Carmen's integration of reality and imagination. The metaphors often operate on two levels, like the "cuarto de atrás" that refers on the literal level to the playroom in Martín Gaite's childhood home, and on the metaphoric level to her creative state of mind.[5]

Perhaps of even more importance in Martín Gaite's novel is the metonymic suggestion that motivates both the protagonist and the readers to expand their imaginative horizons. The metonymic linking of opposing ideas and objects allows the protagonist to create new and unforeseen possibilities. Further, the lack of resolved,

125

incontrovertible metaphors at the end of the novel permits readers to form their own conclusions, or to continue further linking, and gives the novel a feeling of openness and continual process.[6]

Mirror images within the novel also operate as metonymic links, helping Carmen fuse aspects of her past with the magnified self-awareness she experiences in her conversation with the mysterious interlocutor. When Carmen looks into a mirror she is reminded of times that she gazed at herself when she was younger. By visualizing these former reflections, Carmen is able to integrate positive moments of self-identity from her past with her on-going identity formation. This process makes her individuality fluid and changing, instead of static or regressive like Elia's in *El amor es un juego solitario,* or like Matia's in *Primera memoria.* At the same time, the augmentation and blending realized in this mirroring eliminates a complete return to a former self, as when the six-year-old "Julita" took control of Julia's personality in Moix's novel.

Like *Julia,* however, *El cuarto de atrás* begins with the protagonist's insomnia. Carmen's mind and bedroom are cluttered with reminders of books she wants to write—memoirs about postwar Spain and a fantastic novel. Just as she falls asleep the phone rings and an unknown man asks for the interview she promised him. Carmen dresses and, after seeing a huge, black cockroach on the way to the door, lets a man dressed in black enter. As he questions Carmen about her latest writing project, she begins to relax and converse with him. Carmen notices a stack of pages next to her typewriter that she does not remember being there, but their conversation is so compelling that she is distracted from her curiosity. The intimate discussion with the visitor dispels most of the doubts Carmen has about him. Suddenly, a gust of wind scatters the now towering stack of papers, and the stranger offers to rearrange them while Carmen rests on the sofa. Carmen awakes later, fully dressed and in her own bed. Although the conversation seems like a dream, Carmen finds a little gold box given to her by the man in black, as well as the typed pages of her completed fantastic-memoir novel, *El cuarto de atrás.* The opening words of Carmen's novel are identical to those of the novel the readers have just finished.

The aura of wonder and fantasy in *El cuarto de atrás* is foregrounded in the opening pages of the novel, when Carmen's description of the phase between sleeping and waking is expressed in poetic, metaphoric terms. Carmen's words—like the emotive portrayal of Julia's disposition after her nightmare—create a connotative mood that tempers the reader's expectations. But Carmen's word portrait is of a positive dreamlike state rather than a nightmare:

> . . . if I close my eyes . . . a familiar, unchanging apparition visits me: a parade of stars with clowns' faces that soar up like balloons that have escaped and laugh with frozen grins, in a zigzag pattern, one after the other, like spirals of smoke that gradually become thicker.[7]

The apparition that visits Carmen every night, instead of frightening her with its ghostlike presence, exhibits qualities of an awaited adventure. The parade of stars, the clowns' faces, and the balloons all suggest the exciting, imaginative anticipation felt by a child at a carnival or circus.

While the feeling is positive, it still can contain unexpected or unnerving elements like getting lost "amid the confusion" or watching "the lions or the trapeze artist falling from the very highest point" (10). Carmen describes the feeling as a "a melody that can't be heard . . . a strange silence like the prelude of something that's about to happen" (9), suggesting the unexpected eccentricity of a surrealist work of art. This metaphorical representation of Carmen's state between sleeping and waking prepares the readers to suspend their own concepts about the real and the oneiric world and to accept the protagonist's imaginative anticipation as normal.

Carmen elicits what Samuel Levin describes as a special reaction to a metaphor: "we have in the reader a tacit agreement to contemplate a world different from the actual world, a world of . . . imagining in which novelties of reference and suspension of normal truth conditions will be tolerated."[8] The metaphors provide an important bridge, allowing readers to cross over to Carmen's point of view and to accept events that ordinarily might be dismissed as impossible. The acceptance of the incredible is essential within the parameters of the fantastic mode, thus metaphor plays an important role in creating the ambience for fantasy and the marvelous. Additionally, the oneiric atmosphere emerges as an important subconscious metaphor expressing aspects of Carmen's identity.[9]

While metaphor is integral to the chimerical mood, the use of metonymy early in the novel immediately opens new possibilities. Carmen, in a semioneiric state, visualizes herself on the beach without her glasses, drawing pictures in the sand:

> I'm painting. I'm painting, what am I painting? What color am I using and what letter? With the C of my name, three things with C, first a *casa* (house), then a *cuarto* (room), and then a *cama* (bed). (11)

The repeated words and alliterations are reminiscent of a childhood nursery rhyme, as Carmen metonymically associates things that begin with "c" like her name.[10] Just as the simplistic, poetic words evoke a time when Carmen was free to use her imagination, the three things she thinks of—home, room, and bed—are also indicative of places where she was at liberty to develop her creativity.

Therefore, Carmen not only suggests a metonymic linking of objects but also a linking of past with present time. She remembers her childhood and describes the odd transfer in her dreamlike state from that time into the present: "The shifting back and forth has started, I can't tell any longer if I'm lying in this bed or in that one; I think, rather, that I'm moving from one to the other" (12). Carmen explains the bridging between different periods in her life and foregrounds a technique that allows her to recount past memories as if they were happening at that very moment. Her use of metaphoric and metonymic patterns allows her to enact "splits in [her] personality" and "the rupture of boundaries between time and space" (19).[11]

Readers accept the switches from past to present as normal developments in her dreamlike state, and Carmen's tendency to metonymically link past and present times—as well as entities— acts as a catalyst for readers to do the same. This impetus to participate in the novel by linking ideas, things, and different times ultimately permits the linking of the very different fantastic and historical modes.[12] Just as the readers are crucial in Todorov's definition of the fantastic, their role in this process of metonymic linking is so essential that some critics have identified the reader as the ultimate interlocutor.[13]

After Carmen has initiated the process of metonymic association, the readers soon become aware of the multiple—and often conflicting—connections that are evident within the text. For example, a complicated succession of associations begins to unfold as Carmen hurries to the door with the unnerving premonition that she will see a cockroach:

> I apprehensively turn on the light switch, and scarcely a meter from my feet appears an enormous, totally motionless cockroach, standing out clearly in the center of one of the white tiles, as though certain that it is occupying the space where it belongs on a gigantic chess board. (28)

The metaphor comparing the black-and-white floor tiles to a chessboard conveys the idea that Carmen is beginning a type of game.[14]

With the metaphor of a game board established, further metonymic extensions of game-playing help to explain Carmen's reaction to the cockroach.

At first the two players—Carmen and the roach—remain motionless, "attempting to decipher our respective intentions" (28). Carmen then explains her move and reveals that she wants to continue to participate in the game: "I discard all intention of attacking and opt for fleeing" (28). In a game of chess, the most entertaining and strategic move might well be to escape temporarily rather than to annihilate the opponent. Thus Carmen's reaction is not completely defensive but, rather, she makes a tactical move to prolong the game. She subverts the roach's "plan . . . to curtail my getting past it" by "jumping over its body" (28) and continues on to meet the next opponent in her dream/life game.[15]

Her next adversary, "a man dressed in black . . . wearing a broad-brimmed hat, also black" (29), is revealed via his metonymic connections to the cockroach. The color of his clothing, his hat with "grandes alas" (big wings), his black eyes that "shine like two cockroaches" (30), and the feeling of "anxiety mixed with fright, like before seeing the cockroach appear" (29), undeniably link him with the enemy cockroach. But the mysterious man is also reassuring, telling her that "Cockroaches are harmless . . . and they have a very attractive sheen . . . there are too many prejudices against them" (30). Although the "man dressed in black" is linked to the adversary cockroach, as they begin to talk other metonymic connections suggest he might be an ally—or perhaps another foe.[16]

Throughout the novel the man in black can be metonymically linked with a great number of positive, negative, and ambiguous elements in Carmen's life. For example, before Carmen drifted off to sleep, she had been repeating "I want to see you, I want to see you" (25) to an unknown male with whom she had always wanted to communicate. Waking to the call of a mystery male who wants to talk to her naturally links him to the long-dreamed-of, ideal interlocutor.

In other diverse associations the "man dressed in black" is linked to the thunder and storm outside by his voice that coincides with a flash of lightning, and to Raimundo (the hero of *novelas rosa* [harlequin-type romances] that Carmen enjoyed as a young girl) because of the "sudden languor" (38) he causes Carmen to feel. He also is connected to Todorov himself because of comments he makes about fantastic literature. Later, his question of whether Carmen believes in the devil (as the visitor looks at her engraving of "Luther's Discussion with the Devil") links him with Lucifer.

Additionally, the devil conversing with Luther is "totally black," as are the "two huge wings on his back" (17), echoing the color and shape of the man's hat. But despite the ominous appearance of the devil in the picture, Luther seems to be totally absorbed in conversation with him. Likewise, Carmen becomes immersed in her conversation and in thoughts precipitated by the mysterious man who is metonymically connected to a diverse array of entities and ideas.

Indeed, the strange visitor seems to function for Carmen much in the same disorganized and stimulating way as the colored pills from the little gold box he gives her. His questions and comments—like the pills—"revive memories" (107) and help Carmen to link her past remembrances to her present problem of how to write her book. His effect upon her memories and thoughts links him to the contents of the "cajita de oro" (little gold box), as he invites her to play "an unknown game" (106) and to discard her old, unimaginative rules. Later, when Carmen is awakened by her daughter returning home, the "caja de oro" (gold box) and Carmen's completed creative book act as links to the visit of the "man dressed in black." Just as the man wished, the gold box becomes an "amulet" that links her with the past (as well as with his visit) and makes her memories live again.

The end of the novel, which leaves the visitor ultimately connected to the little gold box, might seem to be a metaphor that resolves the ambiguity suggested by the previous metonymic linking. The imaginative power precipitated by the amulet/gold box/ "man dressed in black," however, permits Carmen to revive the imaginative freedom she had as a child in the "cuarto de atrás." Carmen compares that back room to "an attic of the mind, a type of secret enclosure full of obscure old things" (91). Carmen explains that the "cuarto de atrás" had a "curtain protecting the doorway" (104), screening the room from mind and sight. The pills within the gold box act to lift that concealing curtain.

Thus the little gold box permits Carmen the nearly infinite capacity to pull memories and feelings from her past to reintegrate them into her present state in life, renewing the creative resources she had as a child. It permits a continual process and continuation of identity formation by recycling the knowledge gained from reevaluating the past into her present and by inspiring autonomous creativity. Although the gold box attains metaphoric qualities as a physical symbol of the man in black, its power and magical qualities lie in its metonymic, associative, and imaginative attributes, like that of the "cuarto de atrás."

The gold box demonstrates metonymic continuation and process in another sense also, in that it can be considered as a dialogic response to the situation in Emilia Pardo Bazán's short story "La caja de oro" (The Gold Box).[17] While the owner of the gold box in Pardo Bazán's text loses her health and vigor after revealing its secret to her curious male suitor, Carmen recaptures the power over her own psychic health and autonomy when her mysterious visitor presents her with a similar gold box filled with pills. Like Carmen's intertextual rebuttal to the *novela rosa* (with marriage as its happy ending), the significance of the little gold box is also a subversion. It presents a modern woman regaining the autonomy she had been deceived into handing over to a representative of an untrustworthy patriarchal society. Thus the male figure in Martín Gaite's story is transformed into an idealized man who helps a woman to express herself rather than tricking and taking advantage of her.

But despite all the ambiguous and wondrous qualities of the "man dressed in black," he is really not so unusual after all. In her work with women patients, Jungian analyst Clarissa Pinkola Estés has found that women's dreams about a "dark man" are so common that it is unusual for a woman not to have a "dark man" dream.[18] Like Carmen's "man dressed in black," the role of the "dark man" in women's dreams is often ambiguous. Sometimes, according to Estés, the dream is an indication that a woman is about to liberate "a forgotten and captive function of her psyche"—like the lifting of the curtain that obscured the "cuarto de atrás." At other times, the dream might be indicative of an intolerable situation for a woman. In all cases, however, the dreams indicate a change in a woman's consciousness and her "individuation process." Estés calls the dreams "wake-up calls," while in Martín Gaite's novel, the man in black awakens Carmen with a phone call. Estés speculates that the intruding male represents an opposing and instinctive power within the female psyche.[19]

In *Women Who Run with the Wolves,* Estés attempts to reconnect women with their instinctual selves lost through society's attempt to "civilize" them. She uses fairy tales, folk tales, multicultural myths, and stories that illustrate the "Wild Woman archetype." Estés feels this "wild" and instinctive aspect of femininity is important to identify in order to help modern women who are "pressured to be all things to all people."[20] According to Estés, "Bluebeard" is one of the fairy tales demonstrating women's need to recultivate their inherent instinctual knowledge and power. The young woman who marries Bluebeard originally is afraid of him, but because she has been conditioned by society to be nice to all people, she decides he cannot be so bad and marries him. Later she opens a locked room containing the bones of all his former wives and realizes her first impression of him (her instinctive one) was correct. The young wife undoubtedly would have joined the pile of bones in the locked room if she had not been jolted into defying her husband and escaping.

Interestingly, Carola's phone call interrupting Carmen's conversation with her mysterious visitor also warns Carmen to "Put yourself on guard" (156). Carmen comments that Carola's description of Alejandro (whom Carola is hoping to find) reminds her of the story of Bluebeard (157).[21] This reference to "Bluebeard" not only adds another ambiguous dimension to "the man dressed in black" but also echoes Estés's interpretation of the story of "Bluebeard": It is because of the woman's marriage to Bluebeard that she begins to recultivate her instinctual knowledge.

In a similar manner—because of her visitor—Carmen begins to reexamine the way society shaped her as a young girl: She, too, was "tamed" into being a certain kind of woman. When her visitor compliments her by calling her a rebel (123), she reevaluates her formerly negative impression of women exhibiting "anomalous and defiant behavior" that went against the "strict law of elopement" (125). Also, he encourages Carmen to break away from the path society has encouraged her to follow: "sometimes the little white stones don't only serve to mark the path, but also to make us retreat" (135). He suggests that Hansel and Gretel would have had more possibilities if they had not followed the fixed path of stones leading directly back to their home and helps her to recognize the limitations she has been encouraged to set upon herself.[22] In *El amor es un juego solitario* Elia loses sight of her truth of self precisely because she submits to patriarchal society's order: She acquiesces to Ricardo's desire for her to be a seductress instead of communicating her true personality.

Thus—as a variation of "Bluebeard" and the "dark man" dream—Carmen's "man dressed in black" serves the same function as the fairy tale that acts as a mirror and a model. While many fairy tales contain patriarchal propaganda—like the happy ending of marriage in Cinderella—Estés points out that there are important fairy tales, stories, and images that transmit matriarchal wisdom about the female instinct.[23] These positive fairy tale-type models allow a woman to look at herself through story models in the process of creating a strong and autonomous identity—a function similar to La Belle's conception of the mirror.

Within the mirrorlike function of Carmen's "dark man" dream, the "man dressed in black" would again represent a metaphorical function. He helps her to define a part of herself from a perspective not visible without the aid of a mirror; like Stanton's definition of a metaphor, he is a "tool for transporting meaning beyond the known."[24] But the reflection provided by the strange visitor would ultimately be more metonymic than metaphoric because it does not only reflect a similarity (albeit hidden) but moves on to an associated idea and initiates a change in Carmen. Carmen identifies this contiguous reflective quality when she detains the mysterious visitor from leaving: "No, please, your being here is how I remember things" (139).

His presence acts like a mirror revealing facets of her own personality that were previously hidden to her and helps her to move on to other ideas as she continues to create her self.[25] His negative and ambiguous connotations emphasize that her own past and thoughts have enigmatic effects on her consciousness, causing her to reevaluate her opinion of herself. Carmen reexamines the values imposed upon her by patriarchal society and, specifically, by Franco's propaganda about commendable behavior for women. Thus the man in black reinforces Carmen's instinctive behavior that she has been taught to repress, echoing Estés's ideas about the "dark man."

Because the man in black is metonymically connected to so many other elements within the novel during her dreamlike conversation, the multiple reflective power of all those other elements is magnified. Even before the appearance of her mysterious visitor, Carmen recognizes the mirrorlike effect of her engraving of Luther talking with the devil, which depicts "the same situation that I was in" (17). Later connections between the visitor and the picture intensify the mirroring qualities of both.

Thoughts of the *novelas rosa* (remembered because of the visitor's alluring qualities similar to those of the typical hero Raimundo) reflect the seductive, romantic qualities of those well-read books. But their recollection also embodies the displeasing "happy ending," which reflected Franco's propaganda about woman's role as a happily married wife. Carmen's print of "The World in Reverse," previously linked to "the man dressed in black," depicts the world as if it were reflected and distorted in a mirror, but also intimates that such a reversal and change could be positive. (A similar positive reversal occurs in the intertext with Pardo Bazán's "La caja de oro.") The dream of the stars forming the face of the clown duplicates the anticipation and unknown qualities that

Carmen feels in her interview with the man in black. Even the ending of the novel reflects the words of the beginning—demonstrating the mirrorlike function of the text.[26]

Thus there are a variety of positive and negative ideas metonymically connected to the man in black that also act as mirrors. The divergence of these concepts keeps their ultimate meaning as mirrors ambiguous (like the visitor) and suggests a reflective process that has not been completely resolved. Carmen's gaze into her variety of mirror-objects reveals an expanding cycle of growth that has not yet terminated.

Not only do the "man dressed in black" and the elements connected to his visit serve as mirrors for Carmen, Carmen's use of the mirrors within her home also manifests her self-growth from the reexamination of her past. Carmen's need to reactivate her psychic identity is evident as she dizzily looks into the mirror before the call from her mysterious visitor:

> I stand up and the swing straightens, the roof, the walls, and the elongated frame of the mirror—before which I remain immobile, uncertain—straighten. In the mercury, my room appears fictitious to me in its static reality, it gravitates behind me like a lead weight, and the look returned to me by that excessively vertical figure, with her arms hanging along the sides of her blue pajamas, scares me, completely astonishes me. I turn around anxiously, wanting to recover by surprise the truth of that dislocation observed a few seconds before, but outside the mirror the normality that it was reflecting persists, and perhaps because of that, the reigning disorder is more overwhelmingly evident. (15–16)

Carmen, looking into her mirror as she fights with insomnia, perceives her own displacement within her surroundings. The vertigo she feels is a result of her world moving around her as she stands still. Her immobility and "static reality" indicate the frightening need for her to reevaluate her position in life and to make some changes.

As Carmen surveys the reigning disorder in her bedroom, she sees constant reminders of her past—things that helped to make her what she is. Looking into the mirror again, she sees herself partially as the little girl she once was:

> Now the provincial child that can't fall asleep is looking at me by the light of the little yellow lamp . . . I am seeing her just as she sees me; so that my image repairs itself and isn't carried away by the undertow, I need to ask hospitality from that impatient and sleepless heart, that is to say, from my own heart. (23–24)

To see a true reflection of herself, Carmen realizes that she must not deny that which she has been. Thus she reembraces her past in order to recompose herself before evaluating her present identity that needs growth and expansion. The examination of her "heart"—her own inner sense of self-identity—is more difficult to see by looking into a mirror, but she recognizes that "the important thing is that it does not stop" (24). Carmen then falls asleep, feeling at peace with her past, while sensing that she must brace herself for changes and growth.

After the "man dressed in black" arrives, he continues to aid Carmen to reembrace her former self as she remembers a variety of incidents from her past. One incident she remembers is when she went with her family to a health resort as an adolescent girl and noticed for the first time that she was attractive to young men:

> . . . I took out the little mirror, looked at myself, and found myself within its confines with strange and entranced eyes that I didn't recognize; I noted that the bellboy, a boy of my age, was looking at me smiling and that embarrassed me a little, I pretended that I was taking some soot from my eye, but I thought in distress that it wasn't me. (49)

This past encounter with a mirror is relived by Carmen through the conversation with her visitor, and she remembers another time that a mirror reflected her self-consciousness as she was growing and changing. She feels self-conscious again as the stranger examines her life and writing.

Later in the conversation, Carmen goes to make some tea and glances at herself in an antique mirror hanging in her kitchen. The reflection shows her tidying up, as she humorously remembers her abhorrence of domestic duties:

> My smile imbues itself with a slight jeer upon realizing that I'm carrying a dishcloth in my hand; to tell the truth, the one who is watching me is an eight-year-old girl and then an eighteen-year-old young lady. (74)

As she looks at herself from the perspective of her past, she remembers her "rebellions against order and cleanliness" (75) as symbols of her disgust with the servile role society prescribes for women. The antique mirror she had used all her life and the reflections she remembered in it through various stages in her life help her remember a quality that distinguished her from other females. Her rebellion against order also individualized her from the stereotype that Franco projected for women in "La Sección Femenina" (The Feminine Section).[27]

Carmen communicates with herself in the mirror in the kitchen, reviving the liberated ideas that she held in her past, much in the same way that the man in black awakens forgotten aspects of her being. Again, there is simultaneous metaphoric recognition of similarity and difference between her present and past self and also metonymic contiguity. There is a temporal contiguity of the eight- and eighteen-year-old Carmen with her present self (much like Andrea's various stages of self-observation in *Nada*). Also this scene demonstrates the positional metonymic aspect of judgement of the "other" (like Elia's fear of the judgmental reflection of age in *El amor es un juego solitario*).[28]

In this case, Carmen's past self-images are cynically amused at the picture of domesticity that Carmen presents as she straightens up for her visitor. Carmen reassures her "other" selves, while she is also reminded of why she does not want to be too orderly and domestic. The "cuarto de atrás," with its permitted disorder, was what gave free rein to Carmen's imagination in opposition to the rules for feminine comportment in "La Sección Femenina." Looking into the mirror helps Carmen redefine her present situation by way of her past: She recreates and adjusts her autonomous self.

Other reflections in the looking glass reconfirm the importance of cycling back through the past self to create and expand the present self. For instance, after her disconcerting conversation with Carola, Carmen sits down at the mirror of her vanity table, speechless and afraid to go back into the room with the man in black. As she looks into her mirror she perceives a subtle transformation: "The expression of my face is the same, but it appears surrounded by a lace cap and the dark circles and wrinkles around my eyes have disappeared. On the other hand, the mirror has become oval, smaller" (176). Gazing into the mirror, she relives the first time she acted in the Liceo Theater in Salamanca and was overcome with stage fright just before performing. At that time a friend advised her: "Make up your eyes a little more, seeing yourself beautiful gives security" (176). Just as this advice helped in the past, it again helps Carmen with her newfound insecurity toward her interviewer, who is helping her to expand her horizons.

In each case, when Carmen looks into the mirror—or talks with the stranger who functions as a mirror—visions from her past help her formulate new strategies for the present and future. Carmen does not remain in the past nor exactly repeat her past but, rather, she changes her present state of mind because of what she sees about herself in the past, illustrating the metonymic aspect of her use of the speculum. It is helpful here to recall Jakobson's definition of metaphor as "substitution," while he notes that metonymies "combine and contrast."[29] In Carmen's case, the reflection in the mirror is *temporarily* replaced by a past reflection, but the main emphasis of the temporary substitution is the *contrast* between past and present and the *combination* that results from adopting positive information from the past.

Thus the mirror reflections show the propensity for a continual process of identity formation, as there is always the possibility that past reflections can aid in stratagems for the ever-changing present situation. Like the idea expressed by many fairy tales, Carmen's use of the looking glass reflects a process of rebirth. This rebirth occurs by circling back through the past and creates a new (or renewed) autonomous self.[30]

Writing one's story, too, is a perfect example of cycling back through one's past to create the self. Just as in *Nada*, where Andrea's reexamination and writing of her experiences in Barcelona reflected a positive and creative step beyond self-realization in a mirror, the written pages Carmen finds after her conversation with the man in black serve as a concrete product from her process of self-renewal. The first page of Carmen's novel begins: "...And still, I would swear that my position was the same" (210)—repeating the beginning words of *El cuarto de atrás*—and demonstrating the mirrorlike quality of writing about one's life. The novel—as Carmen's own creative expression—seems to echo her self-reflection through the process of cycling back through itself. The conversation that occurs in the novel is also reminiscent of Natàlia's development demonstrated by her orallike retelling of her story in *La plaça del Diamant,* combining the positive effects of written and spoken discourse.[31]

While metaphors help create the oneiric and gamelike mood of the novel and initiate a suspension of normal rules for the readers, the feeling of continual process is initiated by the metonymic linking of diverse items. The novel retains the aura of openness and perpetuation by never resolving the ambiguity that its metonymic connections present. Even elements that seem to have metaphoric equivalence at the end tend to mean more than one thing, and their meaning reflects the need to continue metonymic linking. For example, the "cuarto de atrás" and the gold box connote the creative imagination and, thus, become perpetual instead of limiting or definitive.

Mirror images demonstrate the same continuous quality, reflecting other things that have multiple meanings. For instance, the man in black—who serves as a mirror for Carmen's thoughts—is echoed in the images of pictures, stories, and objects that also have cryptic significance. Even Carmen's use of the looking glass seems to have a dynamic and metonymic essence. She sees her image in the speculum not only as a reflection of herself but also as a sequence of her past and present selves, using the mirror to judge her need to change. The mysterious pages that Carmen and the readers finally realize is her novel are a tangible reflection of Carmen's process of change.

While the division and separation of the narrators from the protagonists in *Julia* and *El amor es un juego solitario* confirm that Julia and Elia were out of touch with their own psyches, and Matia's writing in *Primera memoria* continues her downward and negative spiraling, the personal attempts at recreating one's life are very positive expressions in the other novels examined. Andrea's contemplative memories in *Nada* and Natàlia's personal oral reflection of her life to an unnamed listener in *La plaça del diamant* both demonstrate positive development of their protagonists. Carmen's self-expression, however, seems to be the most positive in that she retains the power of the gold box—the amulet that enables her to revive the infinite creativity of her source. She seems to understand the key that permits her to revitalize her self.

Yet the possession of this amulet or key does not, by any means, guarantee a "happy ending" but, rather, the need for a continuation of process.[32] For example, only Carmen's childhood is explored in her retelling. Although her relationship with the man in black reflects desire,[33] it is manifested principally in the emotional, intellectual, and imaginative sense. While Elia in *El amor es un juego solitario* begins to explore her physical desires as a woman, she can not divulge her true emotional needs. Thus Elia becomes entrapped in endless repetitions of physical expression that eventually are meaningless. Drawing an analogy on the basis of this observation, one might speculate that without a continuation and expansion of the process Carmen has begun, she could conceivably become entrapped in imaginative endeavors drawn from her childhood without ever reexamining the corporeal desires of her adult life.[34] To truly know herself, it would seem that Carmen's examination of her life as an adult—that differed from her free and creative childhood—would be extremely important. Although Carmen has revived her psychic identity, continuation of her creative process of identity is essential.

While *El cuarto de átras* is often seen as a continuation of the process of identity formation in Martín Gaite's earlier novels,[35] these early novels also show reflections of other novels we have examined. For example, Martín Gaite's first novel, *Entre visillos* (1958, Between curtains) is comparable with Laforet's *Nada* and Matute's *Primera memoria*. One of the main protagonists of the novel is sixteen-year-old Natalia, whose mother died while giving her birth. In *Entre visillos,* the "tower of the Cathedral and the great white sphere of the clock like a gigantic eye" echo the description of Matia's grandmother observing others with her binoculars in *Primera memoria,*[36] and the spine-chilling presence of the "gigantic eye" evokes the sense of a nightmare like in Laforet's *Nada* and Moix's *Julia*. All these images are metaphoric of Franco's domineering presence as dictator of Spain. Similarly, the window curtains (*visillos*) of Natalia's home, behind which she must view the world, are symbolic of the restrictive rules for young women: "It's because there are things that a young lady should not do."[37] This feeling of confinement is analogous to the bed with its cagelike bars that confine Matia in *Primera memoria* and to the rules imposed by Andrea's aunt Angustias in *Nada*.

The narrative voice in *Entre visillos* alternates between a third-person narrator and the first-person narrations of Natalia and Pablo Klein, Natalia's young teacher who has just taken a job in her city. While the third-person narrative transmits an idea of the controlled and stifling atmosphere of the city, the chapters that fluctuate between Natalia's and Pablo's perspective anticipate Martín Gaite's later novels that feature dialogue between a male and female: *El cuarto de atrás* and *Retahílas* (Threads).

Retahílas (1974) consists of a long conversation between Eulalia and her nephew Germán. Eulalia has returned to Galicia after an absence of more than twenty years because her grandmother is dying, and Germán has come to help his aunt. Their conversation begins one evening and ends at five the next morning, much like the nocturnal discourse in *El cuarto de atrás*. While one person is speaking in *Retahílas* the other does not interrupt, giving the novel the appearance of alternating monologues. But each discourse acts as an inspiration to the response of the other, weaving the individual expressions together as if they were threads in a fabric. Just as the image of the curtain serves to express the confinement of Natalia in *Entre visillos,* references to barriers such as "the big step that separates it from the one before" and "a difficult wall to scale" convey the obstacles of true communication.[38] Unlike the psychiatrist "the Magician" in Tusquets's *Para no volver,* Germán is sincerely interested in his aunt and contributes to the mirrorlike interchange of ideas.

Recapturing the idea of communication through monologue inspired by another, *Nubosidad variable* (1992, Variable cloudiness) resumes the search for healing communication. Instead of a conversation between aunt and nephew, or a fantastic "dark man" that acts as a mirror, Sofía and Mariana, the middle-aged coprotagonists of *Nubosidad variable,* discover themselves through a series of letters and diary entries intended for each other. They do not limit themselves mainly to childhood memories, as Carmen does, but also reflect on their adult lives and sexual relationships. In addition to adding another sequence to her own novelistic work, Martín Gaite's *Nubosidad variable* might be considered as a dialogic response to the next novel analyzed, Carme Riera's *Qüestió d'amor propi* (A question of self-pride). While *Qüestió d'amor propi* consists of a single letter from Àngela to her friend Íngrid, *Nubosidad variable* explores the possibilities of considering both perspectives within the friendship.

After having been friends in their youth, Sofía (a housewife and mother) in *Nubosidad variable* and Mariana (a successful psychiatrist) bump into each other at a cocktail party more than thirty years later. Their chance encounter inspires both of them to reexamine their earlier friendship and their separate lives through a series of letters and diary entries. Although their communication is inspired by and directed to the other, their actual interchange of ideas is delayed for several months. Like the positive inspiration that writing to Íngrid provides for Àngela in *Qüestió d'amor propi,* Sofía and Mariana reinforce and reflect each other's strengths by writing to the other. Their interchange reveals that "life is made of fragments of mirror, but in each fragment one can look at one's self,"[39] similar to the way that the past and the "man dressed in black" serve as reconstructive mirrors for Carmen.

The "man dressed in black" confirms Carmen's renewed ability to create from her own imagination: "You don't need for anything to exist, if it doesn't exist, you invent it, and if it does exist, you change it . . . you have spent your life without leaving the refuge, dreaming alone. And in the end, you don't need anyone" (196). Carmen's ideal interlocutor (a reflection of her self) affirms her independence within her own world; she is attaining what many of the protagonists of the aforementioned novels have not attained— self autonomy.[40] In *Nubosidad variable,* however, Mariana's hidden insecurity, even though she is a fashionable psychiatrist, suggests that autonomy and self-identity for women are still prob-

lematic issues that cannot be resolved singlehandedly. Sheila Rowbotham suggests that for a woman to feel she is liberated
is not nearly enough: "the liberation of women necessitates the
liberation of all human beings."[41] For women to be truly liberated, society must be unfettered enough to accept them as
autonomous.[42]

The next novel, Carme Riera's *Qüestió d'amor propi*, serves as
proof that women cannot be truly autonomous without the concur-
rence of others in society. Àngela, the protagonist of Riera's novel,
is also a mature woman writer who feels ontologically secure—as
Carmen does at the end of her novel. But after a romantic encounter with a male author, Àngela finds her self-security stripped by
this man—who professes to be in love with her, but merely uses
her as a mirror to magnify his own image. Àngela expresses herself
through a letter to her friend Íngrid, attempting to procure Íngrid's
help in shifting the patriarchally tilted balance of power that left
Àngela weak and degraded.

7

Mirror Messages that Signal Change in
Qüestió d'amor propi

In several respects, Carme Riera's novel *Qüestió d'amor propi* (A question of self-pride) could be considered a continuation of the protagonist Carmen's situation in *El cuarto de atrás*.[1] Like Carmen at the end of Martín Gaite's novel, Riera's protagonist Àngela is an accomplished writer, as well as a self-assured and autonomous person. Yet when Àngela ventures into an amorous relationship with a male writer (perhaps a variation of the mysterious interlocutor of Martín Gaite's novel), she becomes aware of the fragility of her autonomy. The disastrous affair leaves Àngela nearly as deflated as Julia in Moix's novel or Elia in Tusquets's.

But Àngela's devastating liaison provides her the opportunity to explore the underlying norms of gender identity and relationships within Spanish society. An examination of metaphors and metonymic connections reveals Àngela's subconscious acceptance of the culturally symbolic division of the male as an aggressive master and the female as a submissive victim and her later rejection of these parameters. Àngela's instinctual self-pride and her earlier autonomous experiences help her transgress these standards and fight back. She expresses the need for change through metaphors that adopt the voice of retaliation and aggression usually reserved for males of her cultural background.[2]

Àngela is inspired by a female friend from a different culture, who acts as a mirror and model for her cultural transgression. While the mirror provided by her patriarchally dominated society only ridicules her desire to be autonomous and liberated, her friend's perspective allows her to see herself in a positive light. The possibility of a community that accepts a different role for women helps Àngela to change the parameters of her own identity.

Riera's novel consists of Àngela's long letter to her college friend Íngrid in Denmark. Àngela apologizes for not having written in over a year; the rest of the letter is an explanation of her silence and an appeal for her friend's assistance. Àngela attended a literary conference about the novel *La Regenta* the preceding fall, where she became fascinated with Miquel, another writer. Her relationship with Miquel originated with a difference of opinion about the role of women in literature and evolved into a romantic and physical liaison. In spite of Miquel's many declarations of love, their mutual interests, his flowers and phone calls, their relationship ceased after one night of love making. Although Íngrid has advised that sexual union should be regarded merely as gratification of the appetites, Àngela reveals that she has been emotionally devastated by the affair. Adding to her personal humiliation, Miquel has openly ridiculed her by writing a novel called *El canto del cisne* (The swan's song), apparently based on their romance. The female in Miquel's novel is a ludicrous, older woman who becomes involved with an attractive, vibrant writer. After going through a period of severe depression, Àngela is finally able to write to her friend. She asks Íngrid to supply Miquel with erroneous information about Denmark when he goes there to write a series of articles on the country. Thus Miquel will be publicly embarrassed, and his dream of winning the Nobel Prize will be deflated.

In her letter to Íngrid, Àngela refers metaphorically to the cultural differences between herself and her friend by describing the dissimilar quality of light in Denmark and Spain. Although Íngrid regards Mediterranean light as romantic and erotic, Àngela points out the negative aspects of such intense light:

> that furious southern light . . . becomes an obstacle, not only because it attracts us toward the open countryside, to the terraces of bars in the open air and makes us falsely extroverted, but also because it cruelly shows us edges, cracks, and protrusions, and . . . shows us that objects have rough edges, vegetation has rugged stalks, and everything, or nearly everything, can suggest the traitorous ferocity of the knife, the puncturing hardness of the dagger . . . And because of that powerful light, our surroundings bristle and, as if they were in perpetual erection, become disagreeably phallic.[3]

Spain's light produces an atmosphere of aggressive male sexual power. While the light seductively lures everyone under its control, it also emphasizes the symbolic omnipresence of the phallic domination of power.

In contrast, Àngela perceives that the subdued light of the Scandinavian countries leaves everything less clearly differentiated and rigid:

> The nebulous, misty half-light that invades the northern regions is much more desirable to me, the diffuse tones that make objects nearer

> and shorten distances. The soft paleness of your foggy days seems much more welcoming and affects me positively. (16)

The unyielding image of dominant sexual power conveyed in the description of Mediterranean light is contrasted with the atmosphere of pliability and impartiality of Northern light. While a continual threat to female autonomy is present in the first description, equality, approachability, and ambiguity emanate from the second.

Indeed, Íngrid's previous advice to Àngela indicates that her perspective on life is less differentiated from male attitudes than Àngela's, and that she is more open to change. Àngela remembers her friend's guidance:

> . . . you used to reproach me for my pusillanimous attitude toward love, and you advised me to adopt a much more open posture, that I consider sex as a necessity that must be satisfied in order to maintain physical and mental equilibrium. (22)

While Àngela personally scorns sexual relationships without love, Íngrid uses sex as a pleasurable fulfillment of desires. This non-emotional acceptance of sex is an attitude normally associated with men, who are considered to be less emotional and who might regard sex as a natural requirement of their bodies.

Àngela's comments also intimate that Íngrid and others from her culture do not differentiate greatly between the sexes. Even within her love relationships Íngrid considers men and women equals. Àngela contrasts her old-fashioned view of sex with Íngrid's, who has dedicated a book "'To the men and women of my life,' also giving a long list of names in order . . . of intervention" (22). Thus the tones of Northern light that "make objects nearer and shorten distances" (16)—making men and women more equal—metaphorically illustrate the flexibility of gender roles and self-identity in Íngrid's society. Íngrid already communicates in a way that diminishes distinctions between genders—as illustrated by her "masculine" opinions about sex.

In contrast to Íngrid's view of equality that men and women share, Àngela's affair with Miquel dramatically emphasizes the inequality between the sexes in Spain. In theory, Àngela and Miquel should be considered on an equal level, because both of them are accomplished writers and respected critics of literature. Their similar tastes and age also place them in an analogous position. Àngela describes the affinity she perceived between Miquel and herself after they first met:

> Our concurrences, that could originate from similar experiences— when I was born he was five years old—seemed to me to be one more

indication of our fated predestination. We not only preferred the same authors, painters, and musicians, but . . . our tastes in other more ordinary matters . . . were also similar. (27)

But despite this apparent similitude, Àngela expresses her romantic view of love as an uncontrollable force—a fatal destiny— against which she has no power.

After once feeling equally as accomplished as Miquel, Àngela communicates her acceptance of traditional male superiority when she falls in love with him and submits to the "force of desire" (25). In the 1988 Castilian version, Àngela adds that she succumbs to Miquel with "complete surrender."[4] She relates how love converts her into a victim by employing the conventional romantic metaphor of cupid: "I noted the moment in which the divine archer shot his golden arrows and my missing half, after the catastrophe that condemned us to a very long separation, was welded to my being" (26). After Àngela becomes a willing victim of Cupid's arrow, the man with whom she had previously argued about his erroneous perception of *La Regenta* turns into the omnipotent "magician" (30) of her adolescent longings.

Àngela's metaphor comparing Miquel to a magician "capable of pulling a flock of doves out of his top hat" (30) is reminiscent not only of the superior role of the psychiatrist "Magician" in Tusquets's *Para no volver* but also of the passionate feelings between Natàlia and Quimet in *La plaça del Diamant* and of the control that Quimet has over Natàlia's life. The rest of Àngela's comparison, which describes the magician as being able to "knot and un- knot handkerchiefs in the wink of an eye and, in the final apotheosis, saw the neck of his helper and reunite the head to the torso again, with no other help than a few words" (30), demon- strates the power of the magician and the authority of his words. Learning to use the magician's incantatory utterances might trans- fer some of his power. As it is, the magician's performance (cutting off his helper's head) suggests violence against women, because the helper in such acts tends to be female. This image conveys that women are merely objects that can be assembled and disassembled.

All of Àngela's descriptions of her love affair reflect the highly romantic, but also misogynistic, images of passion from her cul- ture, including "the apotheosis of touch . . . of . . . [the] very slow invasion of daggers" (50), the power of cupid and the magician, and the idea of fatal predestination. These revealing depictions of Àngela's sentiments of powerless submission to love reinforce

Pratt's doubts that Eros and autonomy can be compatible for women.[5]

Indeed, after Àngela falls in love, she apparently rejects her feelings of autonomy in order to position herself in the amorous role encoded into her subconscious.[6] Àngela's metaphors reflect this surrender of liberty: "The telephone was . . . our ally . . . it was converted into a type of umbilical cord that kept us united. Very sweet shackle . . . chain that I wanted to be perpetual." (47–48). Before losing her heart to Miquel, Àngela played power games with him, actively arguing her ideas about literature. But even these games were designed to attract his attention. Yet after surrendering to her emotions she expresses the desire to be completely dependent on and permanently chained to him. While her metaphors transmit closeness, they also convey enslavement.

In fact, Àngela reveals to Íngrid a hidden longing to be treated as a child instead of an independent adult:

> I will add that all my life I have wanted someone to call me "little one" while hugging me, although my feminist principles would have floundered by having accepted that which seemed to me a debasement: to be diminished, treated like a child, almost codified. (24)

This desire, nearly completely hidden in Àngela's subconscious, is reminiscent of Julia's attempt to retreat to her childhood in Moix's novel. But instead of blaming the lack of affection on her mother as Julia does, Àngela speaks of the "always blue paradise of childhood, where any nightmare was immediately frightened away by the warm, caring softness of my mother's voice" (23).

Thus the lack of maternal affection that distressed Julia, as well as Elia and Clara in *El amor es un juego solitario,* does not seem to be the reason for Àngela's desire to return to her childhood and to be embraced. Instead, Àngela speaks of the need for women to be "strong, cold, and self-sufficient, especially in front of men" (24). This puerile need for affection, covered over by an artificial self-sufficiency toward men, would complicate meaningful communication with the other sex. Additionally, she states that "many women of my generation, and especially those considered the most intelligent, are going to understand the embarrassment of this propensity toward tenderness . . . weakness" (23–24), suggesting that female immaturity and insecurity are not only personal problems but also cultural ones.

Nancy Chodorow feels that childlike development of females, as well as production of emotionally insensitive males, is a societal problem stemming from the traditional family structure.[7] Franco's dictatorship in Spain further complicated female maturation by directing special programs at women to instill "a passive attitude and spirit of sacrifice."[8] The qualities of obedience and submission are those normally expected of children. Àngela's metaphor that places her "kneeling in front of the grille" (24) suggests yet another cultural cause for women's subordination. Since the Catholic religion places a male priest as "judge" over intimate confessions of the parishioners, women become accustomed to accepting authority and penance from a male. Although men also confess, they never confess to a female priest. Franco's Sección Femenina (Feminine Section) particularly directed Spain's moral responsibility toward women, keeping them truthful, humble, and compliant.[9]

Indeed Àngela misconstrues Miquel as a benefic confessor. What she mistakenly perceives in him is a variation of the idealistic, mysterious interlocutor in El cuarto de atrás—to whom the protagonist Carmen reveals her most intimate reflections. Àngela anticipates a "magician" who would employ the same responsive voice as her mother scaring away nightmares, a priest, or Martín Gaite's "man dressed in black." Like Elena's hope to hear inspirational words from "the Magician" in Para no volver and like Elia's desire in El amor es un juego solitario to see a lost and unloved characteristic in Ricardo, Àngela is seeking a sensitivity and emotional need in Miquel that is similar to hers. She believes she has discovered that impressionable side of Miquel: "I thought I perceived behind that mask a nearly morbid vulnerability and fragility that were what really seduced me" (84).

Instead of any tenderness or similar feelings, Àngela discovers only an extension of the effects of the metaphoric Mediterranean light: Miquel feigns vulnerability to trick her into submission. His only desire is to see himself in the cultural stereotype of Don Juan, who conquers and then departs unaffected. He boasts of his conquest by writing a distorted account of the affair in his novel El canto del cisne. Unlike Martín Gaite's "man dressed in black" (who inspires Carmen to organize her thoughts and write), Miquel publicly and privately humiliates Àngela, paralyzing her creativity.

After the end of their relationship, Àngela continues to cast herself in the role of the dependent victim, but changes her perspective to regard her feelings as an illness rather than accepting them as positive or normal. She speaks of her age as a detriment in her ability to recover from her "sickness" (20) and says that at forty-eight her body could not develop "a sort of vaccine, the antibodies necessary to combat . . . the virus" (21). Her metaphors again suggest invasion by the male and her complete powerlessness to recover, as well as her own culture's bias against older women. She is reduced to "a disposable container" (73) by Miquel's depletion of her emotions and one-night use of her body. Because she is no longer young, her disposal is more justifiable, even from her perspective.

Àngela's feelings of worthlessness after the affair are reminiscent of Julia's monsters and her "death-in-life" existence in *Julia* and of Elia's catatonic states of depression in *El amor es un juego solitario,* especially in the Castilian version: "they were frightful days, populated by terrors to whose incantations appeared specters that executed macabre dances at my side, monsters who mocked me between guffaws and leaps."[10] Also like Julia and Elia, Àngela considers suicide, calculating how much "alcohol and barbiturates would be ideal for an effective mixture" and measuring the distance needed "between the window and the asphalt in order to obtain the desired result" (20). Àngela submits to Miquel's brutal humiliation and even considers completing the assault herself.

Despite the degree of blame that Àngela confers on herself after her disastrous liaison, her friend Íngrid's divergent opinion helps her recuperate her self-worth. Indeed, metonymic extension of some of Àngela's ideas shows that either she subconsciously has begun to change some of the attitudes inscribed in her by her society or that she instinctively realizes they are harmful. For instance, after their meeting in Valencia, Miquel sent her flowers: "The cadaver of an orchid, perfectly exquisite in its plastic casket, was waiting for me at home on my return from Valencia" (45). In this passage it is impossible to discern whether Àngela formulated the metonymic relationship on receiving the flower or in the process of writing to her friend. Another comment, however, indicates that she subconsciously connected Miquel's orchids with cadavers at the time she was still hoping for the affair to transpire. She relates that before Miquel arrived at her home, she bought "the least cadaverous orchids" (49) to decorate her house. This statement reveals that even before their rendezvous Àngela perceived something slightly repulsive in Miquel's selection of flowers.

Metonymic chaining of the concept of the orchid as a cadaver not only intimates danger for Àngela but also suggests the entrapment of a living death (like that experienced by Julia), with its entombment of a live flower in a plastic coffin. Moreover, Miquel's choice of such a flower for her is indicative of his desire to curtail her natural growth and development within the artificial, cagelike box manufactured by the perpetrators of a throwaway culture.

While, on one level, Àngela readily accepts Miquel's romantic gesture of sending flowers, subconsciously she is also threatened by his choice. Just as aspects of Àngela's metaphors comparing Miquel to a magician, the telephone to a shackle, and Miquel's caresses to an "invasion of daggers" (50) suggest a subconscious deviation from the feeling of emotional closeness she desires, metonymic extension of the orchid helps to reveal Àngela's underlying desire for autonomy.

The disposable plastic coffin that contains the imprisoned orchid can also be linked with Miquel's depersonalization of Àngela within their relationship. For instance, after Miquel leaves, Àngela describes the words he said to her as "still wrapped in cellophane and decorated with a big, pink bow, protected but already contaminated" (57). His words, tinged with artificiality, were so recent they still seemed unused and in their protective wrappers. The words arrived like the orchids—efficiently packaged in a disposable material that seemed to adulterate and depersonalize the contents. Thus veiled, but also polluted by their covering, all sorts of entities can be disposed of easily. In fact, Àngela feels that Miquel has essentially converted her into a disposable object, like "a paper plate, cup, or napkin, that after being used only once, goes directly into the trash can" (58).

Debased and reduced to the status of a piece of trash, Àngela wishes to dispose of herself. Only after help from a psychiatrist can Àngela overcome her feelings of worthlessness and undertake a search for prized possessions and expensive antiques in order to revalue herself: "objects interest me more than people, because of that, I spend whatever I can to surround myself with beautiful things" (78). By collecting things that she values, Àngela unconsciously indicates that objects (like herself) should be treasured. Although this metonymic transfer does not indicate recovery from her debased state (she still isolates herself from others and is unable to write), it demonstrates an improvement over her desire to do away with herself. Her process of recovery also includes caring for her garden, which would return her to Pratt's "green-world," nature's refuge from patriarchal domination.[11]

Within her garden, the soft light of the fall afternoons reminds Àngela of Íngrid: "I am fascinated by those moments when the sky acquires pale tones, diffuse blues and whites with splashes of pink that remind me of your light" (78). The illuminated garden reconnects Àngela with the diffused Northern light that equalizes and the comforting "always blue paradise of childhood" (23), where her mother's voice chased nightmares away. Again—like in *El cua-*

rto de atrás—the importance of the liberty felt during childhood is emphasized.

Therefore, when Íngrid's letter arrives, it functions like Ena's mother's voice for Andrea in *Nada* and contains the power to move Àngela from her lethargic silence.[12] Íngrid's "voice" stimulates Àngela to take up "the pen you gave me" (12) and begin to write again. While Miquel left Àngela incapable of returning to her writing and seduced her into a self-abhorrence that caused her to submit "every page of my books to the most unmerciful scrutiny" (73),[13] Íngrid inspires in Àngela the liberty to write.[14]

In the written pages to her friend, Àngela expands her sensibility and acceptance of self by communicating with her friend through an expressive and intimate letter—a marginalized writing form that is especially appropriate for women.[15] Àngela's words reveal that she does not confine herself to a role normally prescribed to a female letter writer but, rather, transgresses those norms and appropriates the discourse of patriarchal hegemony for her own use, thus intimating a change in power.[16] Just as learning a magician's incantations might usurp some of his power, Àngela demonstrates that she now wishes to control her "male voice" of authority and force.

Although Àngela is still in the process of regaining her self-esteem as she writes to Íngrid, her metaphoric description of fall conveys that she no longer feels constrained by her age and sex. She identifies with autumn's vague and fleeting qualities that "have influenced me to change fall to my favorite season" (18). Although fall reveals "the slowed rhythm and calmed pulse" (17) that coincide with her own aging, Àngela also sees its strength and beauty: "the luxurious generosity of the colors that favor nature—the reds that inflame the branches . . . and the disperse ocher voluptuousness of the thousands of leaves" (17). Moreover, she notes that autumn in Spain is particularly "fleeting" (17), holding the promise of a "winter that unexpectedly arrives with subjugating ferocity, like an army whose strategy consists in a surprise attack" (17–18). Àngela refortifies herself as she writes, knowing her situation—like the autumn—is fleeting and changeable, and that soon she will have immutable and surprising strength.

Formerly, Àngela metaphorically cast herself in the role of the willing prey—"the first foolish lamb that crossed his path, offering itself as a victim"—while designating Miquel as the crafty aggressor "with his portable altar under his arm, ready to prepare the ceremony of sacrifice with extreme meticulousness" (85). But her letter indicates she has reanalyzed what Julia Kristeva calls "the potentialities of *victim/executioner* which characterize each identity, each subject, each sex."[17] Àngela relocates the aggressive, "feral" powers within her own nature and wants to "organize an imaginary line of protection" (13) with Íngrid, instead of willingly submitting as before. While she formerly regarded Miquel as the trickster and magician, the plan she proposes involves tricking him, and she knows that Íngrid (from her previous experiences) already has "some marked cards" that will result in Miquel's losing the "game" (84).

The war and card game metaphors that Àngela uses to describe her plan convey strategies, aggression, and activities that typically have been associated with males. More important, they demonstrate that Àngela no longer considers herself a helpless victim. Her adoption of forceful metaphors occurs after Àngela realizes that the "learned helplessness" ingrained in women of her culture ill-prepares them for survival in times of conflict:[18] "The values that a meticulous and bourgeois education tried to instill in me— loyalty, an obsessive cultivation of truth—aren't useful to me as norms of conduct anymore, they've become extinct, they're obsolete" (76). Like Carmen's rebellion against order in *El cuarto de atrás*, Àngela finally sees the need to spurn the widely accepted ideal of abnegated heroism for women taught by Franco's Sección Femenina.

Ultimately, the affair with Miquel illustrates for Àngela the basic incongruity of her self-annulling love ideal with her desire for autonomy. After overcoming her weakness, she then reflects back to Miquel some of the same aggressive tactics other males might use. This mirrorlike reversal of roles also reflects the need to effect a change in society that would make males and females more equal and, therefore, suggests an unfinished process, somewhat like that in *El cuarto de atrás*.

Although (unlike the previous works examined) Riera's epistolary novel does not reveal any scenes in which Àngela looks directly into a mirror, the use of different types of mirroring is extremely important in the work.[19] In fact, Àngela's close relationship to Íngrid fits within Ciplijauskaité's observation that women's close friends often serve as doubles—or mirrors—in literature written by women.[20] The letter written to her friend is an indication that Àngela is forming her "sense of self in relationship to another," as Johnson has observed, and thus is using her friend as a mirror. The affinity between the two friends demonstrates the metaphorical relationship of simultaneous identity and difference, while Àngela's combination of Íngrid's ideas with hers exemplifies the metonymic, combining aspect of the speculum.[21]

Àngela's comments also illustrate that her friendship with Íngrid provides her with a continuous, even more intimate, mirroring than that reflected in the letter. Àngela has maintained a private dialogue with her absent friend that molds Àngela's self-concept much in the same way that the doll, Gorogó, did for Matia in *Primera memoria*. Àngela writes:

> . . . I've often reread your letters and lots of times I have answered you mentally from the most unexpected places, with the hope that you, as well as you know me, would have to realize . . . that my monologue . . . was directed to you. (12)

Despite the distance between them, Àngela has relied on their friendship even when she did not write.

Moreover, it appears that Àngela has not only "communicated" mentally with Íngrid but also, in a certain sense, received information from Íngrid: "I'm nearly positive that your intuition has already suspected that one of the causes of my delay in answering you has been, precisely, that of appearing nearly defenseless, fragile, full of all my prejudices and, above all, ridiculous in front of you" (14). Àngela's thoughts about what her friend would think of her suggest that she has already assessed herself by her friend's standards. Thus the illusory exchange that Àngela conducts with her absent friend suggests that Íngrid has inspired a dialogue with the animus of the other within Àngela, much as the mysterious interlocutor does for Carmen in *El cuarto de atrás*.[22]

Indeed, the desire to find an ideal interlocutor results in part of Àngela's fascination with Miquel. Àngela describes Miquel's efforts to win her confidence:

> I knew immediately that my life was about to change. Miquel not only saved me a place at his side but also was lavish with compliments: Immediately he let me know that I was the most interesting person he had met at the conference, the first woman that had dotted his *i*'s in a debate and, above all, that he was an enthusiastic admirer of my work. (34)

Like Carmen's visitor, Miquel has read Àngela's work and appears to respect her opinions.

It appears that Riera may have had *El cuarto de atrás* in mind (and perhaps Martín Gaite's theoretical work *La búsqueda de interlocutor* [The search for an interlocutor] as well) when she translated *Qüestió d'amor propi* from Catalan. The Castilian version reveals a significant change from the original in Catalan by adding a specific comment about an interlocutor: "He not only saved me a place at his table but also was lavish with compliments: *I had never found an interlocutor that measured up to him. I was the most interesting person at the conference*" (my underline).[23] The specific reference to the interlocutor creates a more obvious dialogue with Martín Gaite's novel, and like Tusquets's and Martín Gaite's later novels that demonstrate dialogue with earlier ones, Riera's translation also shows a continued evolution of ideas.

Moreover, *Qüestió d'amor propi* denounces the idea of employing a male to be the "ideal interlocutor" and indicates that the male, because of his need to regard women as objects, is not yet trustworthy as a confidante. Martín Gaite's protagonist, Carmen, at times adopts the role of the submissive female that Riera is trying to counteract. For instance, when Carmen lies down to sleep on the couch and allows her visitor to rearrange her written pages, one cannot help but think of the power of the censor suggested by the transcriber who translates and rearranges Pascual's manuscript in Camilo José Cela's novel *La familia de Pascual Duarte (The Family of Pascual Duarte)*. With that in mind, Carmen's submission and trust at that point seem incredibly naive.

Additionally, in contrast with Martín Gaite's novel, where Carmen only explores the intellectual and creative aspects of her personality, in Riera's novel the most fragile point in Àngela's character surfaces in her emotional and physical submission to a male. Thus the notion that love relationships can reveal the weak links in female autonomy is important in order to rectify those weaknesses. While the ideal male of Martín Gaite's novel apparently does not abuse that frailty, the less-than-ideal man in Riera's work takes full advantage of it.

Like Carmen's mysterious visitor, Miquel also seems to serve as a mirror: "we began a narration in which we interchanged paragraphs as if we were projecting ourselves in a game of mirrors" (38). But unlike the positive mirroring that Íngrid affords for her friend, or that the man in black provides for Carmen, Miquel renders a very negative, distorted reflection for Àngela. In fact, he is much more concerned with his own image reflected by her. Àngela served as "a mirror in which he based his strategy as a seducer . . . my nude body served him only to contemplate his own image and his body, in contrast, did not reproduce my image" (73–74). His narcissistic behavior makes her realize that if he really had been in dialogue with her (thereby reaching out to her on an equal level emotionally), it would have destroyed his image of himself. (Recall Spacks's claim that men need to see themselves magnified in the reflection of a woman.)[24] Miquel diminishes Àngela in the warped mirror of his novel to "the character of Olga, the old, provincial writer, pretentious from tip to toe, if it isn't my portrait, it is at least my caricature" (79–80). In the Castilian version Àngela describes Olga as being "as pretentious as a cabbage with a bow,"[25] creating a more visual, objectified image of the ridiculed female. Àngela is transformed "from individual woman into mere symbol, determined by male desire," as Rosemary Lloyd has observed in other literature by men.[26]

While Miquel depersonalizes her, he magnifies himself in the character of Sergio, "a stylish novelist, triumphant, seductive, intelligent . . . adorned with a hagiographic halo" (80). His novel acts as a very debilitating image for Àngela:

> In order to know about myself, in order to partially recuperate a lost year, in order to rescue myself from that death where I am, partially, a survivor, I still search for myself among the pages of *El canto del cisne*. I am enormously interested, Ingrid, in . . . your telling me if the protagonist of the book is really me, or if I'm mistaken in recognizing myself in its mirroring pages. (81–82)

After receiving such a negative reflection from Miquel's novel, Àngela desperately needs Íngrid's supportive and catoptric perspective.

Perhaps an even more ominous effect of Miquel's novel is the rippling aftermath it is sure to have on others. Àngela, being a writer and critic, is already aware of the negative portrayal of women in literature and of the effect that art and literature have within a culture. While speaking to Miquel at the conference, Àngela denounces the lack of feminine heroes over thirty years of age: "Literary conventions assume that, from maturity on, nothing happens that is worth the trouble of telling" (35). She also has noticed "the stupidity that, in general, mature female characters embody" and that older women "nearly always tend to be peevish, hypocritical, miserly" (36).

Despite Àngela's awareness of the prejudice against older women in literature—a detail that many people have not noticed— she demonstrates this subconscious, ingrained bias in her beliefs and opinion of herself. She not only patterns her thoughts after young heroines like the ultimately self-destructive Melibea in *La*

Celestina (48) but also denigrates herself and her accomplishments in her wish to fit the model put forth by literature:

> During that night I would have liked to be Faust in order to sell my soul to Mephistopheles in exchange for him changing me into Marguerite. Soon nothing of what had interested me up until then mattered to me. Neither my desire for knowledge nor my creative possibilities mattered to me but, rather, only to be young, to recuperate beauty and innocence in order to maintain the enchantment of eternal love. (51)

To pattern herself after Goethe's Marguerite would require a self-destructive attitude on Àngela's part. Àngela would not only give up any literary achievements and autonomy she has attained but also renounce her whole existence for Miquel's love. Àngela's inclusion of German and French literature, opera, theater, and film in her examples—past arts as well as contemporary—demonstrates the wide-ranging cultural influence of the literary arts as role models.

Just as Andrea in *Nada* and Matia in *Primera memoria* found negative mirrors within fairy-tale models, Riera's novel expands that idea to include the misogynistic influence in much of Western society's art forms. Àngela's literary models have demonstrated not only the subservient, fatalistic attitude that women should follow in their amorous inclinations but also the disapproving reflection given to older women through literature. Like Elia in *El amor es un juego solitario*, Àngela has internalized the concept that age is a liability for females. Literature that depicts only young women in romantic situations, and older ones as ridiculous, is another way of neutering women.[27] Therefore, Miquel's novel that casts the female protagonist as a "cabbage with a bow" can only perpetuate and reinforce the negative image of older women, augmenting men's mockery of them and causing women to belittle themselves and regard other women as foolish.

In contrast, Àngela's letter—the writing of her self—is positive and is a step toward revitalizing her vocation of writing for others. Through her letter, Àngela examines the cultural bias that allowed her relationship with Miquel to destroy the autonomy she had previously acquired. Her letter illustrates how her various mirrors—both negative and positive—helped reveal to her that she had internalized concepts that demanded subservience to men in matters of the heart. She then combines the positive reflection of a friend with a stronger character and the use of the creative mirror of writing to reverse the domination Miquel exerted over her.

This friend from a different culture—metaphorically differentiated by its light—serves as a model to reform Àngela's subconsciously ingrained concept of the female as victim. Thus Àngela begins to adopt a metaphorical expression that is similar to male expression in her attempt to usurp the balance of power in her relationship with Miquel. Her aggressive metaphors imply she has learned to employ the tools of patriarchal domination in order to reconquer and maintain autonomy. Àngela's metonymic appropriation of metaphoric ideas associated with males and her mirroring of Miquel's subversive tactics demonstrate her efforts to change both herself and her heritage. By adopting a more forceful stance, Àngela hopes to regain her self-worth and peace of mind.

But this same militancy paradoxically begins to bridge the preexisting cultural gap between genders in Spain. An analogous incongruity occurred when 1992 Nobel Peace Prize-winner Rigoberta Menchú learned Spanish to use as a "weapon" to combat her oppression and that of other Quiché Indians.[28] When Menchú mastered and appropriated another language, she broadened her perspective and changed herself, while her book beneficially altered the views of others. Similar to Menchú's effect, Àngela's incorporation of the "male voice" manifests her personal metamorphosis and is also a step toward transforming restrictive societal norms. As Àngela (and others) write literature that places women in positions of dignity, it will have the effect of reducing and negating patriarchal subordination of women, such as that advocated by Miquel's novel.

While Àngela makes new strides in the affirmation of female identity by discarding learned behavioral patterns from her culture and adopting the male perspective as a weapon, Ordóñez feels Riera's first novel, *Una primavera per a Domenico Guarini* (Spring for Domenico Guarini), explores the use of feminine language.[29] The question of masculine and feminine discourse is one that Riera investigates in her article "Literatura femenina: ¿Un lenguaje prestado?" (Feminine literature: A borrowed language?) by asking (among other questions): "Should female writers reject masculine language and find their own language?"[30] Ordóñez argues that the protagonist Clara in *Una primavera* leans to speak the female language of the body.[31]

In *Una primavera per a Domenico Guarini* Clara is a young, single journalist investigating the case of Domenico Guarini's vandalism against Botticelli's *Primavera* for a Barcelona newspaper. As she probes the incident, she becomes intrigued with Guarini's perspective as a way to posit her own identity and to decide whether to abort her pregnancy. While listening to a museum lecture explaining Botticelli's painting she remembers the incidents in her childhood upbringing that favored males over females. Her mother once told her, for instance: "A man can cheat on you, although he loves you he may do it. A woman, no, unless she's a whore."[32] The recollection of other myths also reveals discrimination against females, an influence that causes her to have dreams metaphoric of a poor self-image: "Mutilated creature, butterfly-reptile, hurled toward darkness, magnetized by shadows."[33] The close of the novel, however, finds Clara resolved to accept her pregnancy without the help of her former lovers, and there is a metaphoric birth (and rebirth) into the light: "The train has left the tunnel."[34]

Thus, while Clara in *Primavera* learns to speak with a female voice that improves her sense of identity, Àngela's language crosses gender distinctions as she regains command of her situation. In *Qüestió d'amor propi* Riera combines the reason and order of phallocentric language with feminine intuitive and mythical qualities, so that women can recover "our two voices."[35] Angela's need to alter the status quo of patriarchal domination reflects Rowbotham's claim that women can not be truly autonomous until society as a whole is changed and liberated.[36]

While Martín Gaite's novel affirms woman's independence within her own world and, as Bergmann points out, "offers the possibility of freeing the female imagination,"[37] *Qüestió d'amor propi* demonstrates another woman's step forward in the move toward autonomy. Àngela's progress vows to revive the freedom felt in childhood before the imposition of cultural norms for women. Through her examination of a love relationship, Àngela identifies some of the underlying perpetuators of the standards of inequality and begins to reverse them. Riera's novel, therefore, points the way toward transgression of culturally determined restrictions on both males and females through a revolution that would liberate all of society.

Just as Riera's novel could be a continuation of and response to *El cuarto de atrás*—warning women about their ingrained cultural biases that make them vulnerable to males—Martín Gaite's later novel *Nubosidad variable* continues the dialogue. By illustrating the perspectives of the mirrorlike reflections of both friends, Martín Gaite increases the sense of the metonymic, combining aspect of the speculum through discourse between two friends. And like the situation of her protagonists Sofía and Mariana—who both write inspired by the other, but do not communicate immediately with the other—Martín Gaite appears to reinforce the idea of positive interchange between female writers, even when their communication does not go directly to the other. Martín Gaite's work—like *Qüestió d'amor propi* and the other novels examined here—affirms the importance of written female self-expression to improve woman's role in society.

Conclusion: The Temporal Mirror

The search for identity in the novels of this study—*Nada, Primera memoria, La plaça del Diamant, Julia, El amor es un juego solitario, El cuarto de atrás*, and *Qüestió d'amor propi*—forms a reflective continuum that demonstrates the sociopolitical progress of women in Spain since 1944. Our examination of *Nada* indicated that even shortly after the end of the Spanish Civil War (1936–39) some women aspired toward a more autonomous existence. Franco's dictatorship between the end of the civil war and his death in 1975 stifled women's efforts toward autonomy. Thus the novelistic production as late as the sixties was similar and reflected comparable goals for its female protagonists. There is a distinct change, however, in the narrative expression of the seventies, close to and after Franco's death.

Even though great differences are evident between the novels written in the early years and more contemporary writing, the similarities between all the novels analyzed is perhaps more striking. All are novels of self-discovery that employ metaphorical tropes and mirroring to reveal the identity formation of their female protagonists. There are also comparable images and concepts from one work to another that suggest novelistic dialogue about women's role in society. Additionally, my examination of other novels by each of the seven novelists supports this sense of discourse between novels by the same and different authors.

My analysis of metaphor and metonymy in relation to the female protagonists has illuminated the personalities of these women. Because an author uses metaphor and metonymy to convey subconscious processes at work in the protagonist, these tropes often reveal the protagonist's state of mind to the readers before the protagonist is consciously aware of it. Thus tracing the metamorphoses expressed by metaphor and metonymy throughout a novel demonstrates the process of changing identity that the protagonist undergoes.

Mirror scenes and other mirroring devices (such as writing or telling one's own story and intimate communication with a friend) also serve to illustrate the protagonist's development. Because

159

many women use mirrors to look beyond their physical reflection, assessing and re-forming their personality as they look into a mirror, analysis of mirror images also reveals modifications as they occur. In this sense, mirror images in these works communicate in a manner similar to that of metaphor and metonymy, suggesting that change has occurred prior to the protagonist's awareness of it.

Additionally, a mirror functions like a metaphor in that its reflection both is, and is not, the face looking into it. Like metaphors, mirror images begin with a balance of appositions—the face and its inverted reflection—that interacts to establish communication (in this case, communication with the self).[1] Mirrors also function metonymically because they not only reflect the opinion of the person looking into the mirror, but also are mediums through which women in particular often perceive how others are looking at them; they reflect a combination of opinions. Therefore, mirroring, along with metaphor and metonymy, reveals a very dynamic reflection of the protagonist and her identity formation.

For example in *Nada,* Andrea uses metaphoric expression to convey her aspiration toward liberty as well as her fear of a new situation. She subsequently alters her metaphors because of new metonymic associations, demonstrating a subconscious change in her perceptions. This dynamism and change (like that of the flowing movement between metaphor and metonymy) reveal Andrea's growth and self-discovery. Additionally, the various scenes in which Andrea confronts her image in a mirror demonstrate a gradual maturation and self-acceptance.

In contrast, Matia (in Ana María Matute's *Primera memoria*) does not seem to develop and mature in a positive way. Although she metaphorically expresses similar aspirations toward liberty and fear of her situation, her metonymic associations only intensify the fear she feels. Instead of altering and expanding her original metaphor, she merely exaggerates it and applies it to all aspects of her life. Her static metaphor, therefore, suggests her lack of development. Likewise, Matia's mirror reflections demonstrate a trapped conception of self.

In Mercè Rodoreda's *La plaça del Diamant,* the relatively uneducated and unaspiring Natàlia initially conveys her situation through metaphors that the reader may find slightly humorous or simplistic. These original cliché-like metaphors, however, are renewed and invigorated by their metonymic extension throughout her life. New associations immensely expand the meaning of the metaphors, revealing Natàlia's personal growth and the depth of her sensitivity and producing mythic richness for the reader. Although at first Natàlia is too insecure to examine her own self-reflection, she gradually confronts herself in a mirror, again illustrating progress and development somewhat like that demonstrated by Andrea in *Nada*.

The use of metaphor and metonymy in Ana María Moix's transitional novel, *Julia,* is often more subtle than that of the first three novels. The readers must form their own metaphors and then trace the metonymic progression of Julia's repressed memories of a childhood rape. Later metaphoric expression indicates how Julia's feelings coincide with the characteristics of schizophrenic personalities. The scenes in which Julia regards herself in a looking glass reveal progressive alienation from her own reflection, suggesting a more severe personal deterioration than that of Matia in *Primera memoria.*

The explicit sexual scenes, elaborate use of metaphor, and the older protagonist in *El amor es un juego solitario* by Esther Tusquets show a distinct change from the earlier novels. While baroque metaphorical expressions fleetingly reveal Elia's personal subconscious desires, those same metaphors later disguise her true feelings. Elia plays out predetermined roles to hide her own identity, much like the alternate schizophrenic self in *Julia*. Although Elia takes pleasure in the use of mirrors as she plays her seductive roles, she is frightened whenever she catches an unexpected reflection of her own face. Her fear manifests the damage inflicted on her identity, as well as the vague apprehension that she is harming others.

In contrast, the mature protagonist, Carmen, in Carmen Martín Gaite's *El cuarto de atrás,* demonstrates a definite progression toward autonomy. While metaphors establish the dream-like atmosphere for Carmen's conversation with a strange man dressed in black, metonymic chaining back to her past restores the freedom of imagination Carmen felt as a child. The enigmatic man acts as a mirror for Carmen's thoughts, while written pages of her novel amazingly appear next to the typewriter. Those pages, which later prove to be a duplication of her night with the mysterious interlocutor, provide Carmen with a more productive "mirror" of her identity than a mere reflection in a glass.

Although Carmen progresses in her self-realization in *El cuarto de atrás,* the novel does not reveal any later contact with the outside world. Indeed, the strange man is possibly only a reflection of her own thoughts. However, in Carme Riera's *Qüestió d'amor propi,* the mature, self-sufficient protagonist Àngela (who is also a writer) ventures into a romantic relationship with a man who leaves her emotionally devastated. But her explanation of that disastrous affair in a letter to her friend Íngrid provides Àngela the opportunity to explore her debilitating subconscious concepts about love. While initially she uses commonly accepted metaphors that cast her as the victim in love, she eventually can combine the metaphorical expression of her male conqueror with her own through metonymic transformation. Her letter and her friendship with Íngrid serve as mirrors to aid in her self-recovery; they even act as her impetus to aggressively change her cultural identity.

My analysis of metaphoric tropes and mirrors in these novels not only has demonstrated the process of development of the individual protagonists but also has pointed to a much broader evolution. From 1944, when Carmen Laforet won the Nadal Prize for *Nada,* to 1988, the year Carme Riera published the Castilian version of *Qüestió d'amor propi,* the elements I have examined in novels by Spanish women indicate a change in the status of women in Spain within these years. After the civil war, Franco's regime created a quelling environment for women. Martín Gaite quotes a passage from a correspondent of the *New York Post* in Madrid in the forties who described the predicament of Spanish women:

> The position of Spanish women today is like in the Middle Ages. Franco took away their civil rights and Spanish women cannot possess property or even, when their spouses die, inherit it. . . . Nor can they have public jobs, and, although I do not know if there is a law against it, I still have not seen any woman in Spain driving an automobile.[2]

The fascist ideal role for a woman was to acquire "a sufficient cultural formation so that she knows how to understand her husband and accompany him in all of life's problems."[3] All women were taught to serve as an object to magnify the male ego.

In the novels I have analyzed here, the metaphors, metonymy, and mirror images indicate the protagonists' desire to change the repressive situation of Spanish women. For example, while Andrea in *Nada* expresses the need to break away from the archaic rules of her family—particularly those of her aunt Angustias—she also senses the same repressiveness in other members of society. The unpleasant kiss forced on her by the overprotective and possessive Gerardo—metonymically linked to her aunt Angustias—is indicative of the climate of coercion in which Spanish women lived in the 1940s.

In the other novels, women's resistance and opposition to their unyielding and overpowering surroundings is exemplified in a variety of ways. Matia's depression as she writes and gazes into her green glass in *Primera memoria,* Julia's schizophrenic retreat into her childhood personality in *Julia,* and Elia's rebellion and escape through sexual fantasies in *El amor es un juego solitario* are all examples of women confronting societal repression. Natàlia exhibits the same culturally forced identity in *La plaça del Diamant,* but is finally able to let some of her own personality emerge as she grows older. While Carmen in *El cuarto de atrás* feels the need to reactivate the sense of freedom and imagination she experienced as a child (before Franco's dictatorship), Àngela in *Qüestió d'amor propi* eventually rejects the ladylike comportment she was taught all her life in order to retaliate against the injustices she experiences.

Whereas Zatlin and Bergmann recognize the stylistic changes in contemporary Spanish novels written by women that make readers more aware of the female perspective, and while Ciplijauskaité notices the gradual evolution of the female protagonists, my analysis of this group of novels also points to progress in the sociopolitical status of women.[4] For example, Laforet's metaphors in *Nada* timidly and fleetingly express Andrea's aspirations as drops of water in the current and flickering stars in the sky, whereas Riera's Àngela in *Qüestió d'amor propi* ultimately voices her desires for change in aggressive terms. There are also significant thematic changes from the 1940s to the 1980s (e.g., female insanity, homosexuality, liberal sexual mores, and general expressions of sociopolitical independence for women) that reflect basic societal shifts. Many of the themes found in the recent novels would have been censored during the Franco regime.

The gradual development of the female in these novels is reminiscent of the gradual formation of self-identity recorded by Andrea's successive mirror reflections in *Nada.* As a group, these novels serve as a temporal "mirror" of women's development in Spain since the Spanish civil war. Also, rather than a "happy ending" closure, these novels, as exemplified by Martín Gaite's *El cuarto de atrás,* tend to have open endings that suggest a mere pause before resuming the novelistic, and by extension, social process.

Despite the sociopolitical progress women have made in Spain since 1944, women are still battling for an independent role in society. Catherine Davies cites, for example, that in 1987 50 percent of women between fifteen and twenty-four years of age in Spain were unemployed.[5] She explains that "the impressive achievements of socialism and feminism, of a politics of equality, have not been sufficient to radically displace phallocentricity or to enable the materialization of a new order."[6] The role of women writers who mirror female identity in their writing is still needed and still occurring.

The resumption of this novelistic and social process toward women's autonomy is evident in the recent profusion of novels written by women in Spain. Many of these new novels, just as those I have analyzed, feature female protagonists who are still reaching for and beyond themselves as subjects reclaiming their strength and identity. Akiko Tsuchiya feels, for example, that the ghostlike presence of dead fathers and brothers in Adelaida García Morales's *La lógica del vampiro* (1990, The logic of the vampire) and *El Sur seguido de Bene* (1985, The South, followed by Bene) metaphorically represents the haunting influence of Franco even after his death.[7]

Another popular novel, *Bella y oscura* (1993, Beautiful and dark) by Rosa Montero, presents a young protagonist, Baba, who arrives by train to live with her grandmother, aunt, uncle, and cousin after her mother's death.[8] Baba's situation and her metaphorical expression are hauntingly similar to the ones in *Nada* and *Primera memoria,* but Baba's story occurs in the 1990s and focuses on the problems of modern society (child abuse, poverty, noise pollution, moral decay, etc.) in addition to female identity. Other recent novels that relate different perspectives in the continuing search for female identity include Josefina R. Aldecoa's *Mujeres de negro* (1994, Women in black), Angeles Caso's *El peso de las sombras* (1994, The weight of shadows), Cristina Fernández Cubas's *El columpio* (1995, The swing), Almudena Grandes's *Malena es un nombre de tango* (1994, Malena is a name from tangos), Carmen Martín Gaite's *Lo raro es vivir* (1996, Living is a peculiar thing), Maria Mercè Roca's *Cames de seda* (1992, Legs of silk—translated in 1995 as *Piernas de seda*), and Rosa Montero's *La Hija del Caníbal* (1997, The cannibal's daughter)—to name a few.

The profusion of novels that focus on the female identity process in Spanish society indicates that women still feel repressed. As long as women's efforts to change the social forces that confine them are resisted, these particular novelistic and social processes will continue to mirror one another.

Notes

INTRODUCTION: TOOLS OF SELF-DISCOVERY AND CHANGE

1. Carmen Martín Gaite, *Desde la ventana* (Madrid: Espasa-Calpe, 1987), 108.

2. Biruté Ciplijauskaité, *La novela femenina contemporánea: Hacia una tipología de la narración en primera persona (1970–1985)* (Barcelona: Anthropos, 1988), 13, states that the novel of self-realization is prevalent among feminine authors of many countries between 1970 and 1985, and that the female protagonists are often writers meditating over their identity.

3. Ciplijauskaité, *La novela femenina*, 38; Jenijoy La Belle, *Herself Beheld: The Literature of the Looking Glass* (Ithaca: Cornell University Press, 1988); Patricia Meyers Spacks, *The Female Imagination* (New York: Knopf, 1975), 21.

4. Spacks, *The Female Imagination*, 21.

5. Virginia Woolf, *A Room of One's Own* (New York: Harcourt, 1934), 61.

6. Simone de Beauvoir, *The Second Sex*, trans. and ed. H. M. Parshley (New York: Bantam, 1970), 594.

7. La Belle, *Herself Beheld*, 9 and 42. Robert Rogers, *Metaphor: A Psychoanalytic View* (Berkley: University of California Press, 1978), 19, expresses a parallel idea about metaphors, saying that they simultaneously communicate "analogically"—this is similar to that—and "digitally"—this *is* that.

8. Domna C. Stanton, "Difference on Trial: A Critique of the Maternal Metaphor in Cixous, Irigaray, and Kristeva," *The Poetics of Gender*, ed. Nancy K. Miller (New York: Columbia University Press, 1986), 157–58.

9. De Beauvoir, *The Second Sex*, 596.

10. Aristotle, *Rhetoric III*, trans. W. Rhys Roberts, vol. 11 of *Works*, ed. W. D. Ross (Oxford: n.p., 1924), 1406, refers to metaphor as an "added extra" to language that serves as a decorative device. In contrast, Claude Lévi-Strauss, *The Savage Mind*, trans. George Weidenfeld (Chicago: University of Chicago Press, 1966), sees metaphor as a way of experiencing life, even for the most primitive people. Roman Jakobson, *Fundamentals of Language* by Roman Jakobson and Morris Hale (The Hague: Mouton, 1956), employs metaphor in his dyadic view of the explanation of aphasic disturbances. Other diverse elaborations of metaphor include Roland Barthes's semiological explanations of the trope in *Elementos de semiología*, trans. Alberto Méndez (Madrid: Corazón, n.d.); Jacques Lacan's psychoanalytic perspective in his *Ecrits I* (Paris: Seuil, 1970); and Susan Stanford Friedman's feminist approach in her article "Creativity and the Childbirth Metaphor: Gender Difference in Literary Discourse," *Feminisms: An Anthology of Literary Theory and Criticism*, ed. Robyn R. Warhol and Diane Price Herndl (New Brunswick: Rutgers University Press, 1991). For a basic overview of theoretical explanations and an annotated bibliography for additional reading on metaphor, see Terence Hawkes, *Metaphor* (London: Methuen, 1972).

11. *Fundamentals of Language*, 77.

12. In chapter 2, I deal more specifically with "symbolism." For an explanation of the prototypes of metaphoric expression, see René Wellek and Austin Warren,

Theory of Literature, 3d ed. (San Diego: Harcourt, 1977); or Alex Preminger, ed., *The Encyclopedia of Poetry and Poetics* (Princeton: Princeton University Press, 1965).

13. Umberto Eco, *The Role of the Reader* (Bloomington: Indiana University Press, 1979), 82.

14. Paul de Man, *Allegories of Reading: Figural Language in Rousseau, Nietzsche, Rilke, and Proust* (New Haven: Yale University Press, 1979), 15.

15. Michael Cabot Haley, *The Semeiosis of Poetic Metaphor* (Bloomington: Indiana University Press, 1988), 11.

16. Ibid., 106.

17. *The Role of the Reader,* 68.

18. *Fundamentals of Language,* 77.

19. David Lodge, "The Language of Modernist Fiction: Metaphor and Metonymy," *Modernism,* ed. Malcolm Bradbury and James McFarlane (Hassocks, Sussex: Harvester; Atlantic Highlands, N.J.: Humanities, 1978), 491 and 486.

20. See Hawkes, *Metaphor,* 3–5.

21. Michael Shapiro and Marianne Shapiro, *Figuration in Verbal Art* (Princeton: Princeton University Press, 1988), 34. The Shapiros define metaphor and metonymy in this way: "*Metonymy* is defined as that trope in which a hierarchy of signata is either established or instantiated. Complementarily: *Metaphor* is defined as that trope in which the (simultaneously) established hierarchy of signata is either reversed or neutralized" (27). The Shapiros then explain these two tropes with regard to their "life cycle" or "inherent dynamic." (See *Figuration,* chap. 2.)

22. Ibid., 34–35.

23. Conversely, Lodge, "The Language of Modernist Fiction," 489, suggests that continual use of metonymy without metaphor is equally stagnant, citing that the repetitive, metonymic prose of Gertrude Stein "has the effect of converting the dynamic into the static."

24. Stanton, "Difference on Trial," 175.

25. Judith Kegan Gardiner, "On Female Identity and Writing by Women," *Writing and Sexual Difference,* ed. Elizabeth Abel (Chicago: University of Chicago Press, 1982), 179, points out that "female identity is a process" and that male psychologists fail to recognize female identity as a phenomena distinct from male identity. She also says that female identity is less fixed, less unitary, and more flexible than male identity (183). According to Mary Anne Ferguson, "The Female Novel of Development and the Myth of Psyche," *The Voyage In: Fictions of Female Development,* ed. Elizabeth Abel et al. (Hanover: University Press of New England, 1983), 228, the journey for men in novels of development is usually spiral, while that for women is largely circular. La Belle, *Herself Beheld,* 10, states that Lacan sees the "mirror stage" of self-identification as a single event in childhood (implying linear development); however, La Belle feels that for women it is a continual and shifting process of self-realization (suggesting a circular movement). Annis Pratt, *Archetypal Patterns in Women's Fiction* (Bloomington: Indiana University Press, 1981), 11, also finds that plots in women's literature are cyclical rather than linear, attributing the circular form to women's "alienation from normal concepts of time and space" in their day-to-day life. Another factor that Pratt cites with regard to circular development is that older women have more in common with uninitiated, young girls than with women who are integrated into society's social structure as wives and mothers (169).

26. Elizabeth Ordóñez, *Voices of Their Own: Contemporary Spanish Narrative by Women* (Lewisburg: Bucknell University Press, 1991), 27, considers the theories of French and American feminists to interpret the difference in feminine expression in Spanish novels by women. While she mentions the metaphors, metonymy, and mirror images within many of the novels she examines, she does not specifically analyze those tropes as a way to trace female development. Although her conclusions are similar to mine in some instances, our methods of arriving at them are different.

27. *Ecrits I*, 263–65.

28. John P. Muller, *Lacan and Language* (New York: International University Press, 1982), 17, 68, and 357–58, points out that Lacan's view of the unconscious being structured like a language derives from Strauss's and Jakobson's theories of language and Freud's speculations on the unconscious. Ellie Ragland-Sullivan, *Jacques Lacan and the Philosophy of Psychoanalysis* (Chicago: University of Illinois Press, 1986), 164, clarifies Lacan's idea: "When Lacan said the unconscious is precisely structured—as a language—it is to metaphor and metonymy that he refers." Therefore, the mental structuring of metaphor and metonymy goes on without the awareness of the subject (Muller, *Lacan and Language*, 179).

29. M. M. Bakhtin, *The Dialogic Imagination*, trans. Caryl Emerson and Michael Holquist, ed. Michael Holquist (Austin: University of Texas Press, 1981), 324.

30. Gardnier, "On Female Identity," 179.

31. Ibid.

32. Madonna Kolbenschlag, *Kiss Sleeping Beauty Good-Bye: Breaking the Spell of Feminine Myths and Models* (New York: Bantam, 1981), 35.

33. Marianne Hirsch, *The Mother/Daughter Plot: Narrative, Psychoanalysis, Feminism* (Bloomington: Indiana University Press, 1989), 20; Nancy Friday, *My Mother/My Self: The Daughter's Search for Identity* (New York: Delacorte, 1978); Nancy Chodorow, *The Reproduction of Mothering: Psychoanalysis and the Sociology of Gender* (Berkley: University of California Press, 1978), 93.

34. Hélène Cixous, "The Laugh of the Medusa," trans. Keith Cohen and Paula Cohen, *Signs: Journal of Women in Culture and Society* 1 (1976): 878 and 881. The idea of the intercommunication between a woman as "source" or "locus" and the child who is a product of her body is illustrated very well in *La casa de los espíritus* (Barcelona: Plaza, 1988) by the Chilean author Isabel Allende. In that novel there is actual communication between mother and unborn child. Also it shows that each generation mirrors both the preceding generations and those that are to come. Even the names of the women illustrate a matriarchal continuum symbolized by the synonymic or metonymic names of the successive generations of women, from the great-grandmother Nívea, to Clara, to Blanca, to the great-granddaughter Alba. Each name connotes light and yet is distinct.

35. Clarissa Pinkola Estés, *Women Who Run with the Wolves: Myths and Stories of the Wild Woman Archetype* (New York: Ballantine, 1992), 180.

36. Carmen Martín Gaite, *Usos amorosos de la postguerra española* (Barcelona: Anagrama, 1987), 27 (my translation).

37. Ellen Cronan Rose, "Through the Looking Glass: When Women Tell Fairy Tales," *The Voyage In: Fictions of Female Development*, ed. Elizabeth Abel et al. (Hanover: University Press of New England, 1983); Emilie Bergmann, "Reshaping the Canon: Intertextuality in the Spanish Novel of Female Development," *Anales de la Literatura Española Contemporánea* 12 (1987); Virginia Higginbo-

tham, "*Nada* and the Cinderella Syndrome," *Rendezvous: Journal of Arts and Letters* 22.2 (1986): 17; Kolbenschlag, *Kiss Sleeping Beauty Good-Bye,* 2.

38. See Kolbenschlag, *Kiss Sleeping Beauty Good-Bye,* 65.

39. La Belle, *Herself Beheld,* 180–82.

40. Anaïs Nin, *The Diary of Anaïs Nin,* ed. Gunther Stuhlmann (New York: Harcourt, 1967), 2: 86; Cixous, "The Laugh of the Medusa," 880; Pratt, *Archetypal Patterns,* 177–78.

41. La Belle, *Herself Beheld,* 40.

42. Jakobson, *Fundamentals of Language,* 77.

43. *Archetypal Patterns,* 169.

44. Phyllis Zatlin, "Women Novelists in Democratic Spain: Freedom to Express the Female Perspective," *Anales de la Literatura Española Contemporánea* 12 (1987): 41; Bergmann, "Reshaping the Canon," 154; Ciplijauskaité, *La novela femenina,* 46 and 27.

45. Geraldine Cleary Nichols, "Caída/Re(s)puesta: La narrativa femenina de la posquerra," *Actas de las cuartas jornadas de investigación interdisciplinaria: Literatura y vida cotidiana,* ed. María Angeles Durán and José Antonio Rey (Madrid: Universidad Autónoma de Madrid, 1987), 326.

46. See Rogers, *Metaphor: A Psychoanalytic View,* 19.

47. *Archetypal Patterns,* 177.

CHAPTER 1: SUBJECTIVE DEVICES TO REVEAL THE FEMININE PSYCHE IN CARMEN LAFORET'S *NADA*

1. There are several English translations of *Nada: Nada, A Novel* . . . , trans. Inés Muñoz (London: Weidenfeld and Nicolson, 1958); *Nada,* trans. Glafyra Ennis (New York: Lang, 1993); and *Andrea: A Translation of Carmen Laforet's Novel* Nada, trans. Charles Franklin Payne (New York: Vantage, 1964).

Laforet's other novels include *La isla y los demonios* (1952), *La mujer nueva* (1955)—winner of the Premio Menorca in 1955 and the Premio Nacional in 1956, and *La insolación* (1963)—the first novel of an intended trilogy called *Tres pasos fuera del tiempo.* Laforet has also published *La muerta* (1952)—short stories, *La llamada* (1954)—novelettes, *La niña* (1970)—novelettes and short stories, and *Paralelo 35* (1967)—a log of her travels in the United States.

2. Margaret E. W. Jones, *The Contemporary Spanish Novel, 1939–1975* (Boston: Twayne, 1985), 15.

3. Ibid., 23.

4. Jeffrey Bruner, "Visual Art as Narrative Discourse: The Ekphrastic Dimension of Carmen Laforet's *Nada,*" *Anales de la Literatura Española Contemporánea* 18 (1993): 255, emphasizes that Andrea uses visual art to express her inner self, comparing a scene where Andrea looks at herself in a mirror to Picasso's *Girl Before a Mirror.*

5. Although others have analyzed *Nada* as a novel of initiation, they have not explored the use of metaphoric tropes and mirrors as tools to reveal the developing feminine psyche. Carlos Feal Deibe, "*Nada* de Carmen Laforet: La iniciación de una adolescente," *The Analysis of Hispanic Texts: Current Trends in Methodology: First York College Colloquium,* ed. Mary Ann Beck et al. (New York: Bilingual, 1976), explores Andrea's acceptance of the sexual conduct of adults and her change from pre-oedipal to the oedipal stage. Juan Villegas, "*Nada* de Carmen Laforet, o la infantilización de la aventura legendaria," *La estructura*

mítica del héroe en la novela del siglo XX (Barcelona: Planeta, 1978), investigates the mythic structure that Andrea transgresses as she enters adulthood. Elizabeth Ordóñez, "*Nada:* Initiation into Bourgeois Patriarchy," *The Analysis of Hispanic Texts: Current Trends in Methodology: Second York College Colloquium,* ed. Lisa E. Davis and Isabel C. Taran (New York: Bilingual, 1976), emphasizes that Andrea's initiation leads her into the patriarchal bourgeois, while Marsha S. Collins, "Carmen Laforet's *Nada:* Fictional Form and the Search for Identity," *Symposium* 38.4 (1984–85), elaborates the positive development in the conflict between the Self and the Other. Roberta Johnson, *Carmen Laforet* (Boston: Twayne, 1981), 140, underscores that all of the plot lines in Laforet's longer novels involve a quest of identity. Johnson indicates that the mirror scenes in *Nada* relate that Andrea has changed, but she does not connect this to the subconscious development revealed by metaphor and metonymy. Mariana Petrea, "La promesa del futuro: La dialéctica de la emancipación femenina en *Nada* de Carmen Laforet," *Letras Femeninas* 22.1–2 (1994), shows how Andrea fits Patricia Meyer Spacks' observations about feminine and adolescent development. Stephen Hart, *White Ink: Essays on Twentieth-Century Feminine Fiction in Spain and Latin America* (London: Tamesis; Madrid: Támesis, 1993), 19, classifies the work as a *Bildungsroman,* but clarifies that Andrea's development is limited by being female. Margaret E. W. Jones, "Dialectical Movement as Feminist Technique in the Works of Carmen Laforet," *Studies in Honor of Gerald E. Wade,* ed. Sylvia Bowman et al. (Madrid: Porrúa, 1979), explains that Laforet's writing is normally considered "feminine" rather than "feminist," but that all of her works contain a protagonist who seeks independence and individuality in a society that does not understand her. Sara E. Schyfter, "La mística masculina en *Nada,* de Carmen Laforet," *Novelistas femeninas de la postguerra española,* ed. Janet W. Pérez (Madrid: Porrúa, 1983), explores the interactions between males and females in the novel. She finds that the events leading to Román's death destroy Andrea's false illusions about the male mystique and allow her to conceive of a better relationship between the sexes. Sherman Eoff, "*Nada* by Carmen Laforet: A Venture in Mechanistic Dynamics," *Hispania* 35 (1952): 207, however, imparts an extremely antifeminine outlook to his interpretation by saying: "A prominent aspect of the contemporary Spanish novel is the heavy atmosphere of dispiritment concerning *man's* place in the world" [my underline].

6. JAMES OLNEY, *Metaphors of Self* (Princeton: Princeton University Press, 1972), 31.

7. Currie K. Thompson, "Perception and Art: Water Imagery in *Nada,*" *Romance Quarterly* 32 (1985), gives a detailed explanation of the positive images of water in *Nada.*

8. Ragland-Sullivan, *Jacques Lacan,* 217, explains that Lacan speaks of "desire" as a lack that is joined to a signifier as a symbol in a "prethought 'thought' during the mirror stage," when a child becomes aware that his own identity is distinct from that of others. Lacan defines repression as another point of connection between the conscious and unconscious systems and which resurfaces in repetitions of "heavily charged word nodes" (Ragland-Sullivan, 12–14). Repressed desires are translated to conscious language through metaphor and metonymy (Ragland-Sullivan, 112–15).

9. Carmen Laforet, *Nada* (Barcelona: Destino, 1985), 11. All translations are mine. Subsequent citations indicate the page number in parentheses.

10. J. A. Cuddon, *A Dictionary of Literary Terms and Literary Theory,* (Cambridge: Blackwell, 1991), 443, explains that "many, but not all" images are con-

veyed by figurative language. While Andrea conveys the negative imagery through metaphors, later references to mirror images indicate both metaphoric and literal levels. Scenes with mirror images reveal what is occurring in the plot, while they concurrently have figurative significance in the development of the female character.

11. Ragland-Sullivan, *Jacques Lacan,* 249.

12. "The Laugh of the Medusa," 889.

13. See Toril Moi, *Sexual/Textual Politics* (New York: Methuen, 1985), 107, for an explanation of the astral and aquatic images indicative of the cosmic quality of women in the writing of Cixous. Also see Jean Wyatt, "Avoiding self-definition: In defense of women's right to merge (Julia Kristeva and Mrs. Dalloway)," *The Female Imagination and the Modernist Aesthetic,* ed. Sandra M. Gilbert and Susan Gubar (New York: Gordon, 1986), 117, regarding how water and ocean images reveal change and renewal in literature of feminine development.

14. Michael D. Thomas, "Symbolic Portals in Laforet's *Nada,*" *Anales de la Novela de Posguerra* 3, finds the division of the novel into three parts important in the total concept of the work. He states, however, that part 3 "functions as a stage for the clarification of past questions" (58), while my analysis shows that part 3 calls awareness to Andrea's understanding of the female psyche. Thomas believes the doorways in *Nada* have symbolic importance as Andrea crosses from childhood to adulthood in a gradual process. His article, as well as Thompson's "Perception and Art," elaborates metaphoric and symbolic aspects illustrating Andrea's constructive development.

15. Bergmann, "Reshaping the Canon," 143.

16. Kolbenschlag, *Kiss Sleeping Beauty Good-Bye,* 66.

17. Margaret Jones, "Dialectical Movement," 114, explains that the story with a happy ending "glorifies the traditional role expected of a woman" and that Laforet's protagonists depart from this role. Martín Gaite, *Desde la ventana,* 99, also stresses that Andrea is different from the traditional heroine of the *novela rosa* (harlequin-type romance), with its happy ending.

18. Villegas, "*Nada* de Carmen Laforet," 196, demonstrates the incompatibility between myth and reality by contrasting Cinderella's slippers with Andrea's shoes.

19. Rabindranath Tagore, *Personality* (London: Macmillan, 1917), 47.

20. Thomas, "Symbolic," 67, indicates that Andrea's memory of the fat lady at the party who is about to raise a pastry to her mouth is a symbol of the type of person she does not want to become. The smell of someone with too much jewelry would represent the same idea.

21. See Agustín Cerezales, *Carmen Laforet* (Madrid: Ministerio de Cultura, 1982), 139, for Juan Ramón Jiménez's negative criticism of the chapter of Laforet's novel where Ena's mother and Andrea have their intimate conversation. (Recall that Laforet includes a fragment of Jiménez's poem "Nada" as a prologue to her novel.) Ordóñez, *Voices of Their Own,* 49–51, focuses on the mother-"daughter" relationship between Andrea and Ena's mother as a positive force.

22. "The Laugh of the Medusa," 881.

23. Ibid., 878.

24. See Gardiner, "On Female Identity," 35; Hirsch, *The Mother/Daughter Plot,* 20; Estés, *Women Who Run with the Wolves,* 180; Friday, *My Mother/My Self;* and Chodorow, *The Reproduction of Mothering,* 93; for examples of positive and negative mirroring between mother and daughter. Also see Sandra M. Gilbert and Susan Gubar, "The Queen's Looking Glass: Female Creativity, Male Images

of Women, and the Metaphor of Literary Paternity," *The Madwoman in the Attic: The Woman Writer and the Nineteenth-Century Literary Imagination* (New Haven: Yale University Press, 1979), for negative mirroring between mother and daughter in "Snow White and the Seven Dwarfs." Not all the mother-daughter relationships in *Nada* demonstrate the positive mirroring that Ena and her mother have: Angustias and the other sisters are extremely critical of their mother.

25. Feal Deibe, "*Nada* de Carmen Laforet," 240.

26. "The Laugh of the Medusa," 881.

27. "Reshaping the Canon," 143–44.

28. Bergmann, "Reshaping the Canon," 144, establishes the possibility of incestuous attraction between Andrea and Román. Ruth El Saffar, "Structural and Thematic Tactics of Suppression in Carmen Laforet's *Nada*," *Symposium* 28 (1974): 125, points out other links between the two.

29. *Kiss Sleeping Beauty Good-Bye*, ix.

30. Johnson, *Carmen Laforet*, 61–62.

31. *Kiss Sleeping Beauty Good-Bye*, ix.

32. Because Andrea departs for Madrid with Ena's father, Ordóñez, "*Nada*: Initiation into Bourgeois Patriarchy," 61–77, sees this as a return to bourgeois patriarchy. However, neither Ena's father nor Jaime (her boyfriend) fit completely within the model of bourgeois patriarchy. Neither of them try to completely control the women they love but, rather, allow them space to develop.

33. La Belle, *Herself Beheld*, 39–40.

34. The reflection of the opinion of others that La Belle identifies with regard to the mirror would be a "positional" contiguity according to Jakobson, while the second metonymic aspect of the mirror would be a "temporal" contiguity, similar to Jakobson's explanation of cubism "where the object is transformed into a set of synecdoches" (*Fundamentals of Language*, 77–78).

35. *Herself Beheld*, 111.

36. Similarly, a mirror reveals a truth to Ena's mother after she has cut off her beautiful braid to give it to Román and then realizes how foolish she was. "The following day, upon looking at myself in the mirror, I began to cry" (235).

37. See Rose, "Through the Looking Glass," 226; and La Belle, *Herself Beheld*, 15–19.

38. *Carmen Laforet*, 61.

39. The following critics interpret Andrea's development of self in a negative manner: Barry Jordan, *Laforet: Nada*, (Valencia: Soler-Grant, 1993); "Laforet's *Nada* as Female Bildung?" *Symposium* 46.2 (1992); and "Shifting Generic Boundaries: The Role of Confession and Desire in Laforet's *Nada*," *Neophilologus* 77.3 (1993); Eoff, "*Nada* by Carmen Laforet"; Wilma Newberry, "The Solstitial Holidays in Carmen Laforet's *Nada*: Christmas and Midsummer," *Romance Notes* 17 (1976); El Saffar, "Structural and Thematic Tactics of Suppression in Carmen Laforet's *Nada*"; María Nieves Alonso, "Partir, defender, callar (Tres posibilidades de conclusión en la novela española contemporánea)," *Atenea* 448 (1983); Donna Janine McGiboney, "Paternal Absence and Maternal Repression: The Search for Narrative Authority in Carmen Laforet's *Nada*," *Romance Languages Annual* 6 (1994); and David William Foster, "*Nada*, de Carmen Laforet: Ejemplo de neo-romance en la novela contemporánea," *Novelistas españoles de postguerra*, ed. Rodolfo Cardona (Madrid: Taurus, 1976).

More positive interpretations of Andrea's progress are found in articles by Marsha S. Collins, "Carmen Laforet's *Nada*: Fictional Form and the Search for Identity," *Symposium* 38.4 (1984–85); Bergmann, "Reshaping the Canon"; Petrea,

"La promesa del futuro"; Robert C. Spires, "La experiencia afirmadora de *Nada,*" *La novela española de posguerra: creación artística y experiencia personal* (Madrid: Cupsa, 1978); and "*Nada* y la paradoja de los signos negativos," *Siglo XX/20th Century* 3.1–2 (1985–86); Schyfter, "La mística masculina en *Nada*"; and Villegas, "*Nada* de Carmen Laforet."

40. El Saffar, "Structural and Thematic Tactics of Suppression," feels Andrea's reevaluation of her situation though writing is negative and is proof that she did not make any progress. On a more emotive level, Jones, *The Contemporary Spanish Novel,* 23, states that the temporal separation causes the reader to sense the conflict between Andrea the narrator and Andrea the character and helps create a mood of "existential tension."

41. See La Belle, *Herself Beheld,* 180–82; and Cixous, "The Laugh of the Medusa," 880.

42. Carmen Laforet, *La isla y los demonios* (Barcelona: Destino, 1970), 118. The translation is mine.

43. Ibid., 29.

44. Gustavo Pérez Firmat, "Carmen Laforet: The Dilemma of Artistic Vocation," *Women Writers of Contemporary Spain: Exiles in the Homeland,* ed. Joan L. Brown (Newark: University of Delaware Press, 1991), 39.

45. See Martín Gaite, *Usos amorosos,* chap. 1.

46. Carmen Laforet, *La mujer nueva* (Barcelona: Destino, 1967), 290. The translation is mine.

47. Ibid.

48. José María Martínez Cachero, Introducción, *La insolación,* by Carmen Laforet (Madrid: Castalia, 1992), 36 and 39.

49. Carmen Laforet, *La insolación* (Barcelona: Planeta, 1967), 379. The translation is mine.

50. *La novela femenina contemporánea,* 20.

Chapter 2: The Entrapment of the Distorted Mirror in *Primera memoria*

1. *Primera memoria,* like *Nada,* is available in several English translations: *School of the Sun,* trans. Elaine Kerrigan (New York: Pantheon, 1963; New York: Columbia University Press, 1989; London: Quartet, 1991); and *Awakening,* trans. James Holman Mason (London: Hutchinson, 1963).

Although *Primera memoria* is the first novel of the trilogy entitled *Los mercaderes* (The merchants), in an introductory note to the novel, Matute stresses that all three novels have "rigurosa independencia argumental" (strict separation of plots). The trilogy is completed by *Los soldados lloran de noche* (1964, *Soldiers Cry by Night*) and *La trampa* (1969, *The Trap*). Both of these novels have also been translated to English: *Soldiers Cry by Night,* trans. Robert Nugent and María del Carmen (Pittsburg Pa.: Latin American Literary Review Press, 1995); and *The Trap,* trans. María José de la Cámara and Robert Nugent (Pittsburg Pa.: Latin American Literary Review Press, 1996).

Matute's other novels include *Los Abel* (1945), Premio Café Guijón winner *Fiesta al noroeste* (1952), Premio Planeta winner *Pequeño teatro* (1954), *En esta tierra*—the rewritten version of her censored novel *Las luciérnagas*—(1955), Spanish Critics's best novel and Cervantes prizewinner *Los hijos muertos* (1958), *La torre vigía* (1971), and *Olvidado Rey Gudú* (1997). In 1951 Matute won her first literary prize for the short story "No hacer nada" and has published several collections of short stories: *Los niños tontos* (1956), *El tiempo* (1957), *El arrepentido* (1961), *Historias de la Artámila* (1961), *Algunos muchachos* (1968), and *La virgen de Antioquía y otros relatos* (1990). *Tres y un sueño* (1961) consists of three fantastic narrations, *Libro de juegos para los niños de los otros* (1961) is a brief ironic text with poignant pictures of children, *El río* (1963) is usually described as a book of memoirs, and *A la mitad del camino* (1961) is a collection of articles and sketches. Matute's fiction written for children includes *El país de la pizarra* (1956), *Paulina, el mundo y las estrellas* (1960), *El saltamontes verde* (1960), *Caballito loco* (1962), and Premio Lazarillo winner *El polizón del "Ulises"* (1965).

2. "Reshaping the Canon," 146.

3. Margaret E. W. Jones, "Temporal Patterns in the Works of Ana María Matute," *Romance Notes* 12 (1970): 286. Other critics who describe Matia's negative transition into the adult world are Christopher L. Anderson, "Andersen's 'The Snow Queen' and Matute's *Primera memoria:* To the Victor Go the Spoils," *Crítica Hispánica* 14.1–2 (1992); Michael D. Thomas, "The Rite of Initiation in Matute's *Primera memoria*," *Kentucky Romance Quarterly* 25 (1978); James R. Stevens, "Myth and Memory: Ana María Matute's *Primera memoria*," *Symposium* 25 (1971); Nieves Alonso, "Partir, defender, callar"; Ricardo Gullón, *La novela lírica* (Madrid: Cáthedra, 1984); Lucy Lee-Bonanno, "From Freedom to Enclosure: 'Growing Down' in Matute's *Primera memoria*," *Kentucky Philological Review* 13 (1986); and Janet Winecoff (Díaz) (Pérez), "Style and Solitude in the Works of Ana María Matute," *Hispania* 49.1 (1966). Winecoff calls Matute's novels "Odysseys of loss" (62). Rosa Roma, *Ana María Matute*, (Madrid: EPESA, 1971), 80–81, mentions the work's haunting effect.

4. Geraldine Cleary Nichols, "Codes of Exclusion, Modes of Equivocation: Matute's *Primera memoria*," *Ideologies & Literature* 1 (1985): 160, states that Doña Práxedes becomes "the patriarch in the absence of a suitable male." Seemingly, she would expect Borja to take over her role some day. Winecoff, "Style and Solitude," 68, finds Borja reminiscent of Román in *Nada* because of his desire to manipulate others.

5. See the following regarding the existential characteristics of *Primera memoria:* Winecoff, "Style and Solitude," 62 and 68; Javier Martínez Palacio, "Una trilogía novelística de Ana María Matute," *Insula* 219 (1965): 6; and Margaret E. W. Jones, "Antipathetic Fallacy: The Hostile World of Ana María Matute's Novels," *Kentucky Foreign Language Quarterly* 23 Supplement (1967): 14.

6. Ana María Matute, *Primera memoria* (Barcelona: Destino, 1975), 14. All translations are mine. Subsequent citations indicate the page number in parentheses.

Nichols, "Codes of Exclusion," 159, notes that the island is both a metaphor and metonym of Matia's existence. It is used metaphorically, she says, to express Matia's isolated adolescence and metonymically because it is "contiguous and co-extensive with her adolescence" (182).

7. Stevens, "Myth and Memory," 201, associates Doña Práxedes with pre-Aryan Minoan deities, while Thomas, "The Rite of Initiation," interprets the novel in terms of the steps of initiation rites of primitive tribes—each section marks a step in the process. Both articles emphasize the primordial aspect I have mentioned.

8. Following the Spanish civil war, Pope Pius XII expressed his support of Francisco Franco and his regime, an occurrence leading to some of the animosity

and distrust of the Catholic Church in Spain. See Martín Gaite, *Usos amorosos,* chap. 1.

9. J. A. Cuddon, *A Dictionary of Literary Terms and Literary Theory* (Cambridge: Blackwell, 1991), 939, defines symbol as an object that represents or "stands for" something else. The definition explains that a symbol often combines an image with a concept. Michael Riffaterre, *Fictional Truth* (Baltimore: Johns Hopkins University Press, 1990), 54, defines a symbolic system within a text as a "sustained metaphor." He also links symbolism to metonymic repetition saying: "The consequence of repetition, either of structurally identical elements in the guise of variation or of the same figure (for instance, metonymic reification that equates woman with jeweler's window)" in different situations and contexts is "not unlike a sustained metaphor strewn though the whole novel" (45).

Margaret E. W. Jones, *The Literary World of Ana María Matute* (Lexington: University Press of Kentucky, 1970), 105–19, explains the importance of repetition in the establishment of the meaning of symbols, such as that of the flowers in *Primera memoria.* Celia Berreltini, "Ana María Matute, la novelista pintora," *Cuadernos Hispanoamericanos* 144 (1966): 409, states that colors in the novel become symbolic. Like the flowers, the sun also acquires symbolic characteristics (Jones, *The Literary World of Ana María Matute,* 117–18), and Matia calls it "a red thunder" (80). The sun takes on metonymic characteristics of an animal when Matia says the stained-glass windows of the church are harshly "licked by the sun" (80), and Thomas, "The Rite of Initiation," 154–56, compares the sun to both an animal and a supernatural being. These characteristics also link the sun to Doña Práxedes.

10. For more details on the religious symbolism in *Primera memoria,* see Stevens, "Myth and Memory"; and Margaret E. W. Jones, "Religious Motifs and Biblical Allusions in the Works of Ana María Matute," *Hispania* 51 (1968).

11. "The Rite of Initiation," 155.

12. Gullón, *La novela lírica,* 154, writes of Matia's submerging herself in "el pozo de la vida adulta" (the well of adult life).

13. Stevens, "Myth and Memory," 200, compares Doña Práxedes to a lizard.

14. Nichols, "Codes of Exclusion," 158, also says that Matia's final embrace of Borja is a submission to him.

15. Several critics mention the Cain and Abel theme in *Primera memoria:* Jones, "Religious Motifs"; George Wythe, "The World of Ana María Matute," *Books Abroad* 40.1 (1966): 24–25; Víctor Fuentes, "Notas sobre el mundo novelesco de Ana María Matute," *Novelistas españoles de postguerra,* ed. Rodolfo Cardona (Madrid: Taurus, 1976), 105–9; and Artur Lundkvist, "Mellan Kain och Abel," *Bonniers Litterära Magasin* 31 (1962).

16. The following critics see universal or symbolic meaning to the relatively minor conflicts in the novel: Janet (Winecoff) (Díaz) Pérez, "The Fictional World of Ana María Matute: Solitude, Injustice, and Dreams," *Women Writers of Contemporary Spain: Exiles in the Homeland,* ed. Joan L. Brown (Newark: University of Delaware Press, 1991), 107; Joseph Schraibman, "Two Spanish Civil War Novels: A Woman's Perspective," *The Spanish Civil War in Literature,* ed. Janet Pérez and Wendell Aycock (Lubbock: Texas Tech University Press, 1990); Janet W(inecoff) Díaz (Pérez), *Ana María Matute* (New York: Twayne, 1971), 133; and Jones, "Temporal Patterns," *Romance Notes* 12 (1970): 283.

17. Bergmann, "Reshaping the Canon"; and Suzanne Gross Reed, "Notes on Hans Christian Andersen Tales in Ana María Matute's *Primera memoria,*" *Continental, Latin-American and Francophone Women Writers,* vol. 1, ed. Eunice My-

ers and Ginette Adamson (Lanham: University Press of America, 1987); give interpretations of fairy tales such as "The Snow Queen" and "The Little Mermaid" in *Primera memoria*. Nichols, "Codes of Exclusion," deals with the intertexts of childhood stories, while Stevens, "Myth and Memory," 198, finds that the "mythic scope" of *Primera memoria* is augmented by its references to classic children's literature. Hart, *White Ink*, 67–70, explores ways fairy tales affect Matia's personal development. Anderson, "Andersen's 'The Snow Queen,'" 22, demonstrates that Matia ultimately rejects the mythic model of "The Snow Queen."

18. Hans Christian Andersen, *Andersen's Fairy Tales*, trans. Mrs. E. V. Lucas and Mrs. H. B. Paul (New York: Grosset, n.d.), 108.

19. Winecoff, "Style and Solitude," 61 and 68, calls Matute's use of language "poetic distortion" and "verging on the grotesque," illustrating the qualities of distortion that I have mentioned. This distortion associated with mirrors is reminiscent of Ramón del Valle-Inclán's *esperpento*.

20. Andersen, *Andersen's Fairy Tales*, 109.

21. Ibid., 110. Nichols, "Codes of Exclusion," 177, points out that although the doves in the novel are "symbols of peace, love and freedom," they cause Matia to have a negative change of heart toward Manuel as they fly over her. She connects this change to Kay's pessimistic conversion in the Snow Queen. The passage from *Primera memoria* reads: "Grandmother's doves were returning: at that moment they settled in the almond trees. They were like blue and greenish shadows over our heads. They made strange little cracks. Something vibrated in the air, like drops of very fine crystal" (146).

22. "Reshaping the Canon," 146.

23. Ibid., 148.

24. Andersen, *Andersen's Fairy Tales*, 146.

25. Stevens, "Myth and Memory," 202, calls the "desooter" Gorogó a symbol of childhood innocence.

26. In "The Shepherdess and the Sweep" the china figures of a gilded shepherdess and black chimney sweeper, who were perfectly suited for each other, stood side by side on a table under a looking glass. A larger china figure (the Chinaman) claimed he was the grandfather of the Shepherdess and declared that she should marry a wooden statue named "Major-general-field-sergeant-commander-Billy-goat's-legs. Not wanting to marry him, the Shepherdess escaped up the chimney with her beloved Sweep. After seeing the world outside, the Shepherdess became frightened and asked the Sweep to bring her back to the table, in spite of the possibility she might have to marry the other. When they returned, they found the Chinaman broken, and the Shepherdess asked that he be riveted. By coincidence, his rivet prevented him from nodding his assent to "Billy-goat's-legs," so the Shepherdess and Sweep were permitted to stay on the table, loving each other "till they were broken to pieces" (*Andersen's Fairy Tales*, 232).

Nichols, "Codes of Exclusion," 184, observes that the "Major-general-field-sergeant-commander-Billy-goat's-legs" in Andersen's fairy tale might be compared to the type of person whom Matia says she would be afraid of marrying, like her uncle Alvaro. While Borja would embody some of the same characteristics as his father, Manuel would be the antithesis of that negative prototype.

27. Recall that the reflection of others' opinions in a mirror is a positional contiguity, and the reflection over time is a temporal contiguity (see my chap. 1).

28. Fuentes, "Notas sobre el mundo novelesco," 107, mentions the element of fatality in Matute's works.

29. *Herself Beheld,* 100–101.

30. Ibid., 113–28.

31. "The Laugh of the Medusa," 878.

32. Margaret Jones, "Temporal Patterns," notes that in some of Matute's works human nature "traps" the individual into repeating the same actions that were unfavorable for others (284), also suggesting a negative spiral.

33. María del Carmen Riddel, *La novela femenina de formación en la postguerra española* (New York: Lang, 1995), 85.

34. See Pratt, *Archetypal Patterns,* 10 and 169, regarding rebirth in midlife. See Anne E. Brown and Marjanne E. Goozé, "Introduction: Placing Identity in Cross-Cultural Perspective," *International Women's Writing: New Landscapes of Identity,* ed. Anne E. Brown and Marjanne E. Goozé (Westport, Conn.: Greenwood, 1995), xiv; and Riddel, *La novela femenina,* 167–68, regarding the empowerment of writing.

35. Ana María Matute, "Prólogo," vol. 2 of *Obra completa* (Barcelona: Destino, 1975), 7 (my translation).

36. Joan Lipman Brown, "Unidad y diversidad en *Los mercaderes,* de Ana María Matute," *Novelistas femeninas de la postguerra español,* ed. Janet W. Pérez (Madrid: Turanzas, 1983), explores how Matute's three novels conform to and differ from the traditional concept of the trilogy.

37. Ana María Matute, *Los soldados lloran de noche, Obra completa,* vol. 4 (Barcelona: Destino, 1975), 220 (my translation).

38. Ana María Matute, *La trampa,* (Barcelona: Destino, 1987), 152. The translation is mine.

39. Ibid., 30 and 240.

40. In contrast, Martín Gaite, *Desde la ventana,* 88–89, classifies Andrea as "una luchadora" (a fighter) and "diferente de los demás" (different from the rest).

Chapter 3: Metaphor and Metonymy: A Bridge Between the Gaps in *La plaça del Diamant*

1. There are two English translations of *La plaça del Diamant: The Time of the Doves,* trans. David H. Rosenthal (London: Arrow Books, 1981, 1986; New York: Taplinger, 1980, 1981; Saint Paul, Minn.: Graywolf, 1981, 1986); and *The Pigeon Girl,* trans. Eda O'Shiel (London: Deutsch, 1967). In 1982, director Francesc Betriu released the film *La plaça del Diamant,* based on Rodoreda's novel.

Rodoreda's other novels include *¿Sóc una dona honrada?* (1932), *Del que home no pot fugir* (1934), *Un dia en la vida d'un home* (1934), *Crim* (1936), Crexells prizewinning *Aloma* (1938), Sant Jordi and Critics prizewinning *El carrer de les Camèlies* (1966), *Jardí vora el mar* (1967), *Mirall trencat* (1974), and *Quanta, quanta guerra* (1980). Her collections of short stories include Víctor Català prizewinning *Vint-i-dos contes* (1958) and *La meva Cristina i altres contes* (1967). *Semblava de seda i altres contes* (1878) and *Viatges i flors* (1980) are collections of mixed genres. Rodoreda died in 1983, but some of her writing was published posthumously, including a later edition of *Meva Cristina* (1984), *Una campana de vidre* (1984), *El torrent de las flors* (1993), a collection of letters titled *Cartes a Anna Murià* (1984), and two novels: *La mort i la primavera* (1986) and *Isabel i Maria* (1991). *Contes de guerra i revolució (1936–39),* vol. 1 & 2, edited by María

Campillo, contains nine narrations previously published in periodicals. Rodoreda's exile from Spain began in 1939.

2. As with *Nada,* critical opinions of Natàlia's position vary. The following critics sight lack of development. Frances Wyers, "A Woman's Voices: Mercè Rodoreda's *La plaça del Diamant," Kentucky Romance Quarterly* 30 (1983): 307, finds the form of the novel like "a closed circle of enormous sadness," saying Natàlia never categorizes, judges, or reflects on her position as a woman. Kimberly Nance, "Things Fall Apart: Images of Disintegration in Mercè Rodoreda's *La plaça de Diamant," Hispanófila* 101 (1991): 67–76, sees Natàlia's life as perseverance rather than progress and notes an overall negative feeling in the novel. Mario Lucarda, "Mercè Rodoreda y el buen salvaje," *Quimera* 62: 38 and 35, suggests that Natàlia's survival instinct is the most redeeming quality of a nearly autistic heroine; and Roberto Manteiga, "From Empathy to Detachment: The Author-Narrator Relationship in Several Spanish Novels by Women," *Monographic Review/Revista Monográfica* 8 (1992): 30, feels her scream toward the end of the novel is one of "frustration."

Others perceive more positive development. Bergmann, "Reshaping the Canon," 154, says Natàlia's scream at the end of the novel is one "of a woman learning to speak." Likewise, Kathleen Glenn, "*La plaza del Diamante:* The Other Side of the Story," *Letras Femeninas* 12.1–2 (1986): 61, sees progress "from oppression and dispossession to repossession and partial liberation." Carme Arnau, "La obra de Mercè Rodoreda," *Cuadernos Hispanoamericanos* 383 (1982): 241, says Natàlia passes from confinement to liberation, and describes her process of maturation in *Introducció a la narrativa de Mercè Rodoreda: el mite de la infantesa* (Barcelona: Edicions 62, 1982). María del Carmen Porrúa, "Tres novelas de la guerra civil," *Cuadernos Hispanoamericanos* 473–74 (1989): 56, calls Natàlia's scream triumphant and highlights her intimate, feminine perspective of the war. Maryellen Bieder, "The Woman in the Garden: The Problem of Identity in the Novels of Mercè Rodoreda," *Segon Col·loqui d'Estudis Catalans a Nord-Amèrica* (Badalona: Abadia de Montserrat, 1982), 358, finds that Natàlia's communication with nature helps "restore her identity." Kayann Short, "Too Disconnected/Too Bound Up: The Paradox of Identity in Mercè Rodoreda's *The Time of the Doves," International Women's Writing: New Landscapes of Identity,* ed. Anne E. Brown and Marjanne E. Goozé (Westport: Greenwood, 1995), feels that Natàlia's mere survival during the turmoil and destruction of the war shows positive development. Roma Cuismano, "En busca de la tradición literaria femenina: Mercè Rodoreda y *La plaza del Diamante," Literatura femenina contemporánea de España: VII Simposio Internacional de Literatura* (Westminster, Calif.: Instituto Literaria y Cultural Hispánico, 1991), uses Pratt's theories to demonstrate that Natàlia progresses, but only to a certain point. Neus Carbonell, "In the Name of the Mother and the Daughter," *The Garden across the Border: Mercè Rodoreda's Fiction,* ed. Kathleen NcNerney and Nancy Vosburg (Selinsgrove: Susquehanna University Press; London: Associated University Press, 1994), says Natàlia's rebirth subverts phallo-centric, Judeo-Christian tradition; and Enric Bou, "Exile in the City: Mercè Rodoreda's *La plaça del Diamant," The Garden across the Border: Mercè Rodoreda's Fiction,* feels her description of city spaces allegorically shows transformation from domination to control. Loreto Busquets, "El mito de la culpa en *La plaça del Diamant," Cuadernos Hispanoamericanos* 420 (1985), explores how Natàlia progresses from guilt and inferiority to equality and love, explaining Rodoreda's comment that *La plaça del Diamant* is "una novela de amor" (a novel about love) (qtd. in Busquets 117).

3. Critics have identified some of the characteristics that depict Natàlia as an innocent, fairly uneducated woman throughout the entire novel. Wyers, "A Woman's Voices," perceives the novel as spoken rather than written because of its simple linear style and its frequent repetitions of words and ideas (301–2), and notes that Natàlia never refers to anything in writing or print (308). Similarly, Bergmann, "Reshaping the Canon," 153, observes that Natàlia is unfamiliar with the culture around her, including the Bosch print on her friend's wall. Mercè Clarasó, "The Angle of Vision in the Novels of Mercè Rodoreda," *Bulletin of Hispanic Studies* 57 (1980): 149, feels that Natàlia's mixing the order in which things happen is characteristic of an uneducated speaker.

4. Glenn, "The Other Side of the Story," attributes much of the impact of the novel to Rodoreda's "use of an innocent as the center of consciousness" (61), and that Natàlia's repetition of words such as "no saber" (not knowing) and "no (acaber de) entender" (not understanding) maintain the aura of innocence (68). Wyers, "A Woman's Voices," notes that "Rodoreda creates the illusion of speech" (308), alluding to the author's skill. According to Bergmann, "Reshaping the Canon," 153, Rodoreda's exclusion of intertextual references by her protagonist has a similar—but opposite—effect of the many intertexts in other novels, including *Nada* and *Primera memoria*. Patricia V. Lunn and Jane W. Albrecht, "*La Plaça del Diamant:* Linguistic Cause and Literary Effect," *Hispania* 75.3 (1992): 497, emphasize Rodoreda's "absolute narrative control" that draws the reader through the same emotional and cognitive processes as the protagonist. Lucarda, "Mercè Rodoreda y el buen salvaje," 35, expresses wonder that Rodoreda could create such a moving character "de algo tan *nada*" (of something so *nothing*), praising the author's skill while he insults her protagonist.

In *La plaza del Diamante: Edición ilustrada,* trans. Secundí Sañé, intro. Joan Sales, trans. Joaquim Dols (Barcelona: HMB, 1982), 8, twenty years after she wrote the novel, Rodoreda says her novel communicates "With deceptively simple style, with deceptively easy style. . . . A style full of craftiness, of the art of writing, with the unconsicous desire to win over and to seduce" (my translation).

5. "The Other Side of the Story," 61.

6. Wyers, "A Woman's Voices," 301–2, finds the novel's "omissions shine and its silences are eloquent," and that its guarded oral style is indicative of a woman's voice in a restricted patriarchal society.

7. See the following regarding the mythic and allegoric qualities of the work: Carme Arnau, "Introduction," *Obres Completes, 1936–1960* by Mercè Rodoreda, vol. 1 (Barcelona: 62, 1980); Lucarda, "Mercè Rodoreda y el buen salvaje," 38; and Jaume Martí-Olivella, "Bachelardian Myth in Rodoreda's Construction of Identity," *Imagination, Emblems and Expressions: Essays on Latin American, Caribbean and Continental Culture and Identity,* ed. Helen Ryan-Ranson (Bowling Green, Oh.: Bowling Green State University Popular Press, 1993).

8. Hawkes, *Metaphor,* 72. Also see Lunn and Albrecht, "Linguistic Cause and Literary Effect," regarding techniques (including passive constructions that change to active and agentive as the novel progresses) that cause the reader to interpret Natàlia's feelings and to evaluate her character.

9. Mercè Rodoreda, *La plaça del Diamant* (Barcelona: Club, 1979), 22. All translations are mine. Subsequent page numbers are indicated in parentheses. *Colometa* is the diminutive form of *coloma* in Catalan and is derived from the Latin word *colŭmba. Colŭmba* is also the first word in the Latin biological classification system of Order and Family names of pigeons and doves.

10. I have left the words *colom, coloma* and *colomar* in Catalan because of the distinctive connotations of the words *pigeon* and *dove* in English. *Coloma, colom* (the masculine form), and the Spanish word *paloma* can be translated either as "dove" or "pigeon." Although I believe the *coloms* in the novel are domestic pigeons, their proper name is Rock Dove. In English, the word "dove" implies a more romantic or noble bird—a turtledove or the dove of peace—while pigeons in the United States often connote dirty pests, plaguing older buildings in the cities. In contrast, one can purchase *coloms* on Las Ramblas in Barcelona, either as a pet or to breed for food, much in the same manner that rabbits are sometimes raised in the United States.

11. The effect of the war on Natàlia is disputed by several critics. Pérez, *Contemporary Women Writers,* 80, feels that Natàlia suffers nearly as much from her marriage as she does from the civil war, attributing this suffering to the egoism of the patriarchal society, especially Quimet's egoism. In contrast, José Ortega, "Mujer, guerra, y neurosis en dos novelas de M. Rodoreda (*La plaza del Diamante* y *La calle de las Camelias*)," *Novelistas femeninas de la postguerra española,* ed. Janet W. Pérez (Madrid: Porrúa, 1983), 72–73, sees Natàlia's problems as an echo of the neurotic atmosphere of the Spanish civil war. Randolph Pope, "Mercè Rodoreda's Subtle Greatness," *Women Writers of Contemporary Spain: Exiles in the Homeland,* ed. Joan Brown (Newark: University of Delaware Press, 1991), 125, finds it ironic that the war removes all threats to Natàlia's body (Quimet is killed and Antoni is left impotent from the war) and allows her to "move on to a contented mature life."

12. Rodoreda uses many ellipses without spaces (...) as punctuation in Natàlia's discourse. In order to indicate the author's punctuation I will utilize ellipses without spaces whenever she does. For my deletions, however, I will use ellipses with spaces between them (. . .).

13. *The Role of the Reader,* 82.

14. Ibid.

15. Claude Lévi-Strauss, *The Savage Mind,* trans. George Weidenfeld (Chicago: University of Chicago Press, 1966), 212, acknowledges that naming people after flowers, animals, and such has the force and effect of a metaphor.

16. Ibid., 204–5.

17. Loreto Busquets, "El mito de la culpa en *La plaça del Diamant,*" *Cuadernos Hispanoamericanos* 420 (1985): 128, feels the *coloms* represent a territorial battle for psychological space and identity in Natàlia's and Quimet's relationship.

18. *The Savage Mind,* 212.

19. See Hayden White, *Metahistory: The Historical Imagination in Nineteenth-Century Europe,* (Baltimore: Johns Hopkins University Press, 1973), 34–38, for a cyclical quadratic description of metaphor that progresses through four stages (Metaphor, Metonymy, Synecdoche, and Irony) and then cycles back to the first. While White relates these tropes to history, Northrup Frye, *The Anatomy of Criticism: Four Essays* (Princeton: Princeton University Press, 1957), 158–239, delineates a similar four-segment cycle with regard to literary development. Although White's notion of cyclical movement between tropes is similar to the Shapiros's in *Figuration in Verbal Art,* White is more intent on identifying the various stages. In the metaphor Natàlia = *coloma,* White's cyclical concept of Metaphor that progresses to Irony helps reveal change in Rodoreda's original equation.

20. See Nancy Mandlove, "Used Poetry: The Trans-Parent Language of Gloria Fuertes and Angel González," *Revista Canadiense de Estudios Hispánicos* 3 (1983): 306, regarding the renovation of metaphoric language that has become a cliché. Mandlove's comments support the Shapiros's and White's theories that metaphors are cyclical. In "Oral Texts: The Play of Orality and Literacy in the Poetry of Gloria Fuertes," *Siglo XX/20th Century* 5 (1987–88): 16, Mandlove also deals with language (in Gloria Fuertes's poetry) that has an "oral dimension . . . geared to a highly literate public"—similar to Rodoreda's novel.

21. Cuddon, *A Dictionary of Literary Terms and Literary Theory,* 443, explains that images can have both literal and metaphoric levels.

22. Pope, "Mercè Rodoreda's Subtle Greatness," 127, calls the funnel "a symbol of . . . [Natàlia's] increasingly restricted life."

23. Michel Le Guern, *La metáfora y la metonimia,* trans. Augusto de Galvez-Canero y Pidal (Madrid: Cáthedra, 1976), 90, points out the effect of one's reality on mental processes and the ability of metonymy to express the subtleties of a situation.

24. "The Other Side of the Story," 61. Glenn also observes that Natàlia's feeling that her body is not really hers during pregnancy demonstrates the degree of her self-estrangement (67). José Ortega, "Mujer, guerra, y neurosis," 72, speaks of the emptiness in Natàlia's life resulting from her mother's early death; while Pérez, *Contemporary Women Writers,* 80, alludes to her "serious identity problem."

25. "The Laugh of the Medusa," 878.

26. See Kolbenschlag, *Kiss Sleeping Beauty Goodbye,* 64. Kolbenschlag explains that women's acceptance of lowly positions and "virtuous suffering," like that of Cinderella, demonstrates that they have "internalized the consciousness of the victim" (64–65). Although they accept their paltry condition, they passively wait for their "real existence to begin" (5).

27. Arnau, *Obres Completes,* 17, describes the opposition between Quimet and Antoni.

28. Rodoreda, *La plaza del Diamante: Edición ilustrada,* 16, calls this knife a sexual symbol.

29. Natàlia's removal of her stockings after returning home, like a snake shedding its skin, is another metaphoric expression of rebirth. See Richard Callan, "The Archetype of Psychic Renewal in *La vorágine,*" *Woman as Myth and Metaphor in Latin American Literature,* ed. Carmen Virgilio and Naomi Lindstrom (Columbia: University of Missouri Press, 1985), 18, for the symbolic connotations of rebirth of a snake shedding its skin.

30. See Pratt, *Archetypal Patterns,* 10, and Ferguson, "The Female Novel of Development," 228, regarding progressive circular development. See Kolbenschlag, *Kiss Sleeping Beauty Goodbye,* ix, regarding restrictive compulsions and guilt.

31. Clarasó, "The Angle of Vision," 148, mentions Natàlia's "authorial role" in the retelling of her story sometime after the events occurred.

32. See Sharon Magnarelli, *The Lost Rib: Female Characters in the Spanish-American Novel* (Lewisburg: Bucknell University Press, 1985), 68, regarding the silence characteristic of fairy tale heroines.

33. Mercè Rodoreda, *Aloma,* rev. ed. (Barcelona: Edicions 62, 1969).

34. Randolph Pope, "Two Faces and the Character of Her True Nature," *The Garden across the Border: Mercè Rodoreda's Fiction,* ed. Kathleen NcNerney

and Nancy Vosburg (Selinsgrove: Susquehanna University Press; London: Associated University Press, 1994), 146.

35. Mercè Rodoreda, *El carrer de les camèlies* (Barcelona: Club, 1966), 50. The translation is mine.

36. Mercè Rodoreda, *Mirall trencat* (Barcelona: Edicions 62, 1983), 259 and 238. The translation is mine.

CHAPTER 4: THE REFLECTION OF DANGEROUS DIVISION IN *JULIA*

1. There is presently no English translation of *Julia*. In addition to *Julia*, Moix's other narrative publications include two collections of short stories, *Ese chico pelirrojo a quien veo cada día* (1971) and Ciudad de Barcelona prizewinner *Las virtudes peligrosas* (1985); two novels, *Walter, ¿por qué te fuiste?* (1973) and *Vals negro* (1994); and a story for children *La maravillosa colina de las edades primitivas* (1976). She is also well known for her poetry, inspiring Josep María Castellet to include her as one of the new generation of poets in *Nueve novísimos poetas españoles*.

2. Nichols, "Caída/Re(s)puesta," calls the earlier writers (Laforet, Matute, Rodoreda, and Martín Gaite) the "primera generación" (first generation) and distinguishes their works from those written after the death of Franco and dealing principally with older protagonists. She says *Julia* is a "puente" (bridge), as the author's date of birth places her in the second generation, but the theme and style of *Julia* is closer to novels of the first generation (326). In contrast, Isabel Romero, et al., "Feminismo y literatura: La narrativa de los años 70," *Actas de las cuartas jornadas de investigación interdisciplinaria· Literatura y vida cotidiana,* ed. María Angeles Durán and José Antonio Rey (Madrid: Universidad Autónoma de Madrid, 1987), 347 and 351, find aspects of *Julia* comparable to novels written in the seventies (especially those by Tusquets), but they emphasize that it was published earlier. Margaret E. W. Jones, "Del compromiso al egoísmo: La metamorfosis de la protagonista en la novelística femenina de postguerra," *Novelistas femeninas de la postguerra española,* ed. Janet W. Pérez (Madrid: Porrúa, 1983), 128, calls Moix the most important of a new group of writers with common concerns. Linda Gould Levine, "The Censored Sex: Woman as Author and Character in Franco's Spain," *Women in Hispanic Literature: Icons and Fallen Idols,* ed. Beth Miller (Berkeley: University of California Press, 1983), 304–5, concludes that *Julia* (along with Moix's more sexually explicit novel *Walter, ¿por qué te fuiste?*) initiates a break from the preexisting sexual stereotypes about women. Christopher C. Soufas, Jr., "Ana María Moix and the 'Generation of 1968': *Julia* as (Anti-)Generational (Anti-)Manifesto," *Nuevos y novísimos: Algunas perspectivas críticas sobre la narrativa española desde la década de los 60,* ed. Ricardo Landeira and Luis T. González-del-Valle (Boulder: Society of Spanish and Spanish-American Studies, 1978), sees *Julia* as an example of rebellion against ideas and rules of the previous generation.

3. Catherine G. Bellver, "Division, Duplication, and Doubling in the Novels of Ana María Moix," *Nuevos y novísimos: Algunas perspectivas críticas sobre la narrativa española desde la década de los 60,* ed. Ricardo Landeira and Luis T. González-del-Valle (Boulder: Society of Spanish and Spanish American Studies, 1987), identifies four types of doubles in *Julia:* the separate autonomies of "Julia" and "Julita;" the multiplication or "doubling" of Julia's mother figure in her rela-

tionship with other women; Julia's opposite self represented by her grandfather Julio; and the final complete division where "Julita" dominates "Julia." Margaret E. W. Jones, "Ana María Moix: Literary Structures and the Enigmatic Nature of Reality," *Journal of Spanish Studies: Twentieth Century* 4 (1976): 108, believes the "key" to the novel lies in the duality of past and present and the constant shift between the two time periods. Andrew Bush, "Ana María Moix's Silent Calling," *Women Writers of Contemporary Spain: Exiles in the Homeland,* ed. Joan Brown (Newark: University of Delaware Press, 1991), 139, mentions the "subversive interference of Catalan" on Moix's expression in Castilian, and finds that language itself enters into the "doubling or split-identity" in her work. He points out that Julia's rape and her obstructed communication with others "is converted into the symptom, or trope, of stifled breathing" (143). Sara E. Schyfter, "Rites without Passage: The Adolescent World of Ana María Moix's *Julia*," *The Analysis of Literary Texts: Current Trends in Methodology: Third and Fourth York College Colloquia,* ed. Randolph D. Pope (Ypsilanti: Bilingual, 1980), 49, believes Julia's psychological development results in the "double" or "Doppelganger" that leaves her true self unrealized, calling her adolescence one of the "rites without passage." Michael D. Thomas, "El desdoblamiento psíquico como factor dinámico en *Julia,* de Ana María Moix," *Novelistas femeninas de la postguerra española,* ed. Janet W. Pérez (Madrid: Porrúa, 1983), 103–4, regards Julia's psychic doubling as the fundamental dynamic element that draws the reader into the novel, noting chapters where "Julia" dominates and others where "Julita" does. Lucy Lee-Bonnano, *The Quest for Authentic Personhood: An Expression of the Female Tradition in Novels by Moix, Tusquets, Matute and Alós* (Ph.D. diss., University of Kentucky, 1984), identifies Julia as schizophrenic, briefly referring to ideas of Laing, Chesler, and others. She finds *Julia*'s circular form negative in contrast to the male *buildingsroman* that expresses a "progressive expansion of consciousness" (30). As seen in other novels, circularity is not necessarily a criterion for lack of progress in development.

4. La Belle, *Herself Beheld,* 119.

5. Ana María Moix, *Julia* (Barcelona: Barral, 1970), 53. All translations are mine. Subsequent citations indicate the page number in parentheses.

6. R. D. Laing, *The Divided Self* (New York: Pantheon, 1969), 15. Although Laing is not considered a feminist, Barbara Hill Rigney, *Madness and Sexual Politics* (Madison: University of Wisconsin Press, 1978), 8, feels his ideas can aid a feminist psychoanalytic approach to literature because they express that "psychosis, whether in women or in men, is an understandable or even a 'sane' response to life in a destructive society."

7. Benjamin Hrushovski, "Poetic Metaphor and Frames of Reference," *Poetics Today* 5.1 (1984): 6–7.

8. Juliet Michell, *Psychoanalysis and Feminism* (New York: Pantheon, 1974), 10–11 and 260–63, explores the relative difference between "normal" and "abnormal" and "neurotic" and "psychotic."

9. R. D. Laing, *The Politics of the Family and Other Essays* (New York: Pantheon, 1971), 83.

10. Chodorow, *The Reproduction of Mothering,* 93.

11. Laing, *The Divided Self,* 45–46.

12. Ibid., 169, 46, and 47.

13. See Laing, *The Politics of the Family,* 10 and 83–84, regarding transferral of one's feelings to another member of the family, and dreams that transpose outcomes to other family members.

14. See Melanie Klein, *The Psycho-Analysis of Children,* trans. Alix Strachey, revised edition (New York: Delacorte, 1975), 15, regarding children's repressed experiences.

15. A nearly identical passage appears on page 220.

16. Beverly Richard Cook, "Madness as Metaphor in Two Short Stories by Ana María Moix," *Continental, Latin-American and Francophone Women Writers,* vol. 2, ed. Ginette Adamson and Eunice Myers (New York: University Press of America, 1990), 28, discusses the symbolic aspects of the thistle in Moix's short story "Ella comía cardos" (She Ate Thistles), comparing the prickly spurs, and even the flower, to male genitals. When "Ella" eats the thistle, she metaphorically destroys the testicle—"the fertile source of male power, something she lacks in a male-ordered society" (28).

17. *Figuration in Verbal Art,* 34.

18. Moix states that censors made forty-five cuts in her novel *Walter, ¿por qué te fuiste?* before it was published (see Levine, "The Censored Sex," 309).

19. See Cixous, "The Laugh of the Medusa," 889, and Wyatt, "Avoiding self-definition," 117, regarding the sea as a symbol of positive feminine development. See Pratt, *Archetypal Patterns,* 16, regarding nature's "green-world."

20. Soufas, "Ana María Moix and the 'Generation of 1968,'" 219, comments that the physical form of *Julia* (such as the omission of quotation marks) is one of the most rebellious and notable deviations from novels that preceded it. This passage also illustrates the proximity of the first- and third-person narration in *Julia* (Mamá's comments are presented in parentheses—as if they were being relived in Julia's thoughts).

21. Laing, *The Divided Self,* 71.

22. Ibid., 68 and 191.

23. Ibid., 182.

24. Ibid., 80 and 171.

25. Sara E. Schyfter, "The Fragmented Family in the Novels of Contemporary Spanish Women Writers," *Perspectives on Contemporary Literature* 3.1 (1977): 28 and 48, sees the family in various Spanish novels written by women—including Moix's *Julia*—as "a metaphor for a Spain that is constricting, old, decadent, and intolerant" and feels that Julia represents "the existential alienation of modern man and woman" and "the social and spiritual desolation of contemporary Spanish society." Thomas, "El desdoblamiento psíquico," 111, says that *Julia* shows "las causas de la enfermedad nacional" (the causes of the national illness). Likewise, Geraldine Cleary Nichols, "*Julia:* 'This is the way the worlds ends . . . ,'" *Novelistas femeninas de la postguerra española,* ed. Janet W. Pérez (Madrid: Porrúa, 1983), 114, explains that Julia and her brothers are products of "una sociedad hipócrita que rechaza lo vital, lo sexual, negándolo" (a hypocritical society that rejects the vital, the sexual, denying it).

26. *Madness and Sexual Politics,* 11–12.

27. See R. D. Laing, *The Politics of Experience* (New York: Ballentine, 1978), 79.

28. Hirsch, *The Mother Daughter Plot,* 48; Rigney, *Madness and Sexual Politics,* 11–12.

29. "Division, Duplication, and Doubling," 33.

30. Nichols, "*Julia:* 'This is the way the world ends . . . ,'" discusses various sexual maladjustments in Julia's family; while Bush, "Ana María Moix's Silent Calling," 147, states that Julia has a "lesbian relationship with Eva." Schyfter, "Rites without Passage," 43–44, uses ideas from Charlotte Wolff's *Love between*

Women to explain how Julia's relationship with her mother is typical of girls who become lesbians. Levine, "The Censored Sex," 306 and 304, notes that Julia has "not totally come to terms with her lesbianism," but Eva "represents the mother, friend, and lover that Julia actively seeks," and this female homosexuality theme "radically deviates" from topics of earlier writers. Anny Brooksbank Jones, "The Incubus and I: Unbalancing Acts in Moix's *Julia*," *Bulletin of Hispanic Studies* 72 (1995): 84, suggests that Julia's "self-mutilating 'balanceo'" (vacillation) demonstrates that she does not fit completely into either homosexuality or heterosexuality.

31. Karen Horney, *Feminine Psychology* (New York: Norton, 1976), 234–35. Also see Horney (236–37) for more information about adolescent girls exhibiting homosexual symptoms, lesbian tendencies as "reproaches against the mother," and the ensuing guilt. Laing, *The Divided Self*, 169–70, explores the homosexual attitude of schizophrenics.

32. Nichols, "*Julia*: 'This is the way the world ends . . . ,'" 120–22, feels Julia is abnormally attracted to her brother Rafael and finds Rafael's death symbolic because he is the only sibling who has the potential for a life without homosexual attractions.

33. "Division, Duplication, and Doubling," 39.

34. See Laing, *The Divided Self*, 100.

35. In contrast, other critics see Don Julio's influence as positive. Juan Antonio Masoliver Rodenas, "La base sexta contra Ana María Moix," *Camp de l'Arpa* 9 (1974): 9–12, regards Don Julio as an ideal and compares him with the kindly grandfather in *Heidi*. Likewise, Bergmann, "Reshaping the Canon," 149, sees Julia's grandfather as a representation of liberty, saying that Julia "denies herself the autonomy exemplified and offered by her grandfather." Thomas, "El desdoblamiento psíquico," 108, feels that Don Julio exerts a positive influence over Julia. Lee-Bonnano, *The Quest for Authentic Personhood*, 34, says Don Julio puts Julia in touch with nature, comparing the mountain atmosphere of his home with Pratt's "green-world."

36. Phyllis Chesler, *Women and Madness* (New York: Avon, 1973), 31.

37. "The Censored Sex," 310.

38. Ana María Moix, *Walter ¿por qué te fuiste?* (Barcelona: Barral, 1972), 43. The translation is mine.

39. Ibid., 155.

40. Ibid., 196.

41. Because the sexual themes and the negative development in *El amor es un juego solitario* are similar to those in *Julia*, I analyze it next, even though Carmen Martín Gaite's *El cuarto de atrás* was published in 1978, the year before Tusquets's novel.

42. Barbara F. Ichiishi, *The Apple of Earthly Love: Female Development in Esther Tusquets' Fiction* (New York: Lang, 1994), 18, refers to the textual dialogues and personal relationship between Moix and Tusquets.

43. Ibid., 93.

CHAPTER 5: *EL AMOR ES UN JUEGO SOLITARIO:* LOSS OF TRUTH THROUGH BAROQUE METAPHORS AND PROVOCATIVE MIRRORS

1. *El amor es un juego solitario* received the Premio Ciudad de Barcelona in 1979. It is the second novel in a trilogy and has been translated into English by

Bruce Penman as *Love Is a Solitary Game* (London: J. Calder; New York: Riverrun Press, 1985). *El mismo mar de todos los veranos* (1978, *The Same Sea as Every Summer*) and *Varada tras el último naufragio* (1980, Beaching after the last shipwreck) complete the trilogy, and are available in English translation as *The Same Sea as Every Summer*, trans. Margaret E. W. Jones (Lincoln: University of Nebraska Press, 1990) and *Stranded*, trans. Susan E. Clark (Elmwood Park, Ill: Dalkey Archive Press, 1991). Tusquets has published two other novels, *Para no volver* (1985) and *Con miel en los labios (1997); a* novel for children, *La conejita Marcela* (1983); and two books of short stories, *Siete miradas en un mismo paisaje* (1981) and *La niña lunática y otros cuentos* (1996).

2. Nichols, "Caída/Re(s)puesta," 326, refers to a first and second generation of women writers, with Tusquets clearly in the latter. Isabel Romero et al., "Feminismo y literatura," also find novels by women written in the Seventies distinct from earlier ones and repeatedly mention Tusquets. Margaret E. W. Jones, "Different Wor(l)ds: Modes of Women's Communication in Spain's *Narrativa Femenina*," *Monographic Review/Revista Monográfica* 8 (1992): 58, names Tusquets as one of the writers who "[detach] communication from the dominant male discourse and . . . [displace] binary hierarchies." Also see Phyllis Zatlin, "Women Novelists in Democratic Spain: Freedom to Express the Female Perspective," *Anales de la Literatura Española Contemporánea* 12 (1987): 29; Santos Alonso, "Novela en la transición, transición en la novela (1975–80)," *Nueva Estafeta* 31–32 (1981); Catherine G. Bellver, "The Language of Eroticism in the Novels of Esther Tusquets," *Anales de la Literatura Española Contemporánea* 9.1–3 (1984); Marie Murphy, "Metafictional and Erotic Games: *El amor es un juego solitario*," *La escritora hispánica*, ed. Nora Erro-Orthmann and Juan Cruz Mendizíbal (Miami. Universal, 1990); and Stephen Hart, "Esther Tusquets: Sex, Excess and the Dangerous Supplement of Language," *Antípodas: Journal of Hispanic Studies* 3 (1991).

3. Hart, "Esther Tusquets: Sex, Excess"; and Bellver, "The Language of Eroticism"; explore the metaphors in the novel as expressions of sexuality and eroticism, but do not show how metaphors are used to reveal—and then hide—the identity. Mary S. Vásquez, "Tusquets, Fitzgerald and the Redemptive Power of Love," *Letras Femeninas* 14.1–2 (1988): 18, suggests that the novels in Tusquets's trilogy depict women who are "lost inside."

4. Lodge, "The Language of Modernist Fiction," 491, observes an opposite but similar interchange between metaphor and metonymy in the "essentially metonymic style" of Gertrude Stein's writing, that "is made to serve the purposes of metaphor." Conversely, Tusquets's metaphoric style seems to convey metonymic associations rather than expressions of equivalence.

5. Ibid., 486.

6. Ibid.

7. Tusquets has mentioned that her writing style is baroque (see Stacey L. Dolgin, "Conversación con Esther Tusquets: 'Para salir de tanta miseria,'" *Anales de la Literatura Española Contemporánea* 13 [1988]: 401).

8. Ichiishi, *The Apple of Earthly Love,* 18.

9. Esther Tusquets, *El amor es un juego solitario* (Barcelona: Lumen, 1982), 7. All translations are mine. Subsequent citations indicate page numbers within parentheses.

10. Nina L. Molinaro, *Foucault, Feminism, and Power: Reading Esther Tusquets* (Lewisburg: Bucknell University Press, 1991), 47, points out that the narration of the adventure text is ambiguous within the context of Elia's experience:

"It remains undecidable whether the act of reading proceeds from a direct reproduction via the original text, from an indirect reproduction via Elia's consciousness, or from an even more indirect reproduction via the narrator's mediation of
Elia's thoughts." Whatever the case, there is already metaphoric and metonymic
suggestion in the text before Elia metaphorically and metonymically connects it
to her relationship with Ricardo.

11. Mercedes Mazquiarán de Rodríquez, "Narrative Strategies in the Novels
of Esther Tusquets," *Monographic Review/Revista Monográfica* 7 (1991); and
Linda Gould Levine, "Reading, Rereading, Misreading and Rewriting the Male
Canon: The Narrative Web of Esther Tusquets' Trilogy," *Anales de la Literatura
Española Contemporánea* 12 (1987); discuss the uses of intertexts in *El amor.*

12. In classical mythology, Danae's father, Acrisius, confined her to a tower so
she could not conceive a child, after an oracle warned him he would be slain by
her son. While sequestered, Danae was raped and impregnated by Zeus, who
entered the tower as a golden rain. Patricia Monaghan, *The Book of Goddesses
and Heroines* (St. Paul: Llewellyn, 1990), 89, also points out a relationship between Danae and the Danaids, who were water goddesses, and calls attention to
the idea that Danae means "dawn." (See Monaghan and Pierre Grimal, *A Concise
Dictionary of Classical Mythology,* ed. Stephen Kreshaw, trans. A. R. Maxwell-
Hyslop [Oxford: Blackwell, 1986].)

13. See J. Hillis Miller, *Versions of Pygmalion* (Cambridge: Harvard University
Press, 1990), 3–5, for the ironic and narcissistic aspects of Pygmalion's creation
of Galatea in Ovid's *Metamorphoses.* Although Elia does not explicitly refer to
herself as Pygmalion in her relationship with Ricardo, Ricardo and Elia decide
"to act as Pygmalion . . . and Clara is now, in a certain sense, the work of the
two of them" (95).

14. See *The Divided Self,* 46–47.

15. Ibid., 45–46.

16. See Laing, *The Divided Self,* 100.

17. Ibid., 191.

18. See Martha A. Ackelsberg, *Free Women of Spain: Anarchism and the
Struggle for the Emancipation of Women* (Bloomington: Indiana University Press,
1991), 88, for an anecdote equating women's liberty with sexual permissiveness;
and Zatlin, "Women Novelists in Democratic Spain," 30, regarding "the false
equation of women's liberation with sexual freedom" that surfaces in novels written by women in the late 1970s and early 1980s.

19. See Catherine Davies, "Feminist Writers in Spain Since 1900: From Political Strategy to Personal Inquiry," *Textual Liberation: European Feminist Writing
in the Twentieth Century,* ed. Helena Forsas-Scott (London: Routledge, 1991),
207; and Martín Gaite, *Usos amorosos,* 91–115.

20. Stacey L. Dolgin, "The Aesthetic of Eroticism in *Love Is a Solitary Game,*"
The Sea of Becoming: Approaches to the Fiction of Esther Tusquets, ed. Mary
S. Vásquez (Westport, Conn.: Greenwood, 1991), 81. Dolgin compares *El amor*
to the "New Novel" as defined by Alain Robbe-Grillet, stating that "Tusquets's
erotic aesthetic sabotages the notion of a fixed reality" and that the novel is a
protest of Franco's rules (86).

21. Jacques Derrida, "White Mythology: Metaphor in the Text of Philosophy,"
trans. F. C. T. Moore, *New Literary History* 6.11: 26.

22. *Herself Beheld,* 179–80.

23. See Martín Gaite, *Usos amorosos,* 45; and La Belle, *Herself Beheld,* 51.

24. Mary S. Vásquez, "Actor and Spectator in the Fiction of Esther Tusquets," *The Sea of Becoming: Approaches to the Fiction of Esther Tusquets,* ed. Mary S. Vásquez (Westport, Conn.: Greenwood Press, 1991), explores the roles of actor and spectator in Tusquets's fiction, identifying *El amor* as the most extreme example of Tusquets's theatrical style. Mirella d'Ambrosio Servodidio, "Perverse Pairings and Corrupted Codes: *El amor es un juego solitario,*" *Anales de la Literatura Española Contemporánea* 11.3 (1986): 247 and 252, sees the novel as "a self-reflexive artifact intent on staging and testing its own illusions" and "an elaborate hoax." D'Ambrosio calls it "deliberately programmed decadence" in her article "Esther Tusquets's Fiction: The Spinning of a Narrative Web," *Women Writers of Contemporary Spain: Exiles in the Homeland,* ed. Joan Brown (Newark: University of Delaware Press, 1991), 163. Similarly, Janet N. Gold, "Reading the Love Myth: Tusquets with the Help of Barthes," *Hispanic Review* 55 (1987): 345, focuses on the "artificial, programmed" duplicity in the novel. Hart, "Esther Tusquets: Sex, Excess," 97, feels the excessive metaphoric language "renders nothing" in the end. Geraldine Cleary Nichols, "Minding Her P's and Q's: The Fiction of Esther Tusquets," *Indiana Journal of Hispanic Literature* 2.1 (1993): 169, states that Tusquets's fiction raises feminist issues, but "provides no empowering message."

25. See Horney, *Feminine Psychology,* 236–37, regarding reasons for homosexual tendencies in adolescent girls and their guilt after becoming aware of the sexual nature of their feelings.

26. Linda Gould Levine, "Reading, Rereading, Misreading and Rewriting the Male Canon: The Narrative Web of Esther Tusquets' Trilogy," *Anales de la Literatura Española Contemporánea* 12 (1987): 209, feels the texts that compose Elia's life are not of an ideal nature and that they have not been revised by her, but she notes that the last novel of the trilogy, *Varada tras el último naufragio,* does a better job of breaking from patriarchal tradition. Mary S. Vásquez, *The Sea of Becoming: Approaches to the Fiction of Esther Tusquets,* ed. Mary S. Vásquez (Westport, Conn.: Greenwood, 1991), 3, states that "Myth evolved, mocked, shattered and remade is . . . central to Tusquets' work."

27. Kolbenschlag, *Kiss Sleeping Beauty Goodbye,* 2.

28. See Zatlin, "Women Novelists," 30, regarding the increase in narrative dealing with female eroticism after Franco's death. Luis F. Costa, "*Para no volver:* Women in Franco's Spain," *The Sea of Becoming: Approaches to the Fiction of Esther Tusquets,* ed. Mary S. Vásquez (Westport, Conn.: Greenwood, 1991), explains some of the problems of women's new "freedom" resulting from the submissive attitude that had been ingrained in women by Franco's programs to "educate" women to be good wives and mothers.

29. Molinaro, *Foucault, Feminism, Power,* 55. Molinaro partially bases her analysis on Jean Baudrillard's theory of simulacra as expression of postmodernism and Michel Foucault's concept of power as explained in *The History of Sexuality.*

30. See Laing, *The Divided Self,* 100 and 182.

31. See Laing, *The Divided Self,* 40, regarding ontological insecurity. Servodidio, "Perverse Pairings," 239–41, points out the traits in each of the three characters that "mirror" their maternal rejection which, in turn, is reflected by their abnormal behavior.

32. See Chodorow, *The Reproduction of Mothering,* 176.

33. See Laing, *The Politics of Experience,* 115.

34. La Belle, *Herself Beheld*, 76. Also see *Herself Beheld*, 44–46; and Pratt, *Archetypal Patterns*, 10–11; regarding midlife as a turning point for women's identity.

35. Elissa Melamed, *Mirror Mirror: The Terror of Not Being Young* (New York: Simon, 1983), explains how aging is a liability for all females in patriarchal cultures. She indicates that women are made to feel invisible and neutered by society, especially as—and after—their years of reproductive activity cease.

36. *Herself Beheld*, 180.

37. *Foucault, Feminism, and Power*, 52.

38. See Mary S. Vásquez, "Esther Tusquets and the Trilogy which Isn't," *La Chispa 1986: Selected Proceedings*, ed. Alfredo Lozada (Baton Rouge: Louisiana State University, 1987), for a discussion of the concept of trilogy in Tusquets's work.

39. Mirella d'Ambrosio Servodidio, "A Case of Pre-oedipal and Narrative Fixation: *El mismo mar de todos los veranos*," *Anales de la Literatura Española Contemporánea* 12.1–2 (1987): 160.

40. Esther Tusquets, *El mismo mar de todos los veranos* (Barcelona: Anagrama, 1990), 10. The translation is mine.

41. Ibid., 65.

42. Ibid., 87–89.

43. Mary S. Vásquez, "Tusquets, Fitzgerald and the Redemptive Power of Love," *Letras Femeninas* 14.1–2 (1988): 19.

44. Esther Tusquets, *Varada tras el último naufragio* (Barcelona: Lumen, 1980).

45. Esther Tusquets, *Para no volver* (Barcelona: Lumen, 1985), 111. The translation is mine.

46. *The Apple of Earthly Love*, 119–20.

47. Ibid., 120. Also see Nichols, "Minding Her P's and Q's," regarding repetitive elements in Tusquets's work.

48. Elizabeth Ordóñez, "The Barcelona Group: The Fiction of Alós, Moix, and Tusquets," *Letras Femeninas* 6.1 (1980).

CHAPTER 6: METONYMY AND MIRRORS AS PROCESS OF IDENTITY IN *EL CUARTO DE ATRÁS*

1. *El cuarto de atrás* (National Prize for Literature, 1979) was published in English as *The Back Room*, trans. Helen R. Lane (New York: Columbia University Press, 1983). Martín Gaite's other novels are *Entre visillos* (Nadal Prize, 1958), *Ritmo lento* (1962), *Retahílas* (1974), *Fragmentos de interior* (1976), *Nubosidad variable* (1992), *La Reina de las Nieves* (1994), and *Lo raro es vivir* (1996). Her novellas and short stories include *El balneario* (Café Gijón Prize, 1954), *Las ataduras* (1960), and *Cuentos completos* (1978).

Her work also includes poetry: *A rachas* (1976), *Poesía (1931-1991)* (1992); a play: *A palo seco* (1987); and children's literature: *El castillo de las tres murallas* (1981) and *Pastel del diablo* (1985)—published together as *Dos relatos fantásticos* (1986). Her nonfiction works include *El proceso de Macanaz: Historia de un empapelamiento* (1970—reissued as *Macanaz como otro paciente de la Inquisición* in 1975), *Usos amorosos del dieciocho en España* (1972), *Ocho siglos de poesía gallega: Antología bilingüe* (coauthored with Andrés Ruiz Tarazona, 1972), *La búsqueda de interlocutor y otras búsquedas* (1973), *El conde de Guadalhorce, su época y su labor* (1977), *El cuento de nunca acabar* (1983), *Usos amorosos de la postguerra española* (1987), *Desde la ventana* (1987), and *Agua pasada* (1993).

Joan L. Brown, "Carmen Martín Gaite: Reaffirming the Pact between Reader and Writer," *Women Writers of Contemporary Spain: Exiles in the Homeland*, ed. Joan L. Brown (Newark: University of Delaware Press, 1991), 86, notes that *El cuarto de atrás* is clearly Martín Gaite's most studied novel and is the most frequently analyzed novel by a contemporary female Spanish author over the past decade. Isabel M. Roger, "Carmen Martín Gaite: Una trayectoria novelística y su bibliografía," *Anales de la Literatura Española Contemporánea* 13 (1988), published a bibliography of her works and all the criticism written about them up to that date.

2. Many critics have dealt with the metafictional/autobiographic convergence of the author Carmen Martín Gaite and the narrator/ protagonist Carmen. Critics that stress the metafictional essence of the protagonist Carmen are Kathleen M. Glenn, "From Social Realism to Self-Reflection: Carmen Martín Gaite and the Postwar Novel," *Letras Femeninas* 10 (1984): 25; and Robert C. Spires, *Beyond the Metafictional Mode: Directions in the Modern Spanish Novel* (Lexington: University Press of Kentucky, 1984), 115.

Other critics highlight the autobiographical aspects: Linda Gould Levine, "Carmen Martín Gaite's *El cuarto de atrás*: A Portrait of the Artist as Woman," *From Fiction to Metafiction: Essays in Honor of Carmen Martín Gaite*, ed. Mirella Servodidio and Marcia L. Welles (Lincoln: Society of Spanish and Spanish-American Studies, 1983); Jean S. Chittenden, "*El cuarto de atrás* as Autobiography," *Letras Femeninas* 12.1–2 (1986); Linda Chown, "Palimpsestic Biography: *The Back Room*," *Critical Essays on the Literature of Spain and Spanish America*, ed. Luis González-del-Valle and Julio Baena (Boulder: Society of Spanish and Spanish American Studies, 1991); and Concha Alborg, "A Never-Ending Autobiography: The Fiction of Carmen Martín Gaite," *Redefining Autobiography in Twentieth-Century Women's Fiction*, ed. James Morgan and Colette T. Hall (New York: Garland, 1991).

Aleida Anselma Rodríguez, "Todorov in *El cuarto de atrás*," *Prismal/Cabal* 11 (1983), feels the novel is fantastic literature—not autobiographical. Others stress the combination of the two forms: Catherine G. Bellver, "War as Rite of Passage in *El cuarto de atrás*," *Letras Femeninas* 12.1–2 (1986); Manuel Durán, "*El cuarto de atrás*: Imaginación, fantasía, misterio; Todorov y algo más," *From Fiction to Metafiction: Essays in Honor of Carmen Martín Gaite*, ed. Mirella Servodidio and Marcia L. Welles (Lincoln: Society of Spanish and Spanish-American Studies, 1983); and Joan L. Brown, "A Fantastic Memoir: Technique and History in *El cuarto de atrás*," *Anales de la Literatura Española Contemporánea* 6 (1981): 13. Blas Matamoro, "Carmen Martín Gaite: El viaje al cuarto de atrás," *Cuadernos Hispanoamericanos* 351 (1978), feels *El cuarto de atrás* forms a new classification of literature. In a fitting inversion of the fiction/autobiography dilemma, Joan L. Brown named her biography and analysis of Carmen Martín Gaite's work *Secrets from the Back Room: The Fiction of Carmen Martín Gaite* (University, Miss.: Romance Monographs, 1987), echoing the title of the novel.

3. Bellver, "War as Rite of Passage," 70 and 76–77, compares the freedom Carmen associates with "el cuarto de atrás" and writing to Pratt's notion of a "green world," and feels Martín Gaite's writing served as an escape from the war and Franco's dictatorship, aiding her transcendence and self-growth.

4. My use of *process* refers to the process of identity formation by the female protagonist. In contrast, Spires, *Beyond the Metafictional Mode*, 107–24, high-

lights the metafictional element in the novel that offers the reader "product" before the "process" of writing is revealed.

5. More ambiguity and double meanings reside in the metafictional aspect of that room: "el cuarto de atrás" existed both in the life of the author and of the protagonist Carmen in the novel.

6. Ordóñez, *Voices of Their Own,* 98–100, explains how Carmen's role as ideal reader and narrator ruptures the confining parameters of binary opposition that trap readers and writers and eliminates closure.

7. Carmen Martín Gaite, *El cuarto de atrás* (Barcelona: Destino, 1982), 9. All translations are mine. Subsequent citations indicate page numbers in parentheses.

8. Samuel R. Levin, *The Semantic of Metaphor* (Baltimore: Johns Hopkins University Press, 1977), 118.

9. Julian Palley, "Dreams in Two Novels of Carmen Martín Gaite," *From Fiction to Metafiction: Essays in Honor of Carmen Martín Gaite,* ed. Mirella Servodidio and Marcia L. Welles (Lincoln: Society of Spanish and Spanish-American Studies, 1983), 107 and 114, sees the "life-dream" state in *El cuarto de atrás* as an "equation or metaphor" that follows in the tradition of Cervantes, Calderón, and Borges and describes Carmen's dream/metaphor as "a search for identity." Mirella d'Ambrosio Servodidio, "Oneiric Intertextualites," *From Fiction to Metafiction: Essays in Honor of Carmen Martín Gaite,* ed. Mirella Servodidio and Marcia L. Welles (Lincoln: Society of Spanish and Spanish-American Studies, 1983), 122, feels that the identity-search began in Martín Gaite's first novella, *El balneario,* and progresses from the dreams expressed there to the dream in *El cuarto de atrás.*

10. Debra A. Castillo, "Never-Ending Story: Carmen Martín Gaite's *The Back Room,*" *PMLA* 102.5 (1987): 824 and 815, points out that the association of *casa, cuarto,* and *cama* begins a cumulative series and includes many other words that begin with *c,* illustrating metonymic chaining because of visual or auditory similarities and keeping the novel "open-ended." Josefina González, "Dibujo, espacio y ecofeminismo en la C. de *El cuarto de atrás* de Carmen Martín Gaite," *Revista Canadiense de Estudios Hispánicos* 19.1 (1994), sees this same chaining as a force that defies dualism and illustrates "ecofeminism."

11. Stephanie Sieburth, "Memory, Metafiction, and Mass Culture: The Popular Text in *El cuarto de atrás,*" *Revista Hispánica Moderna* 43.1 (1990): 79 and 91, explains that "popular culture is a mediator between the present and the distant past," and that it acts as a "bridge between her [Martín Gaite's] experience and that of other Spaniards who remember the war," giving popular culture a metaphoric-type function in the work.

12. Robert C. Spires, "Intertextuality in *El cuarto de atrás,*" *From Fiction to Metafiction: Essays in Honor of Carmen Martín Gaite,* ed. Mirella Servodidio and Marcia L. Welles (Lincoln: Society of Spanish and Spanish-American Studies, 1983), 114, hints at the metonymic linking in the novel by way of its intertexts when he says "The creative force, therefore, is the network of intertextuality, and one of the threads forming this network extends from the concept of a book of memoirs, to Todorov's theory of the fantastic, and finally to the activity of discourse and the production of texts." The threads he describes act in the same way as metonymy, linking different elements together. Kathleen M. Glenn, "*El cuarto de atrás:* Literature as *juego* and the Self-Reflexive Text," *From Fiction to Metafiction: Essays in Honor of Carmen Martín Gaite,* ed. Mirella Servodidio and Marcia L. Welles (Lincoln: Society of Spanish and Spanish-American Stud-

ies, 1983), 151, points out that Todorov's theory of the fantastic involves the reader identifying with the character.

13. See Glenn, "*El cuarto de atrás:* Literature as *juego*," 153–54; Elizabeth Ordóñez, "Reading, Telling and the Text of Carmen Martín Gaite's *El cuarto de atrás*," *From Fiction to Metafiction: Essays in Honor of Carmen Martín Gaite*, ed. Mirella Servodidio and Marcia L. Welles (Lincoln: Society of Spanish and Spanish-American Studies, 1983), 180; Joan Brown, "Carmen Martín Gaite," 86; and Spires, *Beyond the Metafictional Mode*, 114; regarding the reader's dialogic participation in the novel. However, Brad Epps, "The Space of Sexual History: Reading Positions in *El cuarto de atrás* and *Reivindicación del Conde don Julián*," *Critical Essays on the Literatures of Spain and Spanish America*, ed. Luis T. González-del-Valle and Julio Baena (Boulder: Society of Spanish and Spanish-American Studies, 1991), 84 and 81, feels Martín Gaite "keeps some readers a little further away than others" because of her "subscri[ption] to established gender positions" within the novel. Also see Miguel R. Ruiz-Avilés, "*El cuarto de atrás:* Diferentes vistas según diferentes 'horizontes de experiencias' y 'horizontes de expectativas,'" *Selected Proceedings of the Mid-America Conference on Hispanic Literature*, ed. Luis T. González-del-Valle and Catherine Nickel (Lincoln: Society of Spanish and Spanish-American Studies, 1986), about different readers' reactions to the novel.

14. Glenn, "*El cuarto de atrás:* Literature as *juego*," 155, describes the game-like elements in *El cuarto de atrás*, identifying four different categories of games in the novel: competition, chance, simulation, and vertigo. Glenn does not mention Carmen's feeling of careening between past and present, reality and dream as a type of vertigo, nor the metaphoric chessboard, implying that Carmen has willingly entered into a game of competition when she jumps over the cockroach and opens her door to the man in black.

15. The first and last chapters of the novel posit the dream/life metaphor, making the ambiguous visit of the man in black possible, and the second chapter metaphorically expresses Carmen's agreement to participate in the "game." Other chapters also suggest metaphoric scenarios. For instance "Ven pronto a Cúnigan" (Come soon to Cúnigan), when Carmen goes into the kitchen, suggests a motif like Lewis Carroll's *Through the Looking Glass* where Carmen steps back into her formation as a female child. (Martín Gaite prefaces her novel with a dedication to Lewis Carroll.) The sixth chapter begins with metaphorical allusions to acting. These metaphoric settings are metonymically extended throughout the novel by further references to games, stories, roles, and so on. The metonymic extensions often connect positive, negative, or ambiguous connotations to the original metaphoric concept.

16. See Glenn, "*El cuarto de atrás:* Literature as *juego*," and Ruth El Saffar, "Redeeming Loss: Reflections on Carmen Martín Gaite's *The Back Room*," *Revista de Estudios Hispánicos* 20.1 (1986): 6, for references to games of chance in the novel.

17. In Pardo Bazán's story ("La caja de oro," *Cuentos completos*, vol. 1, ed. Juan Paredes Nuñez [La Coruña: Galicia, 1990]), the male narrator describes his relationship with a woman who mysteriously treasures a little gold box. The man, overcome with curiosity to discover the contents of this box, pretends to be in love with the woman. She submits to his amorous pretenses before giving in to his curiosity, but after a time—declaring that the man's love is more important to her than the power of the secret within the box—she reveals its contents. The box contains pills, purchased from a *curandero* (quack medicine man), that relieve

her attacks and poor health as long as their secret is not revealed to anyone. After the woman expresses that his love will keep her healthy, he decides to continue his love charade, especially as her health begins to decline. Gradually, the woman perceives his duplicity and dies. The man brings the pills to a scientist to have them analyzed. After discovering that the pills are made of bread crumbs, he blames the *curandero* for having deceived the woman.

Marie-Lise Gazarian Gautier, "Conversación con Carmen Martín Gaite en Nueva York," *From Fiction to Metafiction: Essays in Honor of Carmen Martín Gaite,* ed. Mirella Servodidio and Marcia L. Welles (Lincoln: Society of Spanish and Spanish-American Studies, 1983), 33, interviews Martín Gaite, who reclaims the secret of the "caja de oro" lost by Pardo Bazán's character:

> GG:-¿Y llevas la cajita dorada contigo? (And do you carry the little gold box with you?)
> CMG:-Sí, siempre la guardo. (Yes, I always keep it.)
> GG:-¿Pero no aquí? (But not here?)
> CMG:-Eso no se pregunta, no puedo decir donde está. (That's not to be asked, I can't say where it is.)
> GG:-¿Otro misterio? (Another mystery?)
> CMG:-Sí, otro misterio. Tal vez el mayor. (Yes, another mystery. Perhaps the biggest.)

Also see Ordóñez, *Voices of Their Own,* 90–100, for other examples of revised intertexts in the *El cuarto de atrás.*

18. Estés, *Women Who Run with the Wolves,* 66.

19. Ibid., 66–73. Julian Palley, "Dreams in Two Novels," and "El interlocutor soñado de *El cuarto de atrás* de Carmen Martín Gaite," *Insula* 404–5 (1980), investigates dreams and the psyche in *El cuarto de atrás.*

20. *Women Who Run with the Wolves,* 4. Hart, *White Ink,* 71–78, emphasizes that fantasy and the fairy-tale world are mixed with reality and identity throughout *El cuarto de atrás.*

21. Palley, "Dreams in Two Novels," 114, calls Carola Carmen's "female alter ego or Jungian *shadow*" and says Carola and Carmen are both "suffering from ontological doubt."

22. Also see Marcia L. Welles, "Carmen Martín Gaite: Fiction as Desire," *From Fiction to Metafiction: Essays in Honor of Carmen Martín Gaite,* ed. Mirella Servodidio and Marcia L. Welles (Lincoln: Society of Spanish and Spanish-American Studies, 1983), 204, regarding the battle that must be waged against the "Symbolic" and societal order in *El cuarto de atrás.*

23. Estés, *Women Who Run with the Wolves,* 484, points out how some versions of popular fairy tales convey distortions of other versions. Estés's philosophy about the inherent matriarchal wisdom in some fairy tales appears to be in direct opposition to Ellen Cronan Rose's ("Through the Looking Glass," 211): "Women have come to recognize that neither in fairy tales nor in other patriarchal texts can we find true images of ourselves." Examination of different versions of fairy tales might help to pinpoint matriarchal advice to women in contrast to the patriarchal text that Rose notices. Kolbenschlag, *Kiss Sleeping Beauty Goodbye,* 2 and 201, notices the possibility of a matriarchal element: "The fact that most fairy tales embody elements associated with the archetypal 'feminine' points to the possibility that they recapitulate a view of reality that is rooted in the determinism of sex roles." But Kolbenschlag feels that women should "walk out of the fairy tale"—not reconnect themselves with it as Estés proposes.

24. Stanton, "Difference on Trial," 157–58.

25. See Palley, "El interlocutor soñado," 22, regarding the visitor as a mirror and Lacan's theory of mirrored identity. See El Saffar, "Redeeming Loss," 7, about the metonymic mirroring effect of the man in black.

26. Welles, "Fiction as Desire," 202, says the structure of *El cuarto de atrás* "is itself a playful game of mirrors."

27. See Martín Gaite, *Usos amorosos,* for the effects of Franco's propaganda on women.

28. I discuss the "temporal" and "positional" contiguity of the mirror in chapter 1.

29. Jakobson, *Fundamentals of Language,* 77.

30. Pratt, *Archetypal Patterns,* 10, states that women heroes at midlife or later usually go through a process of rebirth. Estés, *Women Who Run with the Wolves,* 130 and 141, explains the importance of renewed life for women with the "Life/Death/Life" cycle as "a cycle of animation, development, decline, and death that is always followed by reanimation" and notes that "woman is a keeper of cycles." Also recall the cyclical development mentioned in my introduction.

31. See Ordóñez, *Voices of Their Own,* 77, about the positive effect of conversation and the approximation of spoken and written discourse in *El cuarto de atrás.*

32. Ordóñez, "Reading, Telling," 182–83, points out that the protagonist has always rejected "happy endings" because there is nothing left to tell. Servodidio, "Oneiric," 125, clarifies the need for a continuation of the process that Carmen has begun in *El cuarto de atrás* when she notes that all details about Carmen's marriage, her role as a mother, and her separation from her husband are "noticeably absent from her account and therefore semiologically present."

33. See Welles, "Carmen Martín Gaite: Fiction as Desire."

34. See Rodríguez, "Todorov in *El cuarto de atrás,*" 80–81, regarding the use of fantastic literature as a medium for authors wishing to explore taboo themes, such as sexual ones, and who censor themselves from directly exploring them. Rodríguez suggests that Martín Gaite's choice to write a fantastic novel is because of self-censorship and an inability to openly express sexual ideas (88). Yet Servodidio, "Oneiric," notes less censorship in *El cuarto de atrás* than in an earlier work by Martín Gaite. This decrease of self-censorship, along with the continual process in the novel, implies that the author is progressing also.

35. See, for example, Joan L. Brown, "One Autobiography Twice Told: Martín Gaite's *Entre visillos* and *El cuarto de atrás,*" *Hispanic Journal* 7 (1986); Manuel Durán, "Carmen Martín Gaite: *Retahílas, El cuarto de atrás,* y el diálogo sin fin," *Revista Iberoamericana* 47.116–17 (1981), and "*El cuarto de atrás:* Imaginación"; Kathleen M. Glenn, "Communication in the Works of Carmen Martín Gaite," *Romance Notes* 19; Palley, "Dreams in Two Novels"; Servodidio, "Oneiric"; and Gonzalo Sobejano, "Enlaces y desenlaces en las novelas de Carmen Martín Gaite," *From Fiction to Metafiction: Essays in Honor of Carmen Martín Gaite,* ed. Mirella Servodidio and Marcia L. Welles (Lincoln: Society of Spanish and Spanish-American Studies, 1983).

36. Carmen Martín Gaite, *Entre visillos* (Barcelona: Destino, 1988), 24. The translation is mine.

37. Ibid., 151.

38. Carmen Martín Gaite, *Retahílas* (Barcelona: Destino, 1974), 47 and 71. The translation is mine.

39. Carmen Martín Gaite, *Nubosidad variable* (Barcelona: Anagrama, 1993), 31. The translation is mine.

40. All the other protagonists either did not have a mother as a role model or had a mother who served as a negative role model. Andrea in *Nada,* Matia in *Primera memoria,* and Natàlia in *La plaça del Diamant* all lamented their lack of a mother figure. Nevertheless, in *Julia* and *El amor es un juego solitario,* Julia and Elia found their attempts at self-identity complicated by mothers who were lost and immature. In contrast, Carmen's mother was supportive, providing the atmosphere for creative and independent development and encouraging Carmen's desire for education, despite the prejudices against scholarly endeavors for girls (*El cuarto de atrás,* 92–93). In this sense, it seems reasonable that Carmen might attain self-autonomy more easily than the other protagonists.

41. Sheila Rowbotham, *Women, Resistance and Revolution* (London: Lane, 1972), 11.

42. Joan L. Brown, "The Challenge of Martín Gaite's Woman Hero," *Feminine Concerns in Contemporary Spanish Fiction by Women,* ed. Roberto C. Manteiga, Carolyn Galerstein, and Kathleen McNerney (Potomac: Scripta Humanistica, 1988), 93–96, points out the importance of social forces in *El cuarto de atrás*" and concludes that "Martín Gaite's novels challenge society to permit them to succeed." Sieburth, "Memory, Metafiction," 78, says that the past Carmen tries to recapture allows "a miraculous recovery of a world erased or obscured by the Franco regime," also underlining the sociopolitical dimension of the novel.

CHAPTER 7: MIRROR MESSAGES THAT SIGNAL CHANGE IN *QÜESTIÓ D'AMOR PROPI*

1. *Qüestió d'amor propi* (1987), like Moix's *Julia,* is not yet available in English. Riera published her own Castilian translation, *Cuestión de amor propio,* in 1988. The translation is an edited version of the original, reflecting stylistic modifications as well as several changes that are significant in my analysis. For that reason, I have used 1988, the date of publication of the Castilian version, as the closing date of my analysis. I also refer to the 1988 version several times.

In addition to *Qüestió d'amor propi,* Riera's novelistic production includes *Una primavera per a Domenico Guarini* (Prudenci Bertrana Prize, 1980), *Joc de miralls* (Ramón Llull Prize, 1989—Riera published her own translation of this novel as *Por persona interpuesta* in 1989), and *Dans el darrer blau* (1994). *Dans el darrer blau,* translated by Riera as *En el último azul,* has won the following prizes: Josep Pla, 1994; Creixells, 1995; Lletra d'Or, 1995; and Nacional de Narrativa, 1995. Riera has also published several collections of short stories: 1974 prize-winning "Te deix, amor, la mar com a penyora," published as the title of a collection in 1975; *Jo pos per testimoni les gavines* (1977); *Palabra de mujer* (1980—Riera's Castilian translation of most of her stories); *Epitelis tendríssims* (1981); and *Contra el amor en compañía: y otros relatos* (1991). She has written critical and historical books: *Els cementiris de Barcelona,* 1980; *Quasi bé un conte, la vida de Ramon Llull,* 1980 (a biography for children); *La escuela de Barcelona: Barral, Gil de Biedma, Goytisolo: el núcleo poético de la generación de los 50,* 1988; *La obra poética de Carlos Barral,* 1990; and *Hay veneno y jazmín en tu tinta: aproximación a la poesía de J. A. Goytisolo,* 1991. She has also published numerous articles.

2. Criticism about Riera's novel focuses on the initial presence of bilateral language in the novel, not the concluding fusion of "masculine" and "feminine" discourse. Roberta Johnson, "Voice and Intersubjectivity in Carme Riera's Narra-

tives," *Critical Essays on the Literatures of Spain and Spanish America,* ed. Luis González-del-Valle and Julio Baena (Boulder: Society of Spanish and Spanish-American Studies, 1991), 157, emphasizes the "sense of female collusion" in Àngela's letter to her friend Íngrid against men's "web of oppression and abuse." Likewise, Emilie Bergmann, "Letters and Diaries as Narrative Strategies in Contemporary Catalan Women's Writing," *Critical Essays on the Literatures of Spain and Spanish America,* ed. Luis González-del-Valle and Julio Baena (Boulder: Society of Spanish and Spanish-American Studies, 1991), explores the letter and diary forms employed by Riera and other Spanish women novelists as being particularly appropriate to express the female voice of marginalization. Akiko Tsuchiya, "The Paradox of Narrative Seduction in Carmen Riera's *Cuestión de amor propio,*" *Hispania* 75.2 (1992), examines the paradoxical "seductive" technique of Àngela's letter to her college friend Íngrid, which hints at the presence of a "male voice" or tactic. Tsuchiya feels Àngela's letter is a "highly self-conscious construct of language through which she seeks to elicit the narratee's sympathy" (282), and that "the novel sees the narrator at the height of her duplicity and at the depth of her self-deception" (286). In contrast, I feel the letter is an intimate, relational communication with Íngrid that demonstrates Àngela's transcendence of the learned submissiveness imperiling her autonomy in a patriarchally oriented society. Kathleen M. Glenn, "Authority and Marginality in Three Contemporary Spanish Narratives," *Romance Languages Annual* 2 (1990): 429, recognizes that Àngela is "empowered" by writing her own story, but does not focus on the type of language that helps her regain power.

3. Carme Riera, *Qüestió d'amor propi* (Barcelona: Planeta, 1987), 15–16. The translation is mine. Subsequent citations indicate page numbers in parentheses.

4. Carme Riera, *Cuestión de amor propio* (Barcelona: Tusquets, 1993), 22 (my translation).

5. See Pratt, *Archetypal Patterns,* 79.

6. Ibid., 6 and 59.

7. See Chodorow, *The Reproduction of Mothering,* 176. Johnson, "Voice and Intersubjectivity," uses Chodorow's theory about the difference between male and female cultural development to show how Riera's narratives demonstrate relational female identification processes.

8. Martín Gaite, *Usos amorosos,* 27 (my translation).

9. Ibid., see chap. 1.

10. Riera, *Cuestión de amor propio,* 62. The Catalan version describes "bitter, viscous, frightful days" full of gruesome, monstrous creatures (72), but omits the description of ghostlike presences and the dance of death in the Castilian version that recall the "life-in-death" state in previously analyzed novels.

11. See Pratt, *Archetypal Patterns,* 22.

12. See Cixous, "The Laugh of the Medusa," 881, regarding the power of woman's voice to inspire other women.

13. The Catalan version says: "I felt completely incapable of attacking it [her writing]" (73). The Castilian version, however, contrasts the influence of Íngrid's support and gift of a pen more directly with Miquel's negative effect: "I felt absolutely incapable of writing a single line" (63).

14. In describing the final relationship of power within Riera's novel, Glenn, "Authority and Marginality," 429, explains that "Angela is empowered to tell her own story, to be the subject of it rather than the object of some *his*tory."

15. See Johnson, "Voice and Intersubjectivity," 153. Bergmann, "Letters and Diaries," explores these writing forms in works by Rodoreda, Riera, and Maria

Mercè Roca and finds them particularly appropriate techniques to express the double marginalization of women writing in a minority language.

16. Nancy Fraser, "The Uses and Abuses of French Discourse Theory for Feminist Politics," *Revaluing French Feminism: Critical Essays on Difference, Agency, & Culture,* ed. Nancy Fraser and Sandra Lee Bartky (Bloomington: Indiana University Press, 1992), 178–80, proposes a theory of discourse that would lead to emancipatory change.

17. Julia Kristeva, "Women's Time," trans. Alice Jardine and Harry Blake, *Signs: Journal of Women in Culture and Society* 7.1 (1981): 34. Fraser, "The Uses and Abuses," (190), and Stanton, "Difference on Trial," criticize feminists who polarize gender qualities; while Kristeva, "Women's Time," 35, wants language to be a "unifying tool." See Estés, *Women Who Run with the Wolves,* 214, concerning women's "feral" qualities.

18. See Estés, *Women Who Run with the Wolves,* 245, regarding the "learned helplessness" imbued in women.

19. Vicente Cabrera, "La imagen en el espejo contemplada por Carme Riera y Cristina Peri Rossi" (paper presented at the annual convention of the Modern Language Association, New York, December 1992), identifies five different types of mirroring in the novel: Àngela as a mirror to magnify Miquel's self-image, Miquel's opaque mirror for Àngela, Íngrid's mirror of feminine solidarity, the reflections of Àngela and Miquel's relationship in *La Regenta* and *El canto del cisne,* and Àngela's creative mirror manifested in her letter. Susan Lucas Dobrian, "Echo's Revenge in Three Spanish Narratives by Women," *Letras Peninsulares* 8.1 (1995): 177, focuses on the "Echo-like protagonist," who mirrors a subversive reflection to her narcissistic lover.

20. Ciplijauskaité, *La novela femenina,* 80.

21. Johnson, "Voice and Intersubjectivity," 153. See La Belle, *Herself Beheld,* 42, for an explanation of the mirror as metaphor. See Jakobson, *Fundamentals of Language,* 77, for a description of metonymy as a combination.

22. See Palley, "Dreams in Two Novels" and "El interlocutor soñado," regarding communication with the animus of the other in *El cuarto de atrás.*

23. Riera, *Cuestión de amor propio,* 30. In the Catalan version, Riera indicates with a colon where Àngela's thoughts end and where the list of compliments that Miquel gives her begins:" . . . es devisqué en gentileses: De seguida em féu saber que jo era la persona més interessant . . ." (. . . he was lavish with compliments: Immediately he let me know that I was the most interesting person . . . , 34). In order to maintain the same indirect style list of compliments in the Castilian version, however, the passage would need to read:" . . . se deshizo en cumplidos: jamás había encontrado un(a) interlocutor(a) tan a *mi* medida" (. . . he was lavish with compliments: he had never met an interlocutor that measured up to me). Instead of "a mi medida" Riera says "a su medida" (30), creating confusion about who is considering whom the exemplary interlocutor. Even if Miquel is complimenting Àngela, telling her that she is the perfect interlocutor, this compliment could make her consider him in a similar way. Since interlocution involves dialogue, both parties would ideally feel trust and intimacy toward the other. But Miquel's untrustworthy conduct reveals that he cannot be confided in: *He* is definitely not the "ideal" interlocutor.

24. See Spacks, *The Female Imagination,* 21.

25. Riera, *Cuestión de amor propio,* 69.

26. Rosemary Lloyd, "Mirroring Difference, Figuring Frames," *Nineteenth-Century French Studies* 19.3 (1991): 347–51.

27. See Melamed, *Mirror Mirror,* 91–112.

28. Elisabeth Burgos-Debray, "Introduction," *I, Rigoberta Menchú: An Indian Woman in Guatemala,* by Rigoberta Menchú, trans. Ann Wright (London: Verso, 1984), xii.

29. Elizabeth Ordóñez, "Beginning to Speak: Carme Riera's *Una primavera para Domenico Guarini,*" *La CHISPA '85: Selected Proceedings,* ed. Gilbert Paolini (New Orleans: Tulane University, 1985). *Una primavera per a Domenico Guarini* was published in 1980 in Catalan, and Luisa Cotoner's Castilian translation came out in 1981.

30. Carme Riera, "Literatura femenina: ¿Un lenguaje prestado?" *Quimera* 18 (1982): 9 (my translation). Ciplijauskaité, *La novela femenina,* investigates the possible existence of "feminine writing" in first-person novels written by women from 1970–85, and mentions Riera's "Palabra de mujer." Also see Margaret Jones's "Different Wor(l)ds" for an overview of the theoretical and literary development of the "feminine voice," and Fraser's introduction to *Revaluing French Feminism* for an account of the controversy involving feminist theory.

31. Ordóñez, "Beginning to Speak."

32. Carme Riera, *Una primavera per a Domenico Guarini* (Barcelona: Edicions 62, 1982), 134. The translation is mine.

33. Ibid., 11.

34. Ibid., 190.

35. Riera, "Literatura femenina," 12 (my translation).

36. Rowbotham, *Women, Resistance and Revolution,* 11.

37. Bergmann, "Reshaping the Canon," 154.

CONCLUSION: THE TEMPORAL MIRROR

1. See La Belle, *Herself Beheld,* chap. 2.

2. Quoted in Martín Gaite, *Usos amorosos,* 30 (my translation).

3. Quoted from Pilar Primo de Rivera in Martín Gaite's *Usos amorosos,* 63 (my translation).

4. See Zatlin, "Women Novelists in Democratic Spain"; Bergmann, "Reshaping the Canon"; and Ciplijauskaité, *La novela femenina.*

5. Catherine Davies, *Contemporary Feminist Fiction in Spain: The Work of Montserrat Roig and Rosa Montero* (Oxford: Berg, 1994), 181.

6. Ibid., 182.

7. Akiko Tsuchiya, "The Phantom of Francoist Culture and the Hermeneutics of Desire in Adelaida García Morales' *La lógica del vampiro,*" paper presented at the annual convention of the Mid-America Conference on Hispanic Literature, Lincoln, Nebraska, Sept. 1996. Also see Mercedes Mazquiarán de Rodríguez, "Gothic Imagery, Dreams, and Vampirism: The Haunting Narrative of Adelaida García Morales," *Monographic Review/Revista Monográfica* 8 (1992); and Kathleen M. Glenn "Gothic Vision in García Morales and Erice's *El Sur,*" *Letras Peninsulares* 7.1 (1994), regarding the haunted females in García Morales's work.

8. Rosa Montero, *Bella y oscura* (Barcelona: Seix Barral, 1993).

Bibliography

Ackelsberg, Martha A. *Free Women of Spain: Anarchism and the Struggle for the Emancipation of Women.* Bloomington: Indiana University Press, 1991.

Alborg, Concha. "A Never-Ending Autobiography: The Fiction of Carmen Martín Gaite." In *Redefining Autobiography in Twentieth-Century Women's Fiction.* Edited by Janice Morgan and Colette T. Hall, 243–60. New York: Garland, 1991.

Allende, Isabel. *La casa de los espíritus.* Barcelona: Plaza, 1988.

Alonso, Santos. "Novela en la transición, transición en la novela (1975–1980)." *Nueva Estafeta* 31–32 (1981): 86–91.

Andersen, Hans Christian. *Andersen's Fairy Tales.* Translated by Mrs. E. V. Lucas and Mrs. H. B. Paul. New York: Grosset, n.d.

Anderson, Christopher L. "Andersen's 'The Snow Queen' and Matute's *Primera memoria:* To the Victor Go the Spoils." *Crítica Hispánica* 14 nos. 1–2 (1992): 13–27.

Aristotle. *Rhetoric III.* Translated by W. Rhys Roberts. Vol. 11 of *Works.* Edited by W. D. Ross. Oxford: n.p., 1924.

Arnau, Carme. *Introducció a la narrativa de Mercè Rodoreda: el mite de la infantesa.* Barcelona: Edicions 62, 1982.

———. Introduction to *Obres Completes, 1936–1960,* by Mercè Rodoreda. Vol. 1. Barcelona: Edicions 62, 1980.

———. "La obra de Mercè Rodoreda." *Cuadernos Hispanoamericanos* 383 (1982): 239–57.

Bakhtin, M. M. *The Dialogic Imagination.* Translated by Caryl Emerson and Michael Holquist. Edited by Michael Holquist. Austin: University of Texas Press, 1981.

Barthes, Roland. *Elementos de semiología.* Translated by Alberto Méndez. Madrid: Corazón, n.d.

Bellver, Catherine G. "Division, Duplication, and Doubling in the Novels of Ana María Moix." In *Nuevos y novísimos: Algunas perspectivas críticas sobre la narrativa española desde la década de los 60.* Edited by Ricardo Landeira and Luis T. González-del-Valle, 29–41. Boulder: Society of Spanish and Spanish-American Studies, 1987.

———. "The Language of Eroticism in the Novels of Esther Tusquets." *Anales de la Literatura Española Contemporánea* 9 nos. 1–3 (1984): 13–27.

———. "War as Rite of Passage in *El cuarto de atrás.*" *Letras Femeninas* 12 nos. 1–2 (1986): 69–77.

Bergmann, Emilie. "Letters and Diaries as Narrative Strategies in Contemporary Catalan Women's Writing." In *Critical Essays on the Literatures of Spain and Spanish America.* Edited by Luis González-del-Valle and Julio Baena, 19–28. Boulder: Society of Spanish and Spanish-American Studies, 1991.

———. "Reshaping the Canon: Intertextuality in the Spanish Novel of Female Development." *Anales de la Literatura Española Contemporánea* 12 (1987): 141–56.

Berreltini, Celia. "Ana María Matute, la novelista pintora." *Cuadernos Hispanoamericanos* 144 (1966): 405–12.

Bieder, Maryellen. "The Woman in the Garden: The Problem of Identity in the Novels of Mercè Rodoreda." In *Segon Col·loqui d'Estudis Catalans a Nord-Amèrica*. Badalona: Abadia de Montserrat, 1982.

Bou, Enric. "Exile in the City: Mercè Rodoreda's *La plaça del Diamant*." *The Garden across the Border: Mercè Rodoreda's Fiction*. Edited by Kathleen NcNerney and Nancy Vosburg, 31–41. Selinsgrove: Susquehanna University Press; London: Associated University Press, 1994.

Brooksbank Jones, Anny. "The Incubus and I: Unbalancing Acts in Moix's *Julia*." *Bulletin of Hispanic Studies* 72 (1995): 73-85.

Brown, Anne E. and Marjanne E. Goozé. "Introduction: Placing Identity in Cross-Cultural Perspective." In *International Women's Writing: New Landscapes of Identity*. Edited by Anne E. Brown and Marjanne E. Goozé, xiii–xxv. Westport, Conn.: Greenwood, 1995.

Brown, Joan L. "A Fantastic Memoir: Technique and History in *El cuarto de atrás*." *Anales de la Literatura Española Contemporánea* 6 (1981): 13–20.

———. "Carmen Martín Gaite: Reaffirming the Pact between Reader and Writer." In *Women Writers of Contemporary Spain: Exiles in the Homeland*. Edited by Joan L. Brown, 72–92. Newark: University of Delaware Press, 1991.

———. "One Autobiography Twice Told: Martín Gaite's *Entre visillos* and *El cuarto de atrás*." *Hispanic Journal* 7 (1986): 37–47.

———. *Secrets from the Back Room: The Fiction of Carmen Martín Gaite*. University, Mississippi: Romance Monographs, 1987.

———. "The Challenge of Martín Gaite's Woman Hero." In *Feminine Concerns in Contemporary Spanish Fiction by Women*. Edited by Roberto C. Manteiga, Carolyn Galerstein, and Kathleen McNerney, 86–98. Potomac: Scripta Humanistica, 1988.

———. "Unidad y diversidad en *Los mercaderes*, de Ana María Matute." In *Novelistas femeninas de la postguerra española*. Edited by Janet W. Pérez, 19–31. Madrid: Turanzas, 1983.

Bruner, Jeffrey. "Visual Art as Narrative Discourse: The Ekphrastic Dimension of Carmen Laforet's *Nada*." *Anales de la Literatura Española Contemporánea* 18 (1993): 247–60.

Burgos-Debray, Elisabeth, ed. "Introduction." In Rigoberta Menchú, *I, Rigoberta Menchú: An Indian Woman in Guatemala*. Translated by Ann Wright, xi–xxi. London: Verso, 1984.

Bush, Andrew. "Ana María Moix's Silent Calling." In *Women Writers of Contemporary Spain: Exiles in the Homeland*. Edited by Joan Brown, 136–58. Newark: University of Delaware Press, 1991.

Busquets, Loreto. "El mito de la culpa en *La plaça del Diamant*." *Cuadernos Hispanoamericanos* 420 (1985): 117–40.

Cabrera, Vicente. "La imagen en el espejo contemplada por Carme Riera y Cristina Peri Rossi." Paper presented at the annual convention of the Modern Language Association, New York, N.Y., December 1992.

Callan, Richard. "The Archetype of Psychic Renewal in *La vorágine.*" In *Woman as Myth and Metaphor in Latin American Literature.* Edited by Carmen Virgilio and Naomi Lindstrom, 15–26. Columbia: University of Missouri Press, 1985.

Carbonell, Neus. "In the Name of the Mother and the Daughter." In *The Garden across the Border: Mercè Rodoreda's Fiction.* Edited by Kathleen NcNerney and Nancy Vosburg, 17–30. Selinsgrove: Susquehanna University Press; London: Associated University Press, 1994.

Castellet, Josep María. *Nueve novísimos poetas españoles.* Barcelona: Barral, 1970.

Castillo, Debra A. "Never-Ending Story: Carmen Martín Gaite's *The Back Room.*" *PMLA* 102 no. 5 (1987): 814–28.

Cerezales, Agustín. *Carmen Laforet.* Madrid: Ministerio de Cultura, 1982.

Chesler, Phyllis. *Women and Madness.* New York: Avon, 1973.

Chittenden, Jean S. "*El cuarto de atrás* as Autobiography." *Letras Femeninas* 12 nos. 1–2 (1986): 78–84.

Chodorow, Nancy. *The Reproduction of Mothering: Psychoanalysis and the Sociology of Gender.* Berkley: University of California Press, 1978.

Chown, Linda. "Palimpsestic Biography: *The Back Room.*" In *Critical Essays on the Literature of Spain and Spanish America.* Edited by Luis González-del-Valle and Julio Baena, 57–64. Boulder: Society of Spanish and Spanish-American Studies, 1991.

Ciplijauskaité, Biruté. *La novela femenina contemporánea: Hacia una tipología de la narración en primera persona (1970-1985).* Barcelona: Anthropos, 1988.

Cixous, Hélène. "The Laugh of the Medusa." Translated by Keith Cohen and Paula Cohen. *Signs: Journal of Women in Culture and Society* 1 (1976): 875–93.

Clarasó, Mercè. "The Angle of Vision in the Novels of Mercè Rodoreda." *Bulletin of Hispanic Studies* 57 (1980): 143–52.

Collins, Marsha S. "Carmen Laforet's *Nada:* Fictional Form and the Search for Identity." *Symposium* 38 no. 4 (1984–85): 298-311.

Cook, Beverly Richard. "Madness as Metaphor in Two Short Stories by Ana María Moix." In *Continental, Latin-American and Francophone Women Writers,* vol. 2. Edited by Ginette Adamson and Eunice Myers, 23–30. New York: University Press of America, 1990.

Costa, Luis F. "*Para no volver:* Women in Franco's Spain." In *The Sea of Becoming: Approaches to the Fiction of Esther Tusquets.* Edited by Mary S. Vásquez, 11–28. Westport, Conn.: Greenwood, 1991.

Cuddon, J. A. *A Dictionary of Literary Terms and Literary Theory.* Cambridge: Blackwell, 1991.

Cuismano, Roma R. "En busca de la tradición literaria femenina: Mercè Rodoreda y *La plaza del Diamante.*" In *Literatura femenina contemporánea de España: VII Simposio Internacional de Literatura.* Westminster, Calif.: Instituto Literaria y Cultural Hispánico, 1991.

Davies, Catherine. *Contemporary Feminist Fiction in Spain: The Work of Montserrat Roig and Rosa Montero.* Oxford: Berg, 1994.

———. "Feminist Writers in Spain Since 1900: From Political Strategy to Personal Inquiry." In *Textual Liberation: European Feminist Writing in the Twentieth Century.* Edited by Helena Forsas-Scott, 192–226. London: Routledge, 1991.

De Beauvoir, Simone. *The Second Sex*. Translated by and edited by H. M. Parshley. New York: Bantam, 1970.

De Man, Paul. *Allegories of Reading: Figural Language in Rousseau, Nietzsche, Rilke, and Proust*. New Haven: Yale University Press, 1979.

Derrida, Jacques. "White Mythology: Metaphor in the Text of Philosophy." Translated by F. C. T. Moore. In *New Literary History* 6 no. 11 (1974): 5–74.

Díaz (Pérez), Janet W(inecoff). *Ana María Matute*. New York: Twayne, 1971.

Dolgin, Stacey L. "Conversación con Esther Tusquets: 'Para salir de tanta miseria.'" *Anales de la Literatura Española Contemporánea* 13 (1988): 397–406.

———. "The Aesthetic of Eroticism in *Love is a Solitary Game*." In *The Sea of Becoming: Approaches to the Fiction of Esther Tusquets*. Edited by Mary S. Vásquez, 79–92. Westport, Conn.: Greenwood, 1991.

Durán, Manuel. "Carmen Martín Gaite: *Retahílas, El cuarto de atrás*, y el diálogo sin fin." *Revista Iberoamericana* 47 no. 116-17 (1981): 233–40.

———. "*El cuarto de atrás:* Imaginación, fantasía, misterio; Todorov y algo más." In *From Fiction to Metafiction: Essays in Honor of Carmen Martín Gaite*. Edited by Mirella Servodidio and Marcia L. Welles, 129–38. Lincoln: Society of Spanish and Spanish-American Studies, 1983.

Eco, Umberto. *The Role of the Reader*. Bloomington: Indiana University Press, 1979.

El Saffar, Ruth. "Liberation and the Labyrinth: A Study of the Works of Carmen Martín Gaite." In *From Fiction to Metafiction: Essays in Honor of Carmen Martín Gaite*. Edited by Mirella Servodidio and Marcia L. Welles, 185–96. Lincoln: Society of Spanish and Spanish-American Studies, 1983.

———. "Redeeming Loss: Reflections on Carmen Martín Gaite's *The Back Room*." *Revista de Estudios Hispánicos* 20 no. 1 (1986): 1-14.

———. "Structural and Thematic Tactics of Suppression in Carmen Laforet's *Nada*." *Symposium* 28 (1974): 119–29.

Eoff, Sherman. "*Nada* by Carmen Laforet: A Venture in Mechanistic Dynamics." *Hispania* 35 (1952): 207–11.

Epps, Brad. "The Space of Sexual History: Reading Positions in *El cuarto de atrás* and *Reivindicación del Conde don Julián*." In *Critical Essays on the Literatures of Spain and Spanish America*. Edited by Luis T. González-del-Valle and Julio Baena, 75–87. Boulder: Society of Spanish and Spanish-American Studies, 1991.

Estés, Clarissa Pinkola. *Women Who Run with the Wolves: Myths and Stories of the Wild Woman Archetype*. New York: Ballantine, 1992.

Feal Deibe, Carlos. "*Nada* de Carmen Laforet: La iniciación de una adolescente." In *The Analysis of Hispanic Texts: Current Trends in Methodology: First York College Colloquium*. Edited by Mary Ann Beck et al., 221–41. New York: Bilingual, 1976.

Ferguson, Mary Anne. "The Female Novel of Development and the Myth of Psyche." In *The Voyage In: Fictions of Female Development*. Edited by Elizabeth Abel et al., 228–43. Hanover: University Press of New England, 1983.

Foster, David William. "*Nada*, de Carmen Laforet: Ejemplo de neo-romance en la novela contemporánea." In *Novelistas españoles de postguerra*. Edited by Rodolfo Cardona, 89–104. Madrid: Taurus, 1976.

Fraser, Nancy. "The Uses and Abuses of French Discourse Theory for Feminist Politics." In *Revaluing French Feminism: Critical Essays on Difference, Agency, & Culture.* Edited by Nancy Fraser and Sandra Lee Bartky, 177–94. Bloomington: Indiana University Press, 1992.

Freidman, Susan Stanford. "Creativity and the Childbirth Metaphor: Gender Difference in Literary Discourse." In *Feminisms: An Anthology of Literary Theory and Criticism.* Edited by Robyn R. Warhol and Diane Price Herndl, 371–96. New Brunswick: Rutgers University Press, 1991.

Friday, Nancy. *My Mother/My Self: The Daughter's Search for Identity.* New York: Delacorte, 1978.

Frye, Northrop. *The Anatomy of Criticism: Four Essays.* Princeton: Princeton University Press, 1957.

Fuentes, Víctor. "Notas sobre el mundo novelesco de Ana María Matute." In *Novelistas españoles de postguerra.* Edited by Rodolfo Cardona, 105–09. Madrid: Taurus, 1976.

Gardiner, Judith Kegan. "On Female Identity and Writing by Women." In *Writing and Sexual Difference.* Edited by Elizabeth Abel, 177–91. Chicago: University of Chicago Press, 1982.

Gazarian Gautier, Marie-Lise. "Conversación con Carmen Martín Gaite en Nueva York." In *From Fiction to Metafiction: Essays in Honor of Carmen Martín Gaite.* Edited by Mirella Servodidio and Marcia L. Welles, 25–33. Lincoln: Society of Spanish and Spanish-American Studies, 1983. (Appeared in *Insula* 411 [1981]: 1 + .)

Gilbert, Sandra M., and Susan Gubar. "The Queen's Looking Glass: Female Creativity, Male Images of Women, and the Metaphor of Literary Paternity." In *The Madwoman in the Attic: The Woman Writer and the Nineteenth-Century Literary Imagination,* 3–44. New Haven: Yale University Press, 1979.

Glenn, Kathleen M. "Authority and Marginality in Three Contemporary Spanish Narratives." *Romance Languages Annual* 2 (1990): 426–30.

———. "Communication in the Works of Carmen Martín Gaite." *Romance Notes* 19: 277–83.

———. "*El cuarto de atrás:* Literature as *juego* and the Self-Reflexive Text." In *From Fiction to Metafiction: Essays in Honor of Carmen Martín Gaite.* Edited by Mirella Servodidio and Marcia L. Welles, 149–60. Lincoln: Society of Spanish and Spanish-American Studies, 1983.

———. "From Social Realism to Self-Reflection: Carmen Martín Gaite and the Postwar Novel." *Letras Femeninas* 10 (1984): 18–26.

———. "Gothic Vision in García Morales and Erice's *El Sur.*" *Letras Peninsulares* 7.1 (1994): 239–50.

———. "*La plaza del Diamante:* The Other Side of the Story." *Letras Femeninas* 12 nos. 1–2 (1986): 60–68.

Gold, Janet N. "Reading the Love Myth: Tusquets with the Help of Barthes." *Hispanic Review* 55 (1987): 337–46.

González, Josefina. "Dibujo, espacio y ecofeminismo en la C. de *El cuarto de atrás* de Carmen Martín Gaite." *Revista Canadiense de Estudios Hispánicos* 19 no. 1 (1994): 83–95.

Grimal, Pierre. *A Concise Dictionary of Classical Mythology.* Ed. Stephen Kreshaw. Translated by A. R. Maxwell-Hyslop. Oxford: Blackwell, 1986.

Gullón, Ricardo. *La novela lírica*. Madrid: Cáthedra, 1984.

Haley, Michael Cabot. *The Semeiosis of Poetic Metaphor*. Bloomington: Indiana University Press, 1988.

Hart, Stephen. "Esther Tusquets: Sex, Excess and the Dangerous Supplement of Language." *Antípodas: Journal of Hispanic Studies* 3 (1991): 85–98.

―――. *White Ink: Essays on Twentieth-Century Feminine Fiction in Spain and Latin America*. London: Tamesis; Madrid: Támesis, 1993.

Hawkes, Terence. *Metaphor*. London: Methuen, 1972.

Higginbotham, Virginia. "*Nada* and the Cinderella Syndrome." *Rendezvous: Journal of Arts and Letters* 22 no. 2 (1986): 17–25.

Hirsch, Marianne. *The Mother/Daughter Plot: Narrative, Psychoanalysis, Feminism*. Bloomington: Indiana University Press, 1989.

Horney, Karen. *Feminine Psychology*. New York: Norton, 1967.

Hrushovski, Benjamin. "Poetic Metaphor and Frames of Reference." *Poetics Today* 5 no. 1 (1984): 5–43.

Ichiishi, Barbara F. *The Apple of Earthly Love: Female Development in Esther Tusquets' Fiction*. New York: Lang, 1994.

Jakobson, Roman, and Morris Hale. *Fundamentals of Language*. The Hague: Mouton, 1956.

Johnson, Roberta. *Carmen Laforet*. Boston: Twayne, 1981.

―――. "Voice and Intersubjectivity in Carme Riera's Narratives." In *Critical Essays on the Literatures of Spain and Spanish America*. Edited by Luis González-del-Valle and Julio Baena, 153–59. Boulder: Society of Spanish and Spanish-American Studies, 1991.

Jones, Margaret E. W. "Ana María Moix: Literary Structures and the Enigmatic Nature of Reality." *Journal of Spanish Studies: Twentieth Century* 4 (1976): 105–16.

―――. "Antipathetic Fallacy: The Hostile World of Ana María Matute's Novels." *Kentucky Foreign Language Quarterly* 23 Supplement (1967): 5–16.

―――. "Del compromiso al egoísmo: La metamorfosis de la protagonista en la novelística femenina de postguerra." In *Novelistas femeninas de la postguerra española*. Edited by Janet W. Pérez, 125–34. Madrid: Porrúa, 1983.

―――. "Dialectical Movement as Feminist Technique in the Works of Carmen Laforet." In *Studies in Honor of Gerald E. Wade*. Edited by Sylvia Bowman et al., 109–20. Madrid: Porrúa, 1979.

―――. "Different Wor(l)ds: Modes of Women's Communication in Spain's *Narrativa Femenina*." *Monographic Review/Revista Monográfica* 8 (1992): 57–69.

―――. "Religious Motifs and Biblical Allusions in the Works of Ana María Matute." *Hispania* 51 (1968): 416–23.

―――. "Temporal Patterns in the Works of Ana María Matute." *Romance Notes* 12 (1970): 282–88.

―――. *The Contemporary Spanish Novel, 1939–1975*. Boston: Twayne, 1985.

―――. *The Literary World of Ana María Matute*. Lexington: University Press of Kentucky, 1970.

Jordan, Barry. *Laforet: Nada*. Valencia: Soler-Grant, 1993.

―――. "Laforet's *Nada* as Female Bildung?" *Symposium* 46 no. 2 (1992): 105–18.

————. "Shifting Generic Boundaries: The Role of Confession and Desire in Laforet's *Nada.*" *Neophilologus* 77 no. 3 (1993): 411-22.

Klein, Melanie. *The Psycho-Analysis of Children.* Translated by Alix Strachey. Revised edition New York: Delacorte, 1975.

Kolbenschlag, Madonna. *Kiss Sleeping Beauty Good-Bye: Breaking the Spell of Feminine Myths and Models.* New York: Bantam, 1981.

Kristeva, Julia. "Women's Time." Translated by Alice Jardine and Harry Blake. *Signs: Journal of Women in Culture and Society* 7 no. 1 (1981): 13–35.

La Belle, Jenijoy. *Herself Beheld: The Literature of the Looking Glass.* Ithaca: Cornell University Press, 1988.

Lacan, Jacques. *Ecrits I.* Paris: Seuil, 1970.

Laforet, Carmen. *La insolación.* Barcelona: Planeta, 1967.

————. *La isla y los demonios.* Barcelona: Destino, 1970.

————. *La mujer nueva.* Barcelona: Destino, 1967.

————. *Nada.* Barcelona: Destino, 1985.

Laing, R. D. *The Divided Self.* New York: Pantheon, 1969.

————. *The Politics of Experience.* New York: Ballantine, 1978.

————. *The Politics of the Family and Other Essays.* New York: Pantheon, 1971.

Lee-Bonanno, Lucy. "From Freedom to Enclosure: 'Growing Down' in Matute's *Primera memoria.*" *Kentucky Philological Review* 13 (1986): 19–25.

————. *The Quest for Authentic Personhood: An Expression of the Female Tradition in Novels by Moix, Tusquets, Matute and Alós.* Diss. University of Kentucky, 1984. Ann Arbor: University of Michigan, 1987. 8510721.

Le Guern, Michel. *La metáfora y la metonimia.* Translated by Augusto de Galvez-Canero y Pidal. Madrid: Cáthedra, 1976.

Levin, Samuel R. *The Semantic of Metaphor.* Baltimore: Johns Hopkins University Press, 1977.

Levine, Linda Gould. "Carmen Martín Gaite's *El cuarto de atrás:* A Portrait of the Artist as Woman." In *From Fiction to Metafiction: Essays in Honor of Carmen Martín Gaite.* Edited by Mirella Servodidio and Marcia L. Welles, 161–72. Lincoln: Society of Spanish and Spanish-American Studies, 1983.

————. "Reading, Rereading, Misreading and Rewriting the Male Canon: The Narrative Web of Esther Tusquets' Trilogy." *Anales de la Literatura Española Contemporánea* 12 (1987): 203–17.

————. "The Censored Sex: Woman as Author and Character in Franco's Spain." In *Women in Hispanic Literature: Icons and Fallen Idols.* Edited by Beth Miller, 289–315. Berkeley: University of California Press, 1983.

Lévi-Strauss, Claude. *The Savage Mind.* Translated by George Weidenfeld. Chicago: University of Chicago Press, 1966.

Lloyd, Rosemary. "Mirroring Difference, Figuring Frames." *Nineteenth-Century French Studies* 19 no. 3 (1991): 343–53.

Lodge, David. "The Language of Modernist Fiction: Metaphor and Metonymy." In *Modernism.* Edited by Malcolm Bradbury and James McFarlane, 481–96. Hassocks, Sussex: Harvester; Atlantic Highlands, N.J.: Humanities, 1978.

Lucarda, Mario. "Mercè Rodoreda y el buen salvaje." *Quimera* 62: 34–39.

Lucas Dobrian, Susan. "Echo's Revenge in Three Spanish Narratives by Women." *Letras Peninsulares* 8 no. 1 (1995): 169–79.

Lundkvist, Artur. "Mellan Kain och Abel." *Bonniers Litterära Magasin* 31 (1962): 692–99.

Lunn, Patricia V., and Jane W. Albrecht. "*La Plaça del Diamant:* Linguistic Cause and Literary Effect." *Hispania* 75 no. 3 (1992): 492–99.

Magnarelli, Sharon. *The Lost Rib: Female Characters in the Spanish-American Novel.* Lewisburg: Bucknell University Press, 1985.

Mandlove, Nancy. "Oral Texts: The Play of Orality and Literacy in the Poetry of Gloria Fuertes." *Siglo XX/20th Century* 5 (1987–88): 11–16.

———. "Used Poetry: The Trans-Parent Language of Gloria Fuertes and Angel González." *Revista Canadiense de Estudios Hispánicos* 3 (1983): 301–6.

Manteiga, Roberto. "From Empathy to Detachment: The Author-Narrator Relationship in Several Spanish Novels by Women." *Monographic Review/Revista Monográfica* 8 (1992): 19–35.

Martínez Cachero, José María. Introducción. *La insolación.* By Carmen Laforet. Madrid: Castalia, 1992.

Martínez Palacio, Javier. "Una trilogía novelística de Ana María Matute." *Insula* 219 (1965): 1+.

Martín Gaite, Carmen. *Desde la ventana.* Madrid: Espasa-Calpe, 1987.

———. *El cuarto de atrás.* Barcelona: Destino, 1982.

———. *Entre visillos.* Barcelona: Destino, 1988.

———. *Nubosidad variable.* Barcelona: Anagrama, 1993.

———. *Retahílas.* Barcelona: Destino, 1974.

———. *Usos amorosos de la postguerra española.* Barcelona: Anagrama, 1987.

Martí-Olivella, Jaume. "Bachelardian Myth in Rodoreda's Construction of Identity." In *Imagination, Emblems and Expressions: Essays on Latin American, Caribbean and Continental Culture and Identity.* Edited by Helen Ryan-Ranson, 315–28. Bowling Green, Oh.: Bowling Green State University Popular Press, 1993.

Masoliver Rodenas, Juan Antonio. "La base sexta contra Ana María Moix." *Camp de l'Arpa* 9 (1974): 9–12.

Matamoro, Blas. "Carmen Martín Gaite: El viaje al cuarto de atrás." *Cuadernos Hispanoamericanos* 351 (1978): 581–605.

Matute, Ana María. *La trampa.* Barcelona: Destino, 1987.

———. *Los soldados lloran de noche.* Barcelona: Destino, 1975. Vol. 4 of *Obra completa.*

———. *Primera memoria.* Barcelona: Destino, 1987.

Mazquiarán de Rodríguez, Mercedes. "Gothic Imagery, Dreams, and Vampirism: The Haunting Narrative of Adelaida García Morales." *Monographic Review/ Revista Monográfica* 8 (1992): 164–82.

———. "Narrative Strategies in the Novels of Esther Tusquets." *Monographic Review/Revista Monográfica* 7 (1991): 124–34.

McGiboney, Donna Janine. "Paternal Absence and Maternal Repression: The Search for Narrative Authority in Carmen Laforet's *Nada.*" *Romance Languages Annual* 6 (1994): 519–24.

Melamed, Elissa. *Mirror Mirror: The Terror of Not Being Young.* New York: Simon, 1983.

Miller, J. Hillis. *Versions of Pygmalion.* Cambridge: Harvard University Press, 1990.

Mitchell, Juliet. *Psychoanalysis and Feminism.* New York: Pantheon, 1974.

Moi, Toril. *Sexual/Textual Politics.* New York: Methuen, 1985.

Moix, Ana María. *Julia.* Barcelona: Barral, 1970.

———. *Walter ¿por qué te fuiste?* Barcelona: Barral, 1972.

Molinaro, Nina L. *Foucault, Feminism, and Power: Reading Esther Tusquets.* Lewisburg: Bucknell University Press, 1991.

Monaghan, Patricia. *The Book of Goddesses and Heroines.* St. Paul: Llewellyn, 1990.

Montero, Rosa. *Bella y oscura.* Barcelona: Seix Barral, 1993.

Muller, John P. *Lacan and Language.* New York: International University Press, 1982.

Murphy, Marie. "Metafictional and Erotic Games: *El amor es un juego solitario.*" In *La escritora hispánica.* Edited by Nora Erro-Orthmann and Juan Cruz Mendizíbal, 251–60. Miami: Universal, 1990.

Nance, Kimberly. "Things Fall Apart: Images of Disintegration in Mercè Rodoreda's *La plaça de Diamant.*" *Hispanófila* 101 (1991): 67–76.

Newberry, Wilma. "The Solstitial Holidays in Carmen Laforet's *Nada:* Christmas and Midsummer." *Romance Notes* 17 (1976): 76–81.

Nichols, Geraldine Cleary. "Caída/Re(s)puesta: La narrativa femenina de la posguerra." In *Actas de las cuartas jornadas de investigación interdisciplinaria: Literatura y vida cotidiana.* Edited by María Angeles Durán and José Antonio Rey, 325–36. Madrid: Universidad Autónoma de Madrid, 1987. (A version appears in Nichols's *Des/cifrar.*)

———. "Codes of Exclusion, Modes of Equivocation: Matute's *Primera memoria.*" *Ideologies & Literature* 1 (1985): 156–88. (A version appears in Nichols's *Des/cifrar.*)

———. *Des/cifrar la diferencia: Narrativa femenina de la España contemporánea.* Madrid: Siglo veintiuno, 1992.

———. *Escribir, espacio propio: Laforet, Matute, Moix, Tusquets, Riera y Roig por sí mismas.* Minneapolis: Institute for the Study of Ideologies and Literature, 1989.

———. "*Julia:* 'This is the way the worlds ends. . . .'" In *Novelistas femeninas de la postguerra española.* Edited by Janet W. Pérez, 113–24. Madrid: Porrúa, 1983.

———. "Minding Her P's and Q's: The Fiction of Esther Tusquets." *Indiana Journal of Hispanic Literature* 2 no. 1 (1993): 159–79.

Nieves Alonso, María. "Partir, defender, callar (Tres posibilidades de conclusión en la novela española contemporánea)." *Atenea* 448 (1983): 101–14.

Nin, Anaïs. *The Diary of Anaïs Nin.* Edited by Gunther Stuhlmann. Vol. 2. New York: Harcourt, 1967.

Olney, James. *Metaphors of Self.* Princeton: Princeton University Press, 1972.

Ordóñez, Elizabeth. "Beginning to Speak: Carme Riera's *Una primavera para Domenico Guarini.*" In *La CHISPA '85: Selected Proceedings.* Edited by Gilbert Paolini, 285–93. New Orleans: Tulane University, 1985.

———. "*Nada:* Initiation into Bourgeois Patriarchy." In *The Analysis of Hispanic Texts: Current Trends in Methodology: Second York College Colloquium.* Edited by Lisa E. Davis and Isabel C. Taran, 61–77. New York: Bilingual, 1976.

———. "Reading, Telling and the Text of Carmen Martín Gaite's *El cuarto de atrás.*" In *From Fiction to Metafiction: Essays in Honor of Carmen Martín Gaite.* Edited by Mirella Servodidio and Marcia L. Welles, 173–84. Lincoln: Society of Spanish and Spanish-American Studies, 1983.

———. "The Barcelona Group: The Fiction of Alós, Moix, and Tusquets." *Letras Femeninas* 6 no. 1 (1980): 38–50.

———. *Voices of Their Own: Contemporary Spanish Narrative by Women.* Lewisburg: Bucknell University Press, 1991.

Ortega, José. "Mujer, guerra, y neurosis en dos novelas de M. Rodoreda (*La plaza del Diamante* y *La calle de las Camelias*)." In *Novelistas femeninas de la postguerra española.* Edited by Janet W. Pérez, 71–83. Madrid: Porrúa, 1983.

Palley, Julian. "Dreams in Two Novels of Carmen Martín Gaite." In *From Fiction to Metafiction: Essays in Honor of Carmen Martín Gaite.* Edited by Mirella Servodidio and Marcia L. Welles, 107–16. Lincoln: Society of Spanish and Spanish-American Studies, 1983.

———. "El interlocutor soñado de *El cuarto de atrás* de Carmen Martín Gaite." *Insula* 404–5 (1980): 22.

Pardo Bazán, Emilia. "La caja de oro." In *Cuentos completos,* vol. 1. Edited by Juan Paredes Núñez, 273–75. La Coruña: Galicia, 1990.

Pérez, Janet (Winecoff) (Díaz). *Contemporary Women Writers of Spain.* Boston: Twayne, 1988.

———. "The Fictional World of Ana María Matute: Solitude, Injustice, and Dreams." In *Women Writers of Contemporary Spain: Exiles in the Homeland.* Edited by Joan L. Brown, 93–115. Newark: University of Delaware Press, 1991.

Pérez Firmat, Gustavo. "Carmen Laforet: The Dilemma of Artistic Vocation." In *Women Writers of Contemporary Spain: Exiles in the Homeland.* Edited by Joan L. Brown, 26–41. Newark: University of Delaware Press, 1991.

Petrea, Mariana. "La promesa del futuro: La dialéctica de la emancipación femenina en *Nada* de Carmen Laforet." *Letras Femeninas* 22 nos. 1–2 (1994): 71–86.

Pope, Randolph. "Mercè Rodoreda's Subtle Greatness." In *Women Writers of Contemporary Spain: Exiles in the Homeland.* Edited by Joan Brown, 116–35. Newark: University of Delaware Press, 1991.

———. "Two Faces and the Character of Her True Nature." In *The Garden across the Border: Mercè Rodoreda's Fiction.* Edited by Kathleen NcNerney and Nancy Vosburg, 135–47. Selinsgrove: Susquehanna University Press; London: Associated University Press, 1994.

Porrúa, María del Carmen. "Tres novelas de la guerra civil." *Cuadernos Hispanoamericanos* 473–74 (1989): 45–57.

Pratt, Annis. *Archetypal Patterns in Women's Fiction.* Bloomington: Indiana University Press, 1981.

Preminger, Alex, ed. *Encyclopedia of Poetry and Poetics.* Princeton: Princeton University Press, 1965.

Ragland-Sullivan, Ellie. *Jacques Lacan and the Philosophy of Psychoanalysis.* Chicago: University of Illinois Press, 1986.

Reed, Suzanne Gross. "Notes on Hans Christian Andersen Tales in Ana María Matute's *Primera memoria.*" In *Continental, Latin-American and Francophone Women Writers,* vol. 1. Edited by Eunice Myers and Ginette Adamson, 177–82. Lanham: University Press of America, 1987.

Riddel, María del Carmen. *La novela femenina de formación en la postguerra española.* New York: Lang, 1995.

Riera, Carme. *Cuestión de amor propio.* Barcelona: Tusquets, 1988.

———. "Literatura femenina: ¿Un lenguaje prestado?" *Quimera* 18 (1982): 9–12.

———. *Qüestió d'amor propi.* Barcelona: Llull, 1987.

———. *Una primavera per a Domenico Guarini.* Barcelona: Edicions 62, 1982.

Riffaterre, Michael. *Fictional Truth.* Baltimore: Johns Hopkins University Press, 1990.

Rigney, Barbara Hill. *Madness and Sexual Politics.* Madison: University of Wisconsin Press, 1978.

Rodoreda, Mercè. *Aloma.* Revised edition. Barcelona: Edicions 62, 1969.

———. *El carrer de les camèlies.* Barcelona: Club, 1966.

———. *La plaça del Diamant.* Barcelona: Club, 1979.

———. *La plaza del Diamante.* Translated by Enrique Sordo. Barcelona: Edhasa, 1988.

———. *La plaza del Diamante: Edición ilustrada.* Translated by Secundí Sañé. Introduction Joan Sales. Translated by Joaquim Dols. Barcelona: HMB, 1982.

———. *Mirall trencat.* Barcelona: Edicions 62, 1983.

Rodríguez, Aleida Anselma. "Todorov in *El cuarto de atrás.*" *Prismal/Cabal* 11 (1983): 76–90.

Roger, Isabel M. "Carmen Martín Gaite: Una trayectoria novelística y su bibliografía." *Anales de la Literatura Española Contemporánea* 13 (1988): 293–317.

Rogers, Robert. *Metaphor: A Psychoanalytic View.* Berkley: University of California Press, 1978.

Roma, Rosa. *Ana María Matute.* Madrid: EPESA, 1971.

Romero, Isabel, et al. "Feminismo y literatura: La narrativa de los años 70." In *Actas de las cuartas jornadas de investigación interdisciplinaria: Literatura y vida cotidiana.* Edited by María Angeles Durán and José Antonio Rey, 337–57. Madrid: Universidad Autónoma de Madrid, 1987.

Rose, Ellen Cronan. "Through the Looking Glass: When Women Tell Fairy Tales." In *The Voyage In: Fictions of Female Development.* Edited by Elizabeth Abel et al., 209–27. Hanover: University Press of New England, 1983.

Rowbotham, Sheila. *Women, Resistance and Revolution.* London: Lane, 1972.

Ruiz-Avilés, Miguel R. "*El cuarto de atrás:* Diferentes vistas según diferentes 'horizontes de experiencias' y 'horizontes de expectativas.'" In *Selected Proceedings of the Mid-America Conference on Hispanic Literature.* Edited by Luis T. González-del-Valle and Catherine Nickel, 147–58. Lincoln: Society of Spanish and Spanish-American Studies, 1986.

Schraibman, Joseph. "Two Spanish Civil War Novels: A Woman's Perspective." In *The Spanish Civil War in Literature.* Edited by Janet Pérez and Wendell Aycock, 149–59. Lubbock: Texas Tech University Press, 1990.

Schyfter, Sara E. "La mística masculina en *Nada*, de Carmen Laforet." In *Novelistas femeninas de la postguerra española*. Edited by Janet W. Pérez, 85–93. Madrid: Porrúa, 1983.

———. "Rites without Passage: The Adolescent World of Ana María Moix's *Julia*." In *The Analysis of Literary Texts: Current Trends in Methodology: Third and Fourth York College Colloquia*. Edited by Randolph D. Pope, 41–50. Ypsilanti: Bilingual, 1980.

———. "The Fragmented Family in the Novels of Contemporary Spanish Women Writers." *Perspectives on Contemporary Literature* 3 no. 1 (1977): 23–29.

Servodidio, Mirella d'Ambrosio. "Esther Tusquets's Fiction: The Spinning of a Narrative Web." In *Women Writers of Contemporary Spain: Exiles in the Homeland*. Edited by Joan Brown, 159–78. Newark: University of Delaware Press, 1991.

———. "Oneiric Intertextualites." In *From Fiction to Metafiction: Essays in Honor of Carmen Martín Gaite*. Edited by Mirella Servodidio and Marcia L. Welles, 117–28. Lincoln: Society of Spanish and Spanish-American Studies, 1983.

———. "Perverse Pairings and Corrupted Codes: *El amor es un juego solitario*." *Anales de la Literatura Española Contemporánea* 11 no. 3 (1986): 237–54.

———. "A Case of Pre-oedipal and Narrative Fixation: *El mismo mar de todos los veranos*." *Anales de la Literatura Española Contemporánea* 12 nos. 1–2 (1987): 157–74.

Shapiro, Michael, and Marianne Shapiro. *Figuration in Verbal Art*. Princeton: Princeton University Press, 1988.

Short, Kayann. "Too Disconnected/Too Bound Up: The Paradox of Identity in Mercè Rodoreda's *The Time of the Doves*." In *International Women's Writing: New Landscapes of Identity*. Edited by Anne E. Brown and Marjanne E. Goozé, 187–95. Westport, Conn.: Greenwood, 1995.

Sieburth, Stephanie. "Memory, Metafiction and Mass Culture: The Popular Text in *El cuarto de atrás*." *Revista Hispánica Moderna* 43 no. 1 (1990): 78–92.

Sobejano, Gonzalo. "Enlaces y desenlaces en las novelas de Carmen Martín Gaite." In *From Fiction to Metafiction: Essays in Honor of Carmen Martín Gaite*. Edited by Mirella Servodidio and Marcia L. Welles, 209–23. Lincoln: Society of Spanish and Spanish-American Studies, 1983.

Soufas, Christopher C., Jr. "Ana María Moix and the 'Generation of 1968': *Julia* as (Anti-)Generational (Anti-)Manifesto." In *Nuevos y novísimos: Algunas perspectivas críticas sobre la narrativa española desde la década de los 60*. Edited by Ricardo Landeira and Luis T. González-del-Valle, 217–28. Boulder: Society of Spanish and Spanish-American Studies, 1978.

Spacks, Patricia Meyer. *The Female Imagination*. New York: Knopf, 1975.

Spires, Robert C. *Beyond the Metafictional Mode: Directions in the Modern Spanish Novel*. Lexington: University Press of Kentucky, 1984.

———. "Intertextuality in *El cuarto de atrás*." In *From Fiction to Metafiction: Essays in Honor of Carmen Martín Gaite*. Edited by Mirella Servodidio and Marcia L. Welles, 139–48. Lincoln: Society of Spanish and Spanish-American Studies, 1983.

———. "La experiencia afirmadora de *Nada*." In *La novela española de posguerra: creación artística y experiencia personal*. Madrid: Cupsa, 1978.

———. "*Nada* y la paradoja de los signos negativos." *Siglo XX/20th Century* 3 nos. 1–2 (1985–86): 31–33.

Stanton, Domna C. "Difference on Trial: A Critique of the Maternal Metaphor in Cixous, Irigaray, and Kristeva." In *The Poetics of Gender*. Edited by Nancy K. Miller, 157–82. New York: Colombia University Press, 1986.

Stevens, James R. "Myth and Memory: Ana María Matute's *Primera memoria*." *Symposium* 25 (1971): 198–203.

Tagore, Rabindranath. *Personality*. London: Macmillan, 1917.

Thomas, Michael D. "El desdoblamiento psíquico como factor dinámico en *Julia, de Ana María Moix*." In *Novelistas femeninas de la postguerra española*. Edited by Janet W. Pérez, 103–12. Madrid: Porrúa, 1983.

———. "Symbolic Portals in Laforet's *Nada*." *Anales de la Novela de Posguerra* 3 (1978): 57–74.

———. "The Rite of Initiation in Matute's *Primera memoria*." *Kentucky Romance Quarterly* 25 (1978): 153–64.

Thompson, Currie K. "Perception and Art: Water Imagery in *Nada*." *Romance Quarterly* 32 (1985): 291–300.

Tsuchiya, Akiko. "The Paradox of Narrative Seduction in Carmen Riera's *Cuestión de amor propio*." *Hispania* 75 no. 2 (1992): 281-86.

———. "The Phantom of Francoist Culture and the Hermeneutics of Desire in Adelaida García Morales' *La lógica del vampiro*." Paper presented at the annual convention of the Mid-America Conference on Hispanic Literature, Lincoln, Nebraska, September 1996.

Tusquets, Esther. *El amor es un juego solitario*. Barcelona: Lumen, 1982.

———. *El mismo mar de todos los veranos*. Barcelona: Anagrama, 1990.

———. *Para no volver*. Barcelona: Lumen, 1985.

———. *Varada tras el último naufragio*. Barcelona: Lumen, 1980.

Vásquez, Mary S. "Actor and Spectator in the Fiction of Esther Tusquets." In *The Sea of Becoming: Approaches to the Fiction of Esther Tusquets*. Edited by Mary S. Vásquez, 157–72. Westport, Conn.: Greenwood, 1991.

———. "Esther Tusquets and the Trilogy which Isn't." In *La Chispa 1986: Selected Proceedings*. Edited by Alfredo Lozada, 243–39. Baton Rouge: Louisiana State University, 1987.

———, ed. *The Sea of Becoming: Approaches to the Fiction of Esther Tusquets*. Westport, Conn.: Greenwood, 1991.

———. "Tusquets, Fitzgerald and the Redemptive Power of Love." *Letras Femeninas* 14 nos. 1–2 (1988): 10–21.

Villegas, Juan. "*Nada* de Carmen Laforet, o la infantilización de la aventura legendaria." In *La estructura mítica del héroe en la novela del siglo XX*. Barcelona: Planeta, 1978.

Wellek, René, and Austin Warren. *Theory of Literature*. 3d ed. San Diego: Harcourt, 1977.

Welles, Marcia L. "Carmen Martín Gaite: Fiction as Desire." In *From Fiction to Metafiction: Essays in Honor of Carmen Martín Gaite*. Edited by Mirella Servodidio and Marcia L. Welles, 197–207. Lincoln: Society of Spanish and Spanish-American Studies, 1983.

White, Hayden. *Metahistory: The Historical Imagination in Nineteenth-Century Europe*. Baltimore: Johns Hopkins University Press, 1973.

Winecoff (Díaz) (Pérez), Janct. "Style and Solitude in the Works of Ana María Matute." *Hispania* 49 no. 1 (1966): 61–69.

Woolf, Virginia. *A Room of One's Own.* New York: Harcourt, 1934.

Wyatt, Jean. "Avoiding self-definition: In defense of women's right to merge (Julia Kristeva and Mrs. Dalloway)." In *The Female Imagination and the Modernist Aesthetic.* Edited by Sandra M. Gilbert and Susan Gubar, 115–26. New York: Gordon, 1986.

Wyers, Frances. "A Woman's Voices: Mercè Rodoreda's *La plaça del Diamant.*" *Kentucky Romance Quarterly* 30 (1983): 301–9.

Wythe, George. "The World of Ana María Matute." *Books Abroad* 40 no. 1 (1966): 24–25.

Zatlin, Phyllis. "Women Novelists in Democratic Spain: Freedom to Express the Female Perspective." *Anales de la Literatura Española Contemporánea* 12 (1987): 29–44.

Index

Ackelsberg, Martha A., 186n 18
adult: children, 106; world, 30, 45, 56.
  See also childlike
aging: as liability for women, 147–48,
  155, 188n 35; in literature about
  women, 154–55; and mirror reflection, 119–20, 136; and older protagonists, 21–22, 124; and women's
  independence, 22. See also *El amor
  es un juego solitario;* older women;
  Qüestió d'amor propi
Alborg, Concha, 189n 2
Aldecoa, Josefina R.: *Mujeres de negro,* 164
allegory. *See* figurative language
Allende, Isabel: *La casa de los espíritus,* 167n 34
Alonso, Santos, 185n 2
Alós, Concha, 124
amor es un juego solitario, El (Tusquets), 13, 21, 106, 107–24, 159, 161,
  163; aging process in, 107, 119, 120,
  121; baroque ornamentation in, 108,
  117, 185n 7; compared with fairy
  tales, 117, 118; compared with *Julia*
  (Moix), 107, 110, 111, 112, 116, 117,
  118, 121; compared with *Nada* (Laforet), 108, 117, 118, 121; compared
  with *La plaça del Diamant* (Rodoreda), 108, 113, 121; compared with
  Primera memoria (Matute), 117,
  123–24; criticism of, 107, 113, 118,
  123, 185n 3, 185–86n 10, 186nn 11,
  20, 187nn 24, 26, 31; Danae intertext
  in, 110–12, 114, 117, 118, 122,
  186n 12; "engulfment" in, 111; eroticism in, 108, 110, 185n 3, 186n 20,
  187n 28; jungle intertext in, 109–13,
  121; lack of autonomy in, 117, 121,
  122; lost child image in, 110–16, 120,
  122; metaphors in, 107–14, 117,

121–22, 185n 3, 186n 10; metonymy
in, 108–15, 117, 122, 185n 4, 186n 10;
mirroring in 108–10, 114, 118, 119–
22; mother-daughter relationship in,
116, 119; nymph image in, 110, 112,
113, 122; Pygmalion role in, 110,
186n 13; reader's role in, 111, 115,
122; rebirth in, 117, 122; reflection of
society in, 119; schizophrenia in,
111–12, 118–19; self-identity in,
107–8, 110, 112, 114–15, 122; sexual
liberation and enslavement in,
113–14, 117–18, 121, 186n 18; staged
roles in, 107–8, 114–17, 119–22,
187n 24; subconscious in, 107, 111;
and trilogy, 122, 188n 38. *See also*
Tusquets, Esther
Andersen, Hans Christian, 57. *See also*
fairy tales
Anderson, Christopher L., 173n 3,
175n 17
"antinarcissism," 19, 36, 155. *See also*
Cixous, Hélène: "antinarcissism";
narcissism
Aristotle, 5, 165n 10
Arnau, Carme: on *La plaça del Diamant,* 177n 2, 178n 7, 180n 27
autonomy for women: as common
theme, 23; as cyclical expansion 22;
fear and guilt in, 36, 37; and Franco,
9, 13, 42, 159; and intense mirroring,
101; loss of in novels, 87; and love
relationships, 145–46, 153; progress
toward in novels, 86, 140, 161; as
quality of identity, 91, 106, 132; and
relationship with society, 141, 157;
and sexual behavior, 113. *See also*
specific novels

Bakhtin, M. M., 18
Barthes, Roland, 165n 10
Bellver, Catherine G.: on *El amor es*

212